With Disastrous Consequences

London Disasters 1830–1917

Wendy Neal

Hisarlik Press
1992

Published by Hisarlik Press, 4 Catisfield Road, Enfield Lock, Middlesex EN3 6BD, UK. Georgina Clark-Mazo and Jeffrey Alan Mazo, publishers.

British Library Cataloguing-in-Publication data available.

ISBN 1 874312 00 1

10 9 8 7 6 5 4 3 2 1

Printed in Great Britain by Broadwater Press, Welwyn Garden City, Hertfordshire.

BASICS LONDON is a voluntary team of doctors who give on the spot medical care to victims of accidents and disasters. This book is dedicated to them, and the author's royalties will go towards providing training and equipment.

Acknowledgements

Many people have helped with the production of this book, and there is no space to mention them all. I am grateful for all the support I have received; without it this book would never have materialised.

I must thank Dr Ken Hines for giving me the initial idea for this book, and for his excellent foreword.

I owe special thanks to Newham Local Studies Librarian Howard Bloch. Howard's contribution has been outstanding. His depth and range of knowlege, enthusiasm and willingness to help have been an invaluable support to my research. Bob Aspinall, of the Museum in Docklands, has also given freely of his time and expertise, and kindly allowed me to use photographic material from the museum's unique collection. I am grateful to staff at local studies libraries and archives across London, and to staff at the Greater London Records Office who brought me countless heavy volumes from their stores without the slightest complaint. I thank the Royal Humane Society for kindly allowing me access to their excellent records. Bill Storey provided most of the photographs of illustrations in the *Illustrated London News* and the *Illustrated Times*. Dave Williams and Adam Pope of Express Photo Services were also a great help in supplying prints. Other photographs came from material held at museums and libraries which have been credited in the captions. I am indebted to Georgina Clark-Mazo of Hisarlik Press for her support and encouragement for the project, and for her useful editorial suggestions.

My husband, Tony, has shown unstinting patience in proof reading and making constructive criticisms of the text. And finally, thanks go to my sons Aidan and Alex who have tolerated my frenetic spells of writing and research with understanding and good humour.

Wendy Neal, April 1992

Contents

SOURCES OF THE ILLUSTRATIONS

Foreword

BY DR KEN HINES

Medical knowledge has expanded enormously in the past century or so. Doctors have access to diagnostic techniques, treatments and life-saving equipment which would bewilder and amaze their turn of the century counterparts. A nineteenth-century GP in the East End would daily witness the grim effects of deprivation—malnutrition, cholera, typhoid and high infant mortality. Much of the workload in an East London surgery today is tackling the stressful effects of a very different lifestyle. In disaster prevention and disaster management it might appear that there is little to learn from our predecessors in the embryo emergency services of the nineteenth century. Yet to err is human—and to do so again and again is more typical of the species. Many of the disasters unfurled in this book bear striking parallels with more modern catastrophes, and show that many lessons of history have still to be learnt.

The sinking of the *Marchioness* in August 1989 shows obvious similarities with the *Princess Alice* disaster of 1878. Both involved Thames pleasure boats being overwhelmed in collisions with much larger, iron-hulled ships. Both incidents were attributed to navigational errors and to the lack of clear guidelines for procedures on the river. Each was followed by those in authority ordering more stringent river regulations. Neither owner knew exactly how many passengers were being carried on board their boats at the time, and in the case of the *Princess Alice* the final death toll was never established. Following the sinking of the *Marchioness* the government at last ordered all boats to maintain accurate records of passenger numbers.

The mid-Victorians were the first to witness Irish terrorism on mainland Britain, and more than a hundred years later the techniques and effects of such outrages remain virtually unchanged. The Fenians, like today's IRA, aimed to cause maximum disruption with minimal effort and risk to themselves. The Fenians chose their targets carefully, preferring national symbols such as the Houses of Parliament, the Tower of London, the Carlton Club and Scotland Yard, where damage would strike at national pride as much as bricks and mortar. The IRA have made carbon copy attacks on these and other buildings. The Fenians opted to leave bombs at London's mainline and underground stations in successful efforts to disrupt communications. Again, the IRA have followed in their footsteps. The simultaneous explosions the Fenians planned at Victoria, Paddington, Charing Cross and Ludgate Hill stations in February 1884 have a curious similarity with the explosions at Paddington and Victoria stations in February 1991. The disruption caused on both dates was enormous as all mainline termini had to be checked for possible explosive devices. The decision to close the stations, despite the socio-economic consequences, was unavoidable; the risk of further death and injury was just too great. In making such decisions the police and railway authorities have a difficult, if not impossible task. They are liable to unfair criticism from some media quarters and from individuals trying to score political points at the expense of somebody's disaster.

Terrorist atrocities have always incited a rush to find, convict and punish the culprits. This haste has led to miscarriages of justice and, again, history has a habit of repeating itself. Recent years have seen the release of the Guildford Four and the Birmingham Six following unsafe convictions and doubtful prosecution evidence. Such episodes create public sympathy that could be utilised to further the aims of the activist groups. Throughout history, however, such opportunities have been squandered. When in 1867 Fenians shot a police sergeant while rescuing colleagues from a prison van, five people were quickly arrested and convicted of murder. Two were reprieved, but the others were hanged despite dubious evidence and an overwhelming surge of public sympathy and support for their case, with mass demonstrations in support of the Fenians. The attack on the Clerkenwell House of Detention followed within a few weeks, and the shock of the carnage brought an instant and absolute turn around for public opinion. To be Irish was to be guilty. Contemporary IRA attacks have similarly incited anti-Irish backlashes which have at times caused much distress to the large contingent of law-abiding Irish men and women who live and work in London. A large section of the nursing profession is Irish, and many have experienced a great deal of distress when faced with the innocent victims of random terrorist bomb attacks.

St Bartholomew's Hospital, in the heart of the City of London, took many of the casualties from Clerkenwell, rapidly preparing extra beds and later boasting all patients were receiving treatment within thirty minutes of their arrival. More recently Bart's dealt with the injured from the explosions at the Tower of London and the Old Bailey. The hospital report for the Old Bailey incident says it happened too quickly for the hospital's major incident plan to be implemented. What the writer meant was that the explosion blew windows out of the hospital itself, and that the casualty staff were still picking themselves up off the floor as the walking wounded began staggering in from the explosion only a hundred yards away.

The IRA, like their Fenian predecessors, plant their bombs in any convenient receptacle and time them to explode when the terrorist is safely away from the scene. In both centuries occasional "own goals" have occurred as terrorists have blown themselves up. The Fenians hid their devices in briefcases, hat boxes and other innocent-looking containers, and made full use of left luggage lockers and other hidey-holes. Terrorist techniques have changed very little, but we still fail to pre-empt them. The 1991 Victoria Station bomb that killed commuter David Corner and injured about thirty-eight others had been concealed in a litter bin. Litter bins were quickly removed from stations, but it was a case of closing the stable door after the horse had bolted. The arrival of cars makes it much easier to abandon a bomb in a vehicle almost anywhere, certainly an easier operation than manhandling a barrel like the Fenians at Clerkenwell.

Train accidents blighted the Victorian years. They caused a staggering 5,231 deaths during the four years 1872 to 1875, a record that today's safety standards will surely prevent ever being challenged. In recent years major accidents on the railway have become relatively rare, but are extremely newsworthy when they do happen. Railway equipment has improved beyond all recognition over the last century, but disasters are still attributable to faulty equipment and human error. Fatalities at three incidents in London during the late 1950s and early 1960s were far higher than those suffered by the Victorians. On 8 October 1952, 112 people died in a crash at Harrow. Only five years later, on 4 December 1957, ninety passengers died in an incident at Lewisham, and in 1967 another forty-nine lost their lives when a diesel electric train hit a broken rail at Hither Green. These railway accidents were dealt with by the emergency services to the best of their abilities, given the equipment and training provided at the time. No one working with rescue teams ever gives less than their best in disaster situations, and there are often amazing stories of courage and skill. Facilities, even at this stage, were limited. The concept of pre-hospital care, with the argument that it is better to stay and stabilise a casualty than to scoop them up and get them to hospital as quickly as possible, was still at an embryo stage. Casualties in the Harrow disaster received unusually good pre-hospital care by chance, as a nearby American air force base provided doctors, nurses and equipment from a field hospital unit, effectively bringing the hospital to the patient. Newspaper photographs showed casualties being tended at the scene with plasma drips established. Usually medical help at this time was restricted, as in Victorian days, to attendance by doctors who happened to live near the scene and were aware their assistance was needed.

More recent major railway disasters include the Moorgate Underground disaster that left forty-three dead and eighty-three injured in February 1975, and the collision that killed thirty-four and injured one hundred at Clapham Junction on 12 December 1988. Train crashes have a unique character, and can cause problems in rescuing casualties that are rarely experienced at other disasters. Accidents often happen at high speed, and the force of the impact can contort metal and debris to entangle the unfortunate passengers in a seemingly impenetrable mass. Victorian carriages were less robust than their modern counterparts, but rescuers lacked modern access to heavy cutting and lifting equipment. The task of freeing those trapped must have been formidable, and the inevitable delays must have cost many lives.

Accidents within the confines of a tunnel are always difficult to deal with. Reading of the 1864 collision in the Charlton Tunnel brings back grim memories of the Moorgate disaster. Rescue workers at Charlton complained of the intense heat and stifling conditions inside the tunnel. The situation at Moorgate was similar, and presented an enormous challenge to emergency services. An underground train had crashed into the blind end of a tunnel. Rescuers had to work in appalling conditions, with little light, excessive heat and reduced oxygen levels. Three major London teaching hospitals were involved. Trapped casualties at least had the benefit of being tended by ambulance staff equipped with pain-relieving gases, airways for unconscious victims and a variety of other life-saving equipment that had not been available only fifteen years earlier. Organised teams of doctors and nurses supported the rescue with more sophisticated resuscitation equipment and Immediate Care skills. The Victorians, of course, had no such luxuries. The best the injured could hope for was a bandage torn from some sheet or clothing, a drink of water and a comfortable cart to wheel them away.

The 1917 Silvertown Explosion, with its horrendous loss of life, illustrates only too clearly the hazards of chemical industries operating within residential areas. Health and Safety regulations, especially the Chemical Industries Major Accident Hazard (CIMAH) regulations, are doing much to minimise any possible similar incident in modern times, but accidents can, and do, still happen. A fire and explosion at a chemical plant in Barking in 1980 led to a major evacuation from the area of some ten thousand people. Fortunately, nobody was seriously hurt. There have been several recent incidents where gas cylinders have exploded, causing havoc in their neighbourhood just like rockets from the Woolwich Arsenal in the nineteenth century.

Design faults, bad workmanship and poor materials combined to cause numerous incidents involving buildings collapsing in the nineteenth century. Today, the construction industry's accident record is still appalling, despite enormous efforts from the Health and Safety Executive to enforce codes of practice. Builders still fall from scaffolding or sustain injuries from falling objects. The industry has an annual death rate of several hundred. Buildings are still known to fall down, as illustrated by the collapse of a house in East Ham during a party in 1984. More than forty of the three hundred party-goers needed hospital treatment.

Some features of disaster persist across centuries. Disasters have a magnetic fascination and attract the public in droves. Major incidents in the nineteenth century attracted vast crowds of spectators long before the days when television brought the drama to the fireside. People would travel miles and endure enormous discomfort for the satisfaction of gazing at a scene where many had died. News of such events spread like wildfire, despite the handicap of rudimentary communication systems. Distraught men, women and children who feared they may have lost friends or relatives in the *Princess Alice* were gathering around the steamship company's offices within hours of the sinking. Milling crowds caused problems for rescue workers, their well-intentioned but inexpert fumbling only serving to add to the dangers faced. Today efficient police cordons keep the public at a safe distance, but difficulties can still arise. When a BEA Trident crashed at Staines in June 1972 emergency services were delayed reaching the scene because all available routes had been blocked by sightseers. When they finally arrived they discovered all 118 people on board had perished. Similarly, at Moorgate a crowd of many hundreds stood around for five days and nights, just watching and waiting for the sight of another body being recovered.

The desire to possess a memento of a disaster has always led to souvenir hunters, and occasionally brazen looters. The *Princess Alice* lost most of her ornamental carvings to scavengers on the foreshore, and at the Lockerbie air crash and other recent incidents arrests have been made for the theft of such relics.

Both then and now, emergency rescue workers are familiar with the additional problems that can be caused by the well-intentioned visits of VIPs. These range from Royalty, Prime Ministers and other Ministers of State to MPs, Bishops, Mayors and other local dignitaries. They can often distract from the work in hand and require extra resources to preserve their safety and security.

Press coverage of major incidents in London was very impressive during the nineteenth century. These were days long before the advent of the communications wizardry that gives us almost instant access to news. There were no fax machines, no computer link-ups, there wasn't even a comprehensive telephone system. Yet when the *Princess Alice* sank with the loss of more than six hundred lives on a September evening in 1878, the papers the next morning carried comprehensive reports, including eyewitness accounts. If the *Princess Alice* went down today it is doubtful if newspaper coverage would be much superior to that of those dedicated, resourceful hacks. Different newspapers often carried the same accounts, sometimes attributed to other publications, but usually appearing as their own work.

Newspapers reflected the middle and upper class attitudes of their readership, and often had more sympathy for victims from their own community. When the *Illustrated London News* reported on the deaths at the launch of the *Albion* in Canning Town, they commented that the East End crowd tended to be more unruly than their West End counterparts. The implication was clear—the people had themselves to blame for ignoring the warning notices. Such a tragedy would not have occurred amongst the higher classes. The forty ice skaters who lost their lives after ignoring warnings at Regent's Park received a much kindlier judgement, with a *Camden and Kentish Town Gazette* leader writer remarking that the country would be without its heroes if everyone gave first priority to safety and took no risks.

Throughout history, most major disasters have been followed by the establishment of a fund to pay compensation both to the survivors and to the families of those who died. Today, the funds are usually well organised and administered, but the same was not always true in the nineteenth century. There were many complaints of unfairness and inefficiency in the distribution of funds. In today's society, the desire to apportion blame and sue for compensation has sometimes led to inflated claims. The recognition of post-traumatic stress syndrome in the rescuers and others affected by a major disaster was long overdue. However, this has led to a growth industry of bodies and individuals claiming to provide an essential counselling support service. Too much may be worse than nothing at all. Disaster seen live on television has even led to compensation claims for post-traumatic stress.

Reading the accounts of different Victorian disasters reveals the almost complete lack of planning on how to deal with major incidents. People closest to the scene managed as well as they were able, but additional resources were few and far between. Ability to cope efficiently under extraordinary circumstances improved with the development of voluntary organisations willing to give their services free of charge when the need arose. By the time of the Silvertown disaster in 1917 these groups had developed sufficiently to provide an effective back-up to the statutory emergency services. It is difficult to see how the authorities would have coped then without help from the Salvation Army, St John Ambulance Corps, the various social settlements and other groups.

The Royal Humane Society, whose doctors were so active at the Regent's Park ice disaster, were the first organisation to perceive the need for medical care at the scene of accidents. In many ways they are the forerunners of today's volunteers in the British Association for Immediate Care (BASICS). Like BASICS, the Royal Humane Society provided a network of volunteer doctors prepared and trained to give on the spot treatment in an emergency. The Society relied on doctors giving their services free of charge, and was totally dependent on voluntary donations. It enjoyed Royal patronage, which brought some material benefits as well as raising esteem.

The impetus for the establishment of the Royal Humane Society came from the large number of accidents on water and ice. The need for BASICS came from the alarming increase in road accident fatalities and serious injuries seen during the 1960s and 1970s. Dr Kenneth Easton, from Catterick, North Yorkshire was the acknowledged father of BASICS. He and his followers argued that if properly trained doctors were called to the scene of serious accidents, then treatment could begin immediately. It did not make sense that you could ask the doctor to visit you if you had bronchitis or a tummy ache, but if you had multiple injuries from a road accident you had to get taken to the doctor. There was a clear need to fill the therapeutic vacuum between the accident happening and definitive medical treatment being started. It was this first hour, the so-called Golden Hour of opportunity, which Easton and his colleagues sought to fill with early effective treatment. It has since been shown that for every twenty-minute delay in starting medical treatment there is a three-fold increase in mortality. The ambulance service of the time was ill-equipped and had little training beyond a basic first aid certificate and a driving licence. They worked on the principle that "Scoop and Run" for help was the best policy. Accident and Emergency departments, or casualties as they were generally known, were also ill-equipped to cope effectively with patients with life-threatening injuries. With a few exceptions, the levels of training and experience of the casualty doctor treating the victims were often inadequate. It was not surprising that for doctors to turn the traditional approach upside down proved difficult in such a conservative and traditional profession. "Scoop and Run" had to be changed to "Stay and Stabilise."

In 1970 a small group of family doctors followed the lead of Kenneth Easton and established themselves as the Chingford and District Accident Unit, the first Immediate Care team for Greater London. Initially they were the only emergency responders equipped with resuscitation equipment to intubate, ventilate and even give an electric shock to restart the heart in a cardiac arrest. Treatment of blood loss and shock could routinely be treated by establishing a drip, and a variety of drugs could be given. Their complementary role to the emergency services quickly became recognised as the number of incidents they attended increased. At first there was considerable hostility from some hospital colleagues and even the ambulance service showed some opposition. Treating casualties properly with pain relief, oxygen, splinting of fractures and the use of a drip meant that equipment was used, got dirty and had to be cleaned afterwards. Gradually the ambulance authorities recognised the message preached by the Immediate Care doctors, and began to press for extended training skills for their ambulance crews.

The Chingford and District Accident Unit—now known as BASICS LONDON to reflect more accurately its area of operation—was involved with its first major incident at the Moorgate train disaster in 1975. The Unit was called upon by Chief Inspector Brian Fisher of the City police, an officer who was well acquainted with Unit doctors from attendance at their regular inter-service meetings. The team, led by Dr Robin Winch, attended on a rota basis from the time of the accident on Friday morning until the following Wednesday, when the last body was recovered and the wreckage was safe. In the report for the Police Commissioner there was specific comment on the need to provide medical cover for the other rescue services even after all live casualties had been removed. Chief Inspector Fisher wrote: "It is of great value that there should be such doctor cover throughout an incident, even after all known survivors have been removed. Without the free and voluntary services of these doctors, casualties amongst the rescue services would not have received such prompt and necessary treatment."

The BASICS LONDON group formed increasingly strong links with their colleagues in the police, fire and ambulance services and with local authority emergency planners. A logical extension of their daily work at road accidents and other incidents was to become involved in disaster response planning. They voluntarily accepted the responsibility for providing a mobile medical team for several hospitals and a specialist Immediate Care team for the London Ambulance Service. They continue to play a key role at London disasters, fully integrated into the capital's emergency services, attending fires, chemical accidents, rail and air accidents in addition to numerous serious road accidents. Often the BASICS doctor has taken on the role of Medical Incident Officer, the doctor responsible for organising medical resources at the scene of a major incident. This was the case at the King's Cross Underground station fire in 1987, when thirty-one people died, including two fire-fighters. Four BASICS members were present until the small hours of the next day. The cause was controversial but, as with many disasters, its effects were far reaching. All smoking was abolished on the

Underground system, a ruling long overdue on health grounds alone. A considerable tightening of the fire safety regulations was also quickly enacted.

Riots and civil disorder of the sort seen at Brixton in 1981 and 1985, Broadwater Farm in Tottenham in 1985, Wapping in 1987 and the Poll Tax riots in Trafalgar Square in 1990 had led to BASICS doctors adapting their role to an altogether different situation. How to recover casualties in a riot, remain neutral and preserve one's safety posed many questions. Special training in protective riot clothing, helmets with visors and new methods of treating victims whilst under attack had to be developed in conjunction with the police.

The train crash at Clapham Junction in December 1988 saw BASICS doctors being flown to the scene in the Metropolitan Police helicopter, the first time this had been used by the doctors in a major accident, although they had been flown to road accidents for some years. BASICS doctors had earned their nickname of "Flying Doctors" long before the Royal London Hospital's Helicopter Emergency Medical Service (HEMS). In his official report on the Clapham disaster, Anthony Hidden QC made specific mention of the role of BASICS and their provision of invaluable medical care on site. He commented that they attended the five casualties who had been trapped the longest, and all five survived. A few months later, in February 1989, the Purley train crash had the emergency services rushing to the scene. It was a reunion for the same team of senior officers and BASICS doctors who had worked together at Clapham.

The sinking of the *Marchioness* presented further challenges to BASICS. Not since the *Princess Alice* disaster had so many people been lost in the river. The search and rescue operation covered a large stretch of the Thames.

In January 1991 the BASICS team were in action again, providing the Medical Incident Officer and a team of doctors at the Cannon Street train crash that killed two passengers and injured more than two hundred. These major incidents, and thousands of less newsworthy accidents, have led to an almost universal acceptance of the importance of pre-hospital care in the work of the emergency ambulance service. Fully-trained paramedics, and BASICS doctors when required, provide a most effective team. The London Ambulance Service publicly acknowledged the importance of pre-hospital care in a statement issued in response to unjustified criticism after the Cannon Street train crash in January 1991:

By ensuring that large numbers of paramedics and ambulance staff reach a major incident within minutes to stabilise casualties and administer life saving treatment before removal to hospital, all injured persons received the best possible level of care in the shortest amount of time.

This was something BASICS doctors had preached and demonstrated at many incidents in the previous twenty years. For far too long, the ambulance service had measured its efficiency at major accidents by recording how quickly the first casualty was removed to hospital. There had been media and public inquiry pressure for this information in the past, and this had added to the haste to get the patient away. It is hopefully now recognised that the first few crews arriving at the scene of an accident should become an on-site treatment team rather than a taxi service. BASICS doctors totally support the concept of extended training for ambulance crews and, together with their hospital colleagues, have been instrumental in establishing training packages for them. The arrival of paramedic trained ambulance crews does not remove the need for a doctor at the scene of some incidents as certain procedures, such as emergency chest drains, the administration of pain-relieving injections, amputations and even confirmation of death can only be carried out by a doctor. The trained Immediate Care doctor and ambulance paramedics working together now give accident victims the best ever chance of survival.

The idea of disaster management has always been slow to gain acceptance in Britain. As recently as the 1960s and 1970s few people in the emergency services and even fewer in the health service had any interest in disasters or major accident planning. The second world war was fading into distant memory, civil defence groups and training had been disbanded. Reorganisation of London boroughs, the formation of the Greater London Council and restructuring of the health service had all contributed to a general apathy about disaster planning. The common attitude was that it is not likely to happen, so why spend time, money and effort in planning how to cope with it?

The one recognised threat to London that did exercise emergency planners' minds was the risk of Thames tidal flooding. The East Coast floods that killed 307 in 1952 were still fresh in the minds of many and the risk of surge floods with the high tides became a greater threat each year. It could have been necessary to evacuate the homes and workplaces of up to a hundred thousand people to non-riparian areas. A special London-wide flood control room was established by the GLC in a tunnel at the Strand. Once the Thames Barrier was completed in 1981 the flood risk to London was supposedly removed, and with the demise of the GLC the underground control was closed down.

In many ways the Moorgate Underground disaster was the jolt needed to make those in authority take action on planning for future emergencies. In 1977, the same year BASICS was founded as an amalgamation of immediate care schemes around the country, the Department of Health issued a guidance document known with affection as HC(77)1. This set out to establish a co-ordinated and standardised response to major accidents and disaster from the Health Service. A few quiet years followed but the series of disasters beginning in 1987 led to further updating and reviewing of plans by all three emergency services, with much better co-operation and standardisation of jargon and procedures. Lessons were learnt at King's Cross, Clapham, Purley and Cannon Street. The Home Office appointed a Civil Emergencies Advisor and the Department of Health produced an updated guide, HC(90)25. Several problems remain unresolved. These include standardisation of the colour of protective clothing worn by rescuers and the method and style of triage labelling—the system of assessing and prioritising casualties according to need.

When it comes to the cause of disasters, be it act of God or human error, lessons from the past are slow to be learnt. Many of our major modern incidents have their forerunners in the nineteenth century. Today's disaster victim can certainly expect better treatment than their unfortunate predecessors.

CHAPTER ONE

The Princess Alice

The *Princess Alice* was the pride of the London Steamboat Company's fleet of pleasure boats. Built in 1865, she was destined for a life of ferrying passengers keen to sample the delights on offer at various pleasure gardens dotted along the banks of the Thames between London and Gravesend. But the flagship's career was dogged by tragedy and in September 1878 she took centre stage in a disaster that holds the grim record of being the worst-ever accident in inland waters in Britain and having the highest death toll of any incident in the country.

Pleasure gardens were a major attraction for the Victorians and the twenty-acre gardens at Rosherville, near Gravesend in Kent, were particularly popular. Attractions included a maze, bear pit, zoo, aviary and botanical gardens. There were slide shows, dances, an indoor theatre seating a thousand people and an open air theatre. The river provided ideal access, and the river trip to the chosen location was seen as part and parcel of the day's fun. Entrance to the gardens cost 6*d* and the boat fare from London, inclusive of entrance fee to the gardens, was a mere 1/9*d*. During the summer season the London Steamboat Company's fleet worked from dawn to dusk and boats were often fully laden with passengers intent on enjoying themselves. During the 1870s the company carried an estimated ten million people each year.

The two hundred-foot long *Princess Alice* was purpose-built for her task. She had been constructed by Caird and Company in 1865 and had undergone various refinements in the years that followed. Early in 1878 she had a complete refit and was licensed to carry a maximum 936 passengers up to Gravesend. This was an unusually large passenger capacity—most pleasure steamers were restricted to around five hundred passengers.

The *Princess Alice* first made newspaper headlines in July 1873, when she was chosen to carry the visiting Shah of Persia on a special tour of the West India Docks. The vessel was bedecked with bunting for the occasion and must have been in pristine condition to be selected for such auspicious duties.

Three months later, in October 1873, she had her first brush with death. A waterman's boat had become lost in dense fog when it was ferrying men from Woolwich to their workplaces on the north side of the river. The little boat suddenly came to the stern of the *Princess Alice*, moored at her usual spot off the shore at Woolwich. Despite the men's frantic efforts to push themselves free of the saloon steamer, the fast-ebbing tide drew them under and the boat capsized.

Nine of the eleven men and boys in the boat were drowned, but it was several weeks before all the bodies were recovered. The workers had undertaken the perilous trip because they had little choice. They needed to reach their workplaces, at the Beckton Gas Works and Henley's Telegraph factory in North Woolwich, as they could ill-afford to lose a day's pay. They would normally have crossed the Thames on the Great Eastern Railway Company's ferry boat, but this never ran when fog made crossing treacherous. So, like hundreds of their colleagues, they paid 2*d* each to a waterman willing to risk his boat and his neck in an attempt to reach the opposite shore in safety.

Only the waterman and one passenger survived and made it to shore. News of the disaster spread rapidly around Woolwich. No one knew the names of those who had been in the boat, and worried families had to wait until the end of the day's work before they knew whether their loved ones were safe. The tight-knit community raised £777 to help bereaved families, and the incident was one of several that eventually led to the construction of the Woolwich foot tunnel.

However, the loss of the workmen was to be eclipsed by the far greater and more horrendous fate that was to befall the *Princess Alice* at Tripcock Point a few years later. The Point was a notorious stretch of the river. In September 1867 it had been the scene of a fatal collision between the Woolwich Steamboat Company's pleasure boat the *Metis* and an iron screw, the *Wentworth*. The *Wentworth* hit the *Metis* on her starboard side, burying the whole of her bows into the pleasure steamer's hull and cutting the vessel in two. Fortunately, the ships were close to land and the *Wentworth* drove the forepart of the stricken *Metis* up to the shore. The aft part of the vessel quickly sank, but the water was relatively shallow and the wreck settled flush with the river's surface. Fortune had placed several small vessels nearby, and rescue efforts were rapid and largely successful. The final death toll was just four, but the incident should have rung warning bells that could have saved the *Princess Alice* and her doomed passengers.

At the subsequent inquest jurors found both vessels to blame. They commented, with commendable foresight:

> The investigation...has brought to light the existence of a state of things on the river which no man in his senses can contemplate without a shudder. It appears there are no rules whatever to guide captains of vessels. All is left to the chapter of accidents—to the chance that vessels will somehow or other manage to pass one another without coming into collision.

The jury stated regulations should be prepared for the navigation of the river, and the coroner, Charles Carttar was instructed to pass on their observations to the Thames Conservancy Board, the body responsible for navigation. Carttar was later to preside over the marathon *Princess Alice* hearing.

The third of September 1878 seemed like a routine Tuesday for the *Princess Alice* and her crew of fifteen men. She left the Old Swan Pier, Woolwich at about 10:30 AM and called at Blackwall, North Woolwich, Rosherville and Gravesend on her way to Sheerness. The trip was problem-free. One passenger, John Eyres, was an able seaman, and despite his lack of experience in navigating the Thames he agreed to take the helmsman's place for the return journey. The helmsman, Hogwood, wished to stay at Gravesend and the stand-in arrangement with Eyres was approved by the captain of the *Princess Alice*, William Grinstead. Eyres expected 4/- for his services.

The paddle steamer left Sheerness at about 4:15 PM with an estimated 487 ticket holders. She picked up more passengers at Gravesend and by the time she left Rosherville Pier at 6:15 PM around 652 tickets had been sold. This figure would not include the many young children who were entitled to travel free of charge. The total number of passengers aboard the *Princess Alice* as she left Rosherville Pier was probably around 750.

It was a perfect September evening, and as dusk fell a band played and passengers sang and danced. Captain Grinstead remained on the bridge, calling out orders to Eyres at the wheel. Eyres had never steered a vessel as long as the *Princess Alice* and was inexperienced at coping with the treacherous Thames waters. All he had to do, however, was to obey the Captain's orders, and Captain Grinstead was a highly skilled and experienced pleasure boat captain. There was some consternation when the steamer encountered a brigantine and was obliged to reverse her engines to avoid a collision. However, the two ships passed safely and the passengers settled to enjoy their cruise. The *Princess Alice* approached Tripcocks Point at about 7:45 PM.

Meanwhile the *Bywell Castle*, an 890-ton collier, left Millwall Dock at about 6:30 PM on the first leg of her trip home to Newcastle. Her regular duties took her on trips between Newcastle and the Eastern Mediterranean, taking coal and returning with cotton, beans and wheat. She had been at Millwall for a repaint and was carrying a load of ballast. The ship was powered by a four-bladed screw. Her master, Captain Harrison, was unfamiliar with the Thames and had hired a pilot, Mr Christopher Dix, to steer the vessel to Gravesend for the fee of £2.4s.2d. She reached Tripcocks Point just as the *Princess Alice* was approaching from the opposite direction.

As the *Princess Alice* and the *Bywell Castle* drew closer the pleasure boat's crew sensed the impending danger. George Long was the first mate on board the *Princess Alice*, and the highest-ranking crew member to survive the collision. He was acting as look-out on the fore saloon. In a deposition made shortly after the disaster to the Receiver of Wrecks for the Port of London, he told how the *Bywell Castle* could be seen advancing ominously in the evening haze as the pleasure steamer rounded Tripcocks Point:

> Our engines were immediately stopped. The other vessel appeared to be coming down upon us stern on, and looming in the evening haze like a great black phantom, gave us a foreboding of the unhappy disaster. She was then about 150 yards distant, and each vessel was of course rapidly nearing the other.

The *Princess Alice* carried just two lifeboats and twelve lifebuoys. Realising collision was unavoidable, Long rushed to free one of the lifeboats. Events moved so rapidly he had no time to cut the ropes before the two ships collided and the *Princess Alice* sank.

Passengers also became aware of their imminent peril as they saw the massive hull of the *Bywell Castle* bearing down on the *Princess Alice*. Peter Haden, an engineer of Cambridge Heath Road, Hackney, was on board with his mother and her servant. He later told the inquest:

> The whistle blew and the people on the fore saloon deck were making a sort of buzz—not actually a screaming or hallooing or anything of that

1   *(Right) William Grinstead, Captain of the Princess Alice*

2   *(Below) The collision between the Princess Alice and the Bywell Castle. Courtesy Museum in Docklands Project.*

sort, but I could hear that there was something going on wrong and I ran forward as far as the steering wheel to see what was the matter.

As soon as I got to the steering wheel I saw the Captain lean forwards and put his hands to his mouth and halloo, 'Where are you coming to?' as loud as ever he could call. I looked ahead and I saw a vessel in the distance. She seemed to be coming straight down the stream. I kept my eye on the vessel and saw that immediately the Captain signalled to her she altered her course instantly and came right fair on us.

The moment she ploughed her way in there seemed to be no shock whatever as she entered us. She came just as you would push your fist through a band box.

The apparent gentleness of the impact belied the devastating effects of the collision. The *Bywell Castle* had ripped through seventeen feet of the *Princess Alice's* twenty-foot breadth with the ease of a knife cutting through a loaf. Many passengers were oblivious to their terrifying plight.

Mr Pittivant of Stoke Newington was sitting in the saloon when the ships collided. He told reporters:

There was a kind of vibration and I could feel the vessels had come together. The tables down below rocked to and fro as if they had been electrified. The glasses tumbled about, and the ornaments came down. The ladies set up screaming, and somebody tried to pacify them by saying that probably the machinery had become deranged

In fact, the *Princess Alice* was rapidly splitting in two. As the *Bywell Castle* reversed away from the stricken pleasure steamer, water rushed into the fatal breach and, within seconds, the extra pressure caused the vessel to break apart. Pittivant rushed to the deck and watched, along with Peter Haden and other horrified passengers, as the forepart of the *Princess Alice* disappeared like a stone. Steam filled the air as water entered the engines and the stern of the vessel sank rapidly. It was all over within four minutes.

Mr George Haynes, of Bow Road, Bow, graphically recalled the nightmare to a reporter from *The Illustrated London News* (14 September):

I cannot describe the scene of confusion and maddening perplexity which seized upon everybody. In a minute or so I could see distinctly the fore part of our vessel sink, the middle going down like a plummet, raising the head of the vessel into the air, and as it sunk the poor people seemed to be shot out as if down a shaft into the gulf below.

Then our part of the vessel went down from the paddle-box aft, the people from the saloon and after deck being also shot into the water, like those at the fore.

Haynes loaned his knife to a crewman desperately trying to release a lifeboat. In the panic, the precious boat was let down into the water without a single passenger and drifted away with the tide. Haynes gripped tightly to the ship's rudder, and was one of the last to fall into the water.

Some passengers managed to save themselves by grabbing a hold on the *Bywell Castle*. Mr John Lesley, of Yorkshire, was close to the spot where the collier had struck the pleasure steamer, and later wrote to the newspaper:

Looking up at the bow of the vessel that had done the mischief, I saw a loop of cable hanging over, and in the hope of reaching it I tried to make my way to the paddle-boxes. The scene on the deck was now one of the greatest confusion, the passengers rushing hither and thither frantic with terror. One woman caught hold of me, and exclaimed, 'Good heavens, what shall I do? Save me!' I told her I could not help her, and, releasing myself with great difficulty from her grasp, I rushed to the paddle-boxes just in time to spring up and catch the cable and climb by its aid on to the deck of the *Bywell Castle*.

Lesley made his escape with seconds to spare. Safely on the larger boat, he threw ropes over the side to assist others trapped on the sinking steamer. "While doing this I saw the fore part of the doomed ship go down," he wrote.

A fearful cry arose from the struggling mass of human beings in the water. The sight was terrible and one that I shall never forget. The stern end of the boat soon followed, and then there was another frightful scene, heart-rending in the extreme.

The river became a mass of writhing humanity, struggling against all odds in hope of salvation. Few Victorians learned to swim and very few passengers could even attempt the three hundred-yard journey that would take them safely to shore. More than seven hundred souls thrashed and choked in the water, grabbing wreckage and each other in frantic efforts to save themselves. Women were clothed in long, cumbersome dresses that must have further reduced their minimal chances of survival. The hopelessly inadequate emergency equipment together with the speed at which the *Princess Alice* sank and the vast number of men, women and children thrown into the river at the same spot ensured an horrendous death toll.

The crew of the *Bywell Castle* threw down ropes, but only a handful were plucked from the seething mass. Henry Totman survived by grasping hold of a buoy thrown from the *Bywell Castle*. He later told a reporter from *The Globe* (4 September):

> The *Bywell Castle* was such a big thing. Looking up at her she seemed to be like a castle. The shrieks were something indescribable. It was something terrible to see 400 or 500 trying to get one rope.

Philip Hilson of Wandsworth Road, Wandsworth, managed to save himself by grasping a rope from the *Bywell Castle*. His wife was less fortunate, as he told a reporter from the *Daily News* (9 September):

> Seeing a rope hanging from the ship I twisted it round my arm and hand. By this time I could feel the ship going out from below us. I swung by the rope in front of the bows of the *Bywell Castle*, my wife still hanging around my neck. I was swinging clear of the water, and slipped to the end of the rope in hope of touching the water, but I was unable to do so.
>
> My wife never said a word all the time I was hanging by the rope. I tried to pull myself up, and I got my foot against the side of the ship and walked up hand over hand. When I had got my right knee on the gunwale I put one hand behind me to support my poor wife, and to give some relief to myself, as I was almost being choked. I said, 'Thank heaven, Polly, we have got to the top.' She then eased herself by releasing hold of my neck. She said 'Oh Philip, I cannot hold on any longer,' and she then dropped back into the water. After I had somewhat recovered, I got hold of the rope and slid down again to the end of it in the hope of seeing my poor wife, but she had disappeared. I cried for help, and I was pulled on board by some members of the crew.

People standing on shore or in a few boats anchored nearby witnessed the disaster. Small boats were launched and set off to rescue survivors. Mr Abraham Dennis saw the end of the *Princess Alice* from his barge, the *Bonetta*. He commented to reporters:

> I hardly know how to describe the scene, it was too dreadful. I can compare the *Princess Alice* to nothing else than a cloud. One moment she was there and the next moment—gone.
>
> I can compare the people to nothing else than a flock of sheep in the water. The river seemed full of drowning people.

The barge master lowered a boat and set off to do what he could to rescue people. "I went in the midst of them," he said,

> but from their frantic exertions to save themselves I hardly thought I should get out again alive. The shrieks and shouts of the people were piteous to hear, and would have quite unnerved me but for my desire to rescue some of the poor creatures.

J.S. Burnett, of the barge *Elizabeth*, also rowed to pick up survivors. He told reporters:

> I immediately launched a boat and rowed to the scene, but was nearly swamped by the crowds, who, shrieking and drowning, made a last struggle for life, and it was necessary to quench their hopes by knocking them off the sides with the oars.

Burnett's men dragged eleven men, women and children into the safety of their boat before making a hasty retreat.

Charles Handley, captain of the barge *Chance*, was alerted to the catastrophe by the screams of those struggling in the water. He set off in a rowing boat with his mate William Robinson. The scene shocked him. "I shall never forget the sight I saw," he said.

> The whole river seemed alive with heads and hair. It looked like a river full of coconuts. Some people were holding on to forms, others to chairs and pieces of wood. A stout gentleman came close to me, and I grabbed at him at once, but he was so heavy that he nearly pulled us over. He was like a madman and would not be quiet. I ordered him to sit down in the boat, but he would not, and my mate and I had to push him down.

> Then another gentleman cried out, 'Twenty pounds to save my life.' The promise of money did not influence me, but I seized hold of him, but he was heavy. We tugged and tugged away and at last we got him in; and whilst we were doing this four little boys floated by us, and the beseeching looks were something dreadful. We saved them, thank God.

> Oh, how I wish I had a bigger boat as I could have saved so many! When we got to the pier the boat was so full of water, and it was with great difficulty we saved her from sinking. So loud were the screams and cries for help that we could not hear ourselves speak.

The stark fact was there were too few boats to cope with the vast number of drowning people. Even the *Bywell Castle*, a large ship on the very spot of the disaster, could only manage to save fifty-odd souls. Some of these, like Eyres the helmsman, climbed onto her as she was

locked into the *Princess Alice*, others hauled themselves up by ropes
thrown over by the crew. The *Bywell Castle* launched three of her own
rescue boats, but the procedure took time—and time was all too scarce
for those struggling in the water. In a statement to the Receiver of
Wrecks, Captain Harrison said:

> The first two boats were immediately swamped by the people, who floated
> round like bees, making the water almost black with their heads and hats
> and clothes. The lifeboat, the last boat launched, was, however, unable to
> save many lives, most of the people having by this time sunk exhausted.
>
> The three boats hold 70 persons but I should say they did not save more
> than 40. They rowed immediately ashore, and afterwards returned to the
> ship, but by this time all was still, and there was nothing to show how
> many hundred death struggles had taken place there just before.

The screams and pleas for help from the hundreds of men, women
and children thrashing for life in the river drifted across to a school
room at Creek Mouth in Barking, where a hundred children were
enjoying a special "treat day" organised by the local curate and Mrs
Bloomfield, wife of the archdeacon. The curate told a newspaper
reporter:

> The screams and shrieks of the poor victims were heard plainly for some
> five minutes by those outside the school room. Those who were on the
> river wall, about 50 yards from the school, distinctly saw arms wildly
> flung up as the moon lighted up the waves, rippling over those who
> should never more see home.

The "treat" was quickly abandoned and the children, offspring of the
three hundred or so employees of Lawes Chemical Manure Factory,
were sent home. The school room was transformed into an emergency
centre, as rescue boats began to land with survivors and the dead. Tea
laid out for the happy youngsters was given instead to the exhausted
survivors, many of whom were grieving for wives, husbands and
children known to be lost. The eighteen to twenty survivors brought in
were given dry clothing from the villagers' meagre stores and sent to
spend the night in the tiny workmen's cottages. Villagers gave up their
beds and their food to their unexpected guests. Thirty bodies were laid
out in a shed at the chemical factory.

At Beckton Gasworks, manager George Trewby and his assistant Mr
Bush also heard the screams and set off in a boat. Trewby took those he

able to save back to his home. Fires were lit, and changes of clothes offered along with brandy and nourishment.

The *Princess Alice*'s sister ship, the *Duke of Teck*, was travelling close behind her and the *Duke*'s passengers and crew witnessed the collision. They arrived at the scene just ten minutes after the incident, but even that was too late to be of much assistance to the drowning mass. The accident happened at the point where the northern and southern outfall sewers discharged into the Thames and the river was full of raw, putrid sewage. The heavy pollution did nothing to improve the chances of those floundering in the water. Within twenty minutes of the collision the Thames had sucked in its victims. All that remained as testament to the horrendous events that had taken place were floating pieces of debris from the ship, and the hats, caps, cloaks and other personal belongings of its unfortunate passengers. Captain Grinstead went down with his ship. His son John, brother Charles and sister-in-law Jane had been on board and drowned with him.

Crew and passengers from the *Duke of Teck* hauled in bodies, dead and alive, and the Captain, a Mr Funge, took them to Woolwich before returning to put his ship on guard over the wreck throughout the night. One of the first to be picked up by the *Duke of Teck* was Mrs Emily Towse, 32, wife of the London Steamboat Company's superintendent, Mr William Towse. The poor lady was barely alive when she was rescued and died before the boat could reach shore. Four of the family's children (Frederick, Edgar, Barnard and Winifred), Mrs Towse's sister Helen Wearing, mother Eliza Hooper, cousin Ellen Warmy and the family nursemaid Mary Barker were also drowned. William Towse had not joined the outing and first heard of the disaster when the *Duke of Teck* arrived at Woolwich with his wife's body on board. During the days that followed he overcame his own grief to help deal with the aftermath of the tragedy.

When the *Duke of Teck* docked at Woolwich the crew told of the *Princess Alice*'s sinking. Despite the lack of television and radio, the news travelled with astonishing speed. Before long the offices of the Steamboat Company at Roff's Wharf in Woolwich and in the City were besieged by anxious crowds desperate for news of their friends and families suspected to have been on the river. Those in charge were forced to set aside their shock and disbelief at the scale of the tragedy and devise a plan for dealing with the consequences. Charles Carttar, the Kent coroner, was immediately notified. The Steamboat Company sent extra staff to Woolwich to help deal with enquiries and extra police were drafted. Plumstead workhouse prepared a hundred beds in readiness to receive survivors, though pitifully few of these were needed. Teams of doctors, including Drs Fullar, Mitchell, Coleman, Howard, Sharpe, Lett and Smith arrived to give any necessary treatment to survivors. Local churchmen made their way to the steamboat offices to give what comfort they could to the distraught relatives.

Initially, and inevitably, the situation was confused, and the true death toll for this disaster will never be known. Around 640 bodies were dragged from the river in the days and weeks that followed, and just over a hundred survivors were accounted for. There were no accurate records to show the number of passengers on board; many survivors may have returned to their homes, their presence on board never recorded. There were no accurate lists of survivors, and the dead were being collected at different spots on both sides of the river.

The boardroom at the Steamboat Company offices at Roff's Wharf was turned into a temporary mortuary, and the floor and balcony were soon covered by bodies. Police officers carefully labelled each corpse with an identification number and the relatives and friends waiting outside were allowed to view the dead in the hope of identifying those feared lost. Bodies continued to be brought to shore throughout the night and were collected in public houses, warehouses, factories, sheds and municipal offices in Kent and Essex; more were brought in by the hour. Crowds jostled to catch a glimpse of partially covered corpses as carts brought them from the shore to their temporary resting places. By the next morning the authorities realised that fears about the scale of the disaster were fully justified.

Lists of known survivors were finally posted on the doors of the Steamboat company. The same lists were published in the *Times* and other newspapers. Those who failed to find the names they sought were forced on a depressing and heart-rending trek around the various temporary "mortuaries." Many friends and relatives had to make the journey repeatedly as more bodies arrived. Ferrymen taking people across the river waived the fares if their passengers appeared too poor or upset to pay.

Something needed to be done to alleviate distress and bring some order to the situation. The solution came from Captain Barrington of the

3 *Recovering bodies from the river. Courtesy Museum in Docklands Project.*
4 *Relatives identifying bodies of victims*

Woolwich Dockyard. He offered the use of large sheds, each capable of holding up to two hundred bodies. This centralised operations and saved relatives the trauma of travelling around in their search. Fortunately, Woolwich was a barrack town, and soldiers from several corps volunteered their services to help deal with the bodies. Many were from the Army Services Corps and the Army Hospital Corps, and had dealt with mass casualties in battles. The army had its own supply of ambulances and bearers, and so coped efficiently with retrieving bodies from the boats.

Some were to profit from the catastrophe. Captain Fitzgerald, the Woolwich harbourmaster, paid watermen £2 per day to join the search for bodies and they received a bonus of 5/– for each corpse recovered. The watermen congregated around the wreck of the *Princess Alice* and used hooks to drag up bodies close to the surface. Others searched further down river for victims who had been washed along by the tide. With such rich pickings on offer there were many unseemly fights over "fishing rights." Bodies recovered by the watermen were loaded onto the tug *Heron* and taken to Woolwich. Still more bodies were taken in by police steamers.

At the Dockyard a grim routine was established. Chief Inspector Lucas was in charge of operations in the sheds allocated to receive the bodies, and he was assisted by Inspectors Phillips and Dawkins. As each body arrived it was numbered and a brief description was recorded in a book. The same number was marked on the clothes and any other property discovered on the body. Smaller items were placed in a box with a glass lid and, again, this was marked with the allocated number before being taken to a separate area to await identification by friends and relatives. The corpse was then washed and taken to another shed and placed in line with scores of others. Relatives and friends walked along the lines hoping to recognise those they were searching for. Bodies which had been claimed were sent to a third shed to await removal for burial.

The tragedy fascinated the country and, for the sightseers at least, a holiday atmosphere soon superseded the initial shock. Crowds rapidly became a major problem, and an extra 230 constables were brought in to maintain order. The collection of bodies attracted ghouls like a magnet, but the police did their best to ensure only those who had lost loved ones in the disaster were allowed access to the makeshift mortuary. Police had less control in the streets of Woolwich, where mobs gathered in hope of catching glimpse of a corpse and to ogle at the distress of the bereaved. Sightseers were also a major problem across the river in North Woolwich, where they flocked by the trainload to gawk at the spot where the *Princess Alice* had sunk, and at the watermen recovering the dead. Policemen were posted at Beckton Gasworks to prevent the mob taking a shortcut along the river bank to Barking Creek.

The calamity did little to deter travellers using the pleasure steamers. Only two days after the sinking the *Princess Alice*'s sister ship, the *Albert Edward*, sailed obligingly close to the spot of the disaster. She was crammed with passengers eager to survey the scene. The problems caused by the inquisitive mobs were to worsen a few days later when the wreck of the *Princess Alice* was finally beached.

The morning after the disaster, Wednesday 4 September, the Board of Trade announced it would be holding an inquiry and sent two officials to Woolwich to take statements. The wreck became the property of the Thames Conservators. It was feared many bodies were trapped inside, and the wreck was clearly a danger to shipping. The Conservators quickly acted to lift her from the river. Mr Charles Wood, Superintendent of the Conservancy, took charge of operations.

Meanwhile, Carttar, the 66-year-old veteran coroner, began to consider the enormous task ahead. It was immediately apparent to him that quick identification and burial of the bodies was essential. The weather was hot, and refrigeration facilities were non-existent. The bodies recovered were already showing signs of decomposition and he knew they could present a very serious health hazard. On Wednesday afternoon he opened the inquest at the Alexandra Hall in Woolwich for the sole purpose of taking identification evidence and allowing at least some burials to take place.

The identification evidence taken revealed the devastation the calamity had brought to hundreds of families. Fifty women, elderly members of a Bible class from the Cowcross Mission in West Smithfield, had been on board. Just one had survived. Alfred Alesbury and his wife Eliza, of Hackney, were enjoying a day out with their five children. All perished. Inspector King, of the Thames Police, was returning from Gravesend with his wife, two children, father, mother and brother. He was thrown into the water and swam for the shore with a woman he believed to be his wife. The woman was, in fact, a stranger. All members of King's family had drowned.

The enormity of the disaster shocked the Victorians. They were accustomed to hearing of large number of fatalities in battles abroad, but these involved soldiers who were expected to risk their life for their Queen and country. Those on board the *Princess Alice* were holiday-makers, women and children. Pleasure steamers were a favoured means of transport and amusement. The Thames was part of everyday life, a well-known and loved feature of London. Familiarity with the river and boats bred contempt and potential danger was overlooked.

On Thursday 5 September, the South Eastern Railway agreed to take claimed bodies direct from the Dockyard to London Bridge free of charge, and many relatives made use of the arrangement. Numerous bodies at the yard, however, remained unclaimed and Carttar and Mr John Taylor, chairman of the local Board of Health, were becoming increasingly concerned with their condition. On Friday Taylor ordered fifty graves to be dug at Plumstead Cemetery, about two miles from Woolwich, and Carttar warned that bodies unclaimed by 10:00 AM the following day would be treated as unknown and buried by the parish. This was a drastic but necessary step. Being "buried by the parish" was seen as the ultimate shame, but it was essential to dispose of the rapidly decomposing bodies as quickly as possible. In many cases whole families had been wiped out in the tragedy and it was clearly unlikely they would be identified until someone realised they were missing and considered the possibility they may have perished on the ill-fated ship. Photographs were taken of the unidentified dead, and each was marked with the number allocated to the body, its clothes and other property. These records were carefully stored to allow identification later. The coffin was marked with the same number and the location where the body had been found. The same details were later inscribed on the cross marking the grave of each unidentified person. Thirty women were brought in from the Woolwich Workhouse and given the unenviable task of placing the unclaimed bodies into "shells"—basic coffins—ready for burial.

The Woolwich Board of Health were responsible for the burials. Board members were anxious to be seen to carry out their duties with a generosity and kindness that reflected public concern towards the victims, a concern not usually evident at "pauper" burials. The first burials for the unidentified took place at Plumstead Cemetery, near Plumstead Common, on Monday 9 September. A mounted policeman led the procession, followed by the churchwarden and overseers of Woolwich and a deputation from the Board of Health. Four military

5   *Wreck of the Princess Alice. Courtesy Museum in Docklands Project.*

6   *Burial of the unknown dead at Woolwich Cemetery. Courtesy Museum in Docklands Project.*

wagons, carrying thirteen coffins, followed behind. The route was lined with an estimated six to seven thousand spectators and the cemetery was packed. The police posted an inspector, five sergeants and fifty constables in the cemetery, but the crowds were quiet and well behaved. The Rector of Woolwich, the Reverend Adelbert Anson, read the burial service, and as the coffins were placed in their graves a kindly Miss Broughton placed a single flower on each. The scene was repeated later in the day and in the days that followed. Altogether 120 victims were buried before being identified. The meticulous police records enabled relatives and friends to claim 103 bodies in the weeks and months that followed, and many were exhumed for re-burial closer to their homes.

Bodies were still being recovered and Carttar was deluged with advice from an obviously intrigued and doubtless well-intentioned public. Many of these letters, along with transcripts of the inquest into the disaster, remain intact at the Greater London Records Office. One helpful soul thought he had the answer to the problem of bodies decomposing. He wrote to Carttar:

> Enclosed I beg to forward particulars of my patent fresh meat preservative, well-known to most butchers at the Metropolitan Meat Market—no doubt many of the bodies could be preserved this way.

Mr Aldridge, a plumber, decorator and wholesale oilman came up with a suggestion to speed up the trickle of bodies coming to the surface. "It occurred to me," he wrote,

> that if a heavy piece of cannon was fired over the river where it is supposed some of the bodies are laying that it might bring some to the surface. I have seen it tried and have seen a body rise almost perpendicular.

Some of the suggestions were helpful, but Carttar had little time to deal with them. On Monday 9 September, the *Globe* reported:

> The coroner said he was overwhelmed with correspondence containing absurd suggestions, and if his correspondents would stop their letters he should be much obliged.

As the funerals for the first unidentified bodies were taking place, the Thames Conservancy men were reaching a crucial stage in their efforts to raise the wreck. By midnight both sections had been beached at Woolwich Arsenal and at daybreak on Tuesday the gruesome task of searching for trapped bodies began. Few were found, because most had been washed into the river by the tides.

Vast crowds now gathered to pore over the wreckage. Hundreds of thousands flocked in trains from London and the mass was liberally laced with pickpockets intent on making the most of the golden opportunity presented. Rowing boats scattered the river, filled with "tourists" desperate for a good view. Passing London Steamboat Company pleasure steamers paused at the scene to ensure fascinated passengers could satisfy their curiosity.

Not everyone in the crowds could contain their excitement, and there were many unruly scenes as people jostled to tear off pieces of the wreck to keep as relics. Arthur Mills and Richard Shephard, both of Millwall, were sentenced to fourteen days' hard labour after being found guilty of violently assaulting two police constables during an attempt to grab mementos from the *Princess Alice*. The men, along with others, had boarded the principal Conservancy barge at the scene and became violent when the two police constables tried to order them off. The *Kentish Independent* later reported (12 October):

> The whole of the ornamental carvings, and nearly everything that could be chipped or wrenched off the saloons, paddle boxes and other parts of the ship, have been carried off as curiosities by visitors and the men who have had charge of the wreck have found the employment so satisfactory that they positively refused on Saturday to resign their duty to the steamboat crew who were sent down to take possession.

By 11 September, eight days after the tragedy, around 630 bodies had been recovered. No post-mortems were held and some locals suspected several foul deeds had escaped detection because of the police force's overwhelming preoccupation with the disaster. We will never know if canny murderers dumped their unfortunate victims in the Thames to be passed off as casualties of the *Princess Alice*.

By 16 September the stream of bodies into the Woolwich Dockyard had almost come to a halt, and Carttar had taken most of the identification evidence. He was a highly competent coroner with more than forty years' experience and determined to stand firm against outside pressure to bring proceedings to a speedy conclusion. This was, after all, no everyday inquest. The list of dead formed a scroll that was yards long. Carttar felt strongly that no stone should be left unturned in pursuing the cause of an accident that killed well over six hundred people. The jury heard 116 witnesses, and the verbatim report of proceedings contain a marathon 600,000-plus words. Carttar's determination to scrutinise every detail, and witness cross-examinations by lawyers representing the *Bywell Castle* and the *Princess Alice* meant proceedings at times seemed interminable. Captain Harrison, of the *Bywell Castle*, wrote up his log soon after the collision, when the collier lay anchored off the wreck. His description of events provide a good and concise summary of the *Bywell Castle*'s view of the affair.

> Being about centre of the reach observed an excursion steamer coming up Barking Reach, showing her red and masthead lights, when we ported our helm to get over towards Tripcocks Point. As the vessels neared, observed that the other steamer had ported, and immediately afterwards saw that she had starboarded and was trying to cross our bows, showing her green light close under the port bow. Seeing collision inevitable, stopped our engine and reversed full speed, when the two vessels collided, the bow of the *Bywell Castle* cutting into the other steamer which was crowded with passengers, with a dreadful crash.

The highest-ranking surviving crew member of the *Princess Alice* was George Long, the chief mate. In a statement to the Board of Trade he said:

> On rounding Tripcocks Point the vessel's helm had been starboarded to pass a screw steamer bound down the river, and we still remained so, and at that moment we saw the vessel which proved to be the *Bywell Castle*. Our engines were immediately stopped. The other vessel appeared to be coming down upon us stern on....

Long stated the *Bywell Castle* ported and came directly towards the *Princess Alice*. He had no doubt the *Bywell Castle*'s decision to port was the sole cause of the accident. He gave the same story at the inquest.

The evidence dragged on. Carttar allowed each witness to be cross-examined by lawyers representing the two ships and by his nineteen-man jury. The jury foreman, a Mr Harrington, became noted for his relentless and often pointless questioning. The inquest papers at the Greater London Records Office contain an anonymous poem that must have been slipped to Carttar:

> The foreman stood at the Town Hall door,
> Smoking a two-penny weed
> When up came the jury and softly said
> You naughty old man take heed.

Oh! When will you stop old man they said
Oh! When will you stop said they
When I've asked 50,000 more
Of the silliest questions hi hi !
Of the silliest questions hi hi !

He talked and he jawed in his grizzling way
Till he couldn't jaw any more
And then the jury boiled him down
And gave him away to the poor
And gave him away to the poor.

Carttar was meticulous. Every aspect had to be painstakingly analysed, every rumour explored. The court spent some time considering the story of a drunken sailor who had turned up at Erith on the night of the disaster and had made wild accusations about drunkenness on board the *Bywell Castle*. He told locals the disaster had been "caused by the booze." The sailor, Purcell, had collapsed in a pub before telling of Captain Harrison's and pilot Dix's alleged drinking session. There was no truth in his story, but Carttar obviously felt he had to prove its fabrication, and called several witnesses to confirm that Harrison and Dix were sober at the time of the collision. Much to Carttar's chagrin, the Board of Trade opened its inquiry on 14 October and its findings, putting the blame firmly on the *Princess Alice*, were announced on 6 November. This was eight days before Carttar's jurors finally left the court to consider their own verdict. Carttar made his anger crystal clear in his summing up. He said it seemed to him it would have been more courteous on the part of the Board of Trade, and more conducive to the administration of justice had its decision, concerned as it was with pounds, shillings and pence, been withheld until the conclusions of his court had been known. He argued he had a right to complain as the action of the Board had in some measure interfered with his court's freedom of judgement.

As the inquest went on it had become obvious Carttar felt the *Princess Alice* was at fault and he pulled no punches in his summing up. He was particularly concerned at the ship's manning levels—fifteen men, including four firemen and two engineers. He told the jury:

The evidence which we have had here has not been for one moment contradicted but, on the contrary, it is evidence given from the ship herself; and I think that a more deplorable or more unfortunate state of things could not possibly have existed elsewhere, or could not possibly have been believed by the public or by anybody travelling by her.

Here is a vessel sent out, I assume and take for granted, fully competent to do the journey, but to do that properly I take for granted it is necessary that she should be properly manned.

He said a perfect stranger had been allowed to take the wheel and those posted on look-out were mere lads of 18 and 21 years. "I apprehend," he went on, "that we should every one of us rather walk away from the ship and stop at home than run so dangerous a risk in the matter."

Carttar finished his summing up by 5:00 PM and the jurors began their deliberations. On several occasions they called for Carttar to clarify points, and as the night wore on it became clear they were having difficulty in reaching a verdict. At 4:30 AM they called again for Carttar's assistance, and he remained with them until 7:10 AM when the verdict was finally given. It was a majority verdict, supported by fifteen of the nineteen jurors. One of the dissenters was Harrington, the jury foreman. The verdict returned was:

> That the deceased William Beachey and others died on the 3rd of September from drowning in the River Thames, occasioned by the collision that took place between the steam vessel called the *Bywell Castle* and the steam vessel called the *Princess Alice*, whereby the *Princess Alice* was cut in two and sank, such collision not being wilful; that the *Bywell Castle* did not take the necessary precautions in time of easing, stopping, and reversing her engines, and also that the *Princess Alice* contributed to the collision by not stopping her engines and going astern; and not by the hands of violence or any person or persons whomsoever. All such collisions, in the opinion of the jury, might be in future avoided if proper and stringent rules and regulations were laid down for the regulation of steam traffic on the River Thames.

There were four riders:

> 1. The jury unanimously consider that the *Princess Alice* was on the 3rd of September last river worthy.
> 2. Also unanimously, that the *Princess Alice* was not properly and efficiently manned.
> 3. Also unanimously, that in the opinion of the jury the number of passengers that were on the *Princess Alice* at the time of the collision was greater than was prudent.

4. Also unanimously, that in the opinion of the jury more appliances for saving life should be provided for passenger steamers of the class of the *Princess Alice.*

The London Steamboat Company brought an action against Messrs Hall of Newcastle, the owners of the *Bywell Castle*, and Messrs Hall made a counter claim against the Steamboat Company. The case was heard by the Court of Admiralty, presided over by Sir Phillimore at Trinity House. The judgement was delivered on 11 December, and blamed both vessels for the collision. The *Princess Alice* was at fault for going starboard, when she should have continued on her course and passed the *Bywell Castle* port to port; and the *Bywell Castle* was at fault because when she saw the *Princess Alice* had starboarded, she ported, putting her on direct collision course with the pleasure steamer. The court agreed the *Bywell Castle* would have hit the *Princess Alice* even if she hadn't ported, but they said the damage would have been far less and would not have caused the vessel to sink. The case went to the Court of Appeal and was heard by Lord Justices James, Brett and Cotton, assisted by two nautical assessors. The verdict came on 15 July 1879, and put the blame squarely on the *Princess Alice*. The appeal judges reached the unanimous decision that although the *Bywell Castle's* last minute manoeuvre, to port, had been a mistake it had not contributed to the catastrophe.

News of the disaster filled papers at home and abroad for days on end, and the episode sparked long and angry arguments into navigation laws on the Thames. So who was to blame? On 6 September, a few days after the tragedy, a leader in the *Times Weekly Edition* had commented:

It seems not unlikely that, however lamentable the event may be, and however certainly it ought to have been avoided, it will yet prove to be of the number of those for which no-one in particular can be held to blame. The wonder indeed is, not that such an accident should have happened, but rather that it should have been so long escaped. Collisions in the Thames are of incessant occurrence. From whatever cause they are brought about, from careless navigation, or whatever else, they are to be counted literally by scores.

The editorial was painfully true. Near misses were part and parcel of life on the Thames. Only days after the sinking of the *Princess Alice* another Steamboat Company paddle steamer, the *Ariel*, was run into by a barge as she was between London Bridge and Cherry Garden Pier on her way to Greenwich. The passengers on the pleasure boat were, understandably, panic-stricken and several jumped overboard into the barge, injuring their legs as they fell. Luckily they were the only casualties. The *Ariel* was badly damaged, but managed to limp to the safety of the Steamboat Company headquarters at Woolwich.

The simple fact was there were no hard and fast laws regulating navigation on the river. The Thames Conservancy Board had brought in regulations to govern navigation in 1872. These stated that when steam vessels met head on, "so as to involve risk of collision, the helms of both shall be put to port, so that each may pass on the port side of the other." Sadly, the regulations were not widely publicised, bore no weight in law and were little regarded even among seasoned riverboat captains. Captains were more likely to follow conventions built up over many years, and one of those established customs and practices was for pleasure steamers rounding Tripcock Point to hug the shoreline. This is exactly what Captain Grinstead was doing, and what he had always done during his many years on the river, even though the action would have caused his ship to pass the *Bywell Castle* starboard to starboard.

Tripcock Point deflected an ebb tide, so that any ship coming upstream around the point met two opposing currents in quick succession. These would carry the ship first midstream, and then swirl her back towards the shore. When the *Bywell Castle* saw the *Princess Alice*'s red light they presumed she had turned to port, towards the north shore. In fact she was being pulled by the tide and the movement was quickly counteracted. The Captain intended to keep to his routine, to hug the south shore. Dix, the *Bywell Castle*'s pilot, should have been well aware of these practices. Clearly, action was needed to make navigation safer. On 18 March 1880, rules and by-laws for navigation on the Thames became law. As the *Port of London Shipmasters' Guide* states:

> Power-driven vessels navigating against the tidal stream are required to proceed with care when approaching a point or sharp bend and likewise when approaching a bridge it must avoid risk of collision with a vessel coming in the opposite direction. The latter vessel has the right of way.

Nearly four hundred families were devastated by the *Princess Alice* disaster and, as usual, a disaster fund was immediately established to alleviate distress. The fund was opened by the Lord Mayor at Mansion House and donations were soon pouring in at a rate approaching £2,000 per day. This was a staggering sum in days when a good wage for a working man would have been around £2 per week. Early donations included £100 from Queen Victoria, £50 from the Prince of Wales and £50 from the French theatre company, Comedie Française. The Australian cricket team were on tour in England at the time, and contributed £100 towards the fund. The military clubbed together to make substantial donations. The thousand-strong Rifle Brigade, stationed at Woolwich, chipped in one shilling each, the officers of the Royal Artillery mess at Woolwich donated £50 and the officers and men of the 1st Brigade Royal Artillery (D) Battery gave up a day's pay to boost the fund. The Steamboat Company superintendent, William Towse, who lost eight relatives in the disaster, including his wife and four children, contributed ten guineas and other officials from the company also made contributions.

In true Victorian fashion, poems on the event were written and sold to raise funds for the appeal. The following ballad is typical of many published:

So sad a disaster ne'er has been told,
As that which I now have just to unfold,
The Thames was the scene of this terrible sight
Where hundreds were drowning, for dear life did fight.
So appalling a tale the papers they tell
Of 600 souls who from life have now fell;
May God in his mercy look down I pray
On the poor creatures who died in so fearful a way.

Chorus...

Six hundred poor souls, whom no one could save
Died in the depths of the Thames, a watery grave;
While those who were saved had all cause to mourn,
The loss of the dear ones who are dead and gone.

The history of this sad tale I'll relate
Showing how dreadful this unlooked for fate
A vessel, the *Princess Alice* by name
A large saloon steamer, and well known to fame
On her return journey from Southend and Sheerness
She ran into and sunk in five minutes or less
By a large iron screw collier, *Bywell Castle*, they say,
That was going down river that fatal day.

On Tuesday evening, September the third,
Rosherville pier the *Princess Alice* steer'd
All hearts were light on that fatal day
Not a thought of danger on the way
About 8 o'clock on that fatal night
With a fearful crash all was afright
Run down were they just off Essex shore,
Hundreds sunk in the deep to rise no more.

The captain was soon at his post on the deck
Directly before this calamitous wreck
Shouting directions his vessel to save
But alas! all is ended in a watery grave
Excitement is raging in Woolwich they say,
Where scores of the bodies lie in a terrible array
May God help all those who suffered such pain
And may we ne'er have such another disaster again.

Can anyone fancy so dreadful a scene,
Hundreds of people in agony seen,
No one to save them so close to home,
Shrieking for help, nothing can be done
Fathers, mothers and children, on a holiday trip
Have enjoyed themselves—the day they've made of it
Homeward on board this vessel they came
Only to suffer, poor souls, both grief and pain.

                              W. Fortey, Steam Printer, Monmouth Court.

One Edwin Guest edited a small book on the disaster, "The Wreck Of the *Princess Alice*", within weeks of the disaster. This was a compilation of newspaper reports and other observations and was published by Weldon and Company. Proceeds from sales went to the Mansion House Fund.

The newspapers carried daily reports of the fund's progress until it was closed on 11 October, as the Lord Mayor and his colleagues believed the £35,000 collected would be sufficient to meet all needs. Money continued to trickle in and the final grand total came to £38,246. The amount sounds large today, and would have seemed a fortune to the Victorians. In fact, it was barely sufficient to meet needs and there is no doubt many survivors and countless dependents suffered long-term severe hardship as a direct result of the tragedy.

Mansion House officials moved swiftly to relieve distress as well as they could. The Reverend Stylemann Herring was put in charge of distribution. He had run several disaster funds and his experience was invaluable in the mammoth task ahead. There were, of course, no social services and the only help available to the destitute was the dreaded workhouse. Application forms were distributed among survivors and relatives within a week of the calamity. The forms were designed to assess the circumstances of each applicant and help ensure the fund was distributed according to need. Just £725 went in providing immediate, emergency relief and another £802 was distributed as gifts to survivors and rescuers.

The bulk of the fund went on helping dependant relatives and on buying admission to orphanages for children whose fathers, and in many cases mothers, had lost their lives when the *Princess Alice* sank. Many sympathetic people wrote to offer homes to orphans and widows. Several wrote to Carttar offering to adopt children. Cabman Mr Sear and his wife offered to take a girl aged under two years, while Mr Wardle-worth the bookseller requested a girl aged between three and eight. Mrs Taylor was more concerned with class than with age. She wanted a middle-class girl. Children's Homes and orphanages offered free places. Mr Freake of the National Orphan Home at Hamm was willing to take two girls aged over six years. Miss Sharman, of the Orphans' Home in Southwark, was even more generous. Seven of her orphans had travelled from Sheerness on board the *Princess Alice* the evening before the disaster. She offered places to seven children as a thanks offering for the good fortune of her charges.

An orphans sub-committee was set up, and members were keen to place all fatherless children into homes. There was a strong feeling that the youngsters would be better off in an orphanage than with a mother who was likely to become poor. Poverty and pauperism were seen as self-perpetuating; if a child lived in poverty then poverty would become a way of life. The sub-committee also suspected some relatives might take on a child in the hope of gaining some financial reward from the fund. As the *Kentish Independent* reported on 2 November:

> In such cases where the ages of the children, or their surroundings, made them eligible for admission into public orphanages, the sub-committee strongly advised that they should be sent into such institutions; but in many instances, especially where the mother of the child was still living, strong affection or in some cases the extreme youth or ill health of the orphan prevented that advice being taken and made it necessary that the child should not be parted with. In some cases, again, where it was obvious that the expectation of receiving money from the fund overrode

the more natural interest in the future of the child, the sub-committee enforced upon the applicants that no grant would be awarded unless the children were taken into institutions or properly provided for.

Around 240 children lost at least one parent in the disaster, and the fund eventually purchased ninety-nine admissions into orphanages. One little lad, John Everist, had been on board the *Princess Alice* with his father, the Inspector of Nuisances at West Ham, his mother and three brothers. Miraculously John and two of the brothers survived, and were sent to the Royal Albert Orphanage at Bagshot in Surrey. John later told his story to the Duke of Connaught and Empress Eugenie. The total cost of placing children in orphanages and making provision for those who remained with relatives came to £17,525. The remaining cash went in grants to widows and other dependant relatives.

Another "sixpenny" subscription was organised to purchase a memorial stone at Plumstead Cemetery to commemorate the disaster. The stone memorial, a large Celtic cross, stands to this day.

In mid-October the London Steamboat Company purchased the wreck of the *Princess Alice* from the Thames Conservators for the sum of £350. As the Conservators had spent £276.4s.0d on raising the boat, plus another £2 per day to pay guards, they certainly made no profit on the deal. The London Steamboat Company salvaged the engines, and the wreck was then broken up in a yard at Greenwich.

The *Bywell Castle* sank with all hands in the Bay of Biscay in 1883.

Carttar, the coroner, was suffering from heart disease at the time of the inquest and the strain of the hearing took its toll. He died at his home in Catherine House, Blackheath Road, Greenwich on 19 March 1880.

The *Princess Alice* had been named after the third daughter of Queen Victoria. Diphtheria broke out in Alice's Royal household in Dormstadt in Autumn 1878. Alice contracted the disease after kissing her young son, and she died on November 6—the day the Board of Trade published its inquiry findings blaming the eponymous pleasure steamer for the country's worst-ever disaster.

CHAPTER TWO

Death by Design

So-called "panics" produced a horrifying death toll in Britain during the nineteenth century. The poor design of public buildings meant that any incident causing a rush to leave was liable to end in a fatal crush. The tragedies usually happened when narrow exits became blocked, either by jammed doors or by the bodies of those who had stumbled in the scramble to escape. Incidents were commonplace and often resulted in multiple deaths. In December 1842 thirty people died while trying to leave Galway Chapel. Seven years later, in February 1849, seventy were killed in a crush at the Glasgow Theatre. In January 1850 thirty men and women died in a panic in Limerick Workhouse, and in 1868 another twenty-three lost their lives at Lang's Victoria Music Hall in Manchester. The Victoria Hall tragedy in Sunderland in June 1883 holds the record for the highest number of deaths caused by a panic. Children leaving a magic show found their exit barred by a heavy door, and 183 youngsters were crushed to death before adult help arrived. The sheer force of a jostling crowd compacted into an insufficient area remains one of the most common causes of multiple fatalities, as the 1989 Hillsborough disaster that saw the deaths of more than ninety football spectators testifies only too well.

Most of the more serious incidents happened in the music halls and theatres which provided one of the greatest sources of entertainment for Victorians. A government select committee appointed in March 1892 found that the thirty-five most popular theatres and music halls in London attracted nightly audiences totalling forty-five thousand—or more than fourteen million per year. At this date there were forty-three licensed theatres and 189 licensed music halls in the capital, plus countless unlicensed "clubs." Amusements on offer ranged over serious performances of classic works, renditions of Shakespeare that would make the bard cringe in his grave and melodramas of dubious artistic merit.

Audiences were invariably enthusiastic, usually vast and all too often crammed into buildings that were little more than deadly fire traps. Between 1830 and 1892 fires gutted twenty London theatres and well over a hundred more suffered serious damage. Captain Eyre Massey Shaw, commander of the Metropolitan Fire Brigade from its formation in 1866 until 1891, was appalled at the dangerous condition of places of entertainment in the capital. He was convinced that laws were needed to ensure audiences had adequate protection from fire and the means to escape, and he led a vociferous campaign to keep the subject in the public eye.

Surprisingly, the majority of serious blazes in London happened outside opening times, with a handful of fatalities almost entirely restricted to firemen and theatre staff. In the capital, at least, a greater loss of life was caused by panics than by fire. Audiences knew the risks of fire and the fear of burning to death overrode the more immediate danger of being crushed and suffocated in the rush for the exits. Fire alarms were well known to provoke pandemonium, and they were often triggered maliciously. Large audiences acted as magnets to pickpockets. Ordinarily the thieves would mingle with the crowd, stealing whatever seemed easily available. Occasionally they decided to go for the jackpot, instigating the chaos that would give them a perfect opportunity for rich pickings. The possibility of detection in such turmoil was remote and the potential rewards enormous. Other panics were caused by individuals or groups acting out of sheer devilment, to add spice to their entertainment or to deliberately disrupt the performance.

The Reverend Charles Spurgeon could be described as the nineteenth-century forerunner to Billy Graham. He galvanised the Baptist Church, blasting it from the doldrums and injecting desperately needed energy and enthusiasm. His father was a coal merchant's clerk who also served as a pastor. Spurgeon was born in 1834 and from his early years displayed a prodigious gift as a church preacher. In 1853, aged just 19, he was given a three-month trial as pastor at the New Park Street Baptist Church in Lambeth, South London. His sermons were in stark contrast to the sombre norm of the period. He brought vitality and extravagance into a church that was thirsting for a livelier, more enjoyable interpretation of Christianity.

When Spurgeon arrived the New Park Street church was filling just one hundred of its twelve hundred seats. News of the exciting young preacher travelled fast and within a few months the congregation was bursting at the seams. Spurgeon decided to move to Exeter Hall, but his flock continued to increase, and quickly outgrew its new home. The church decided that drastic action was essential—they would build a new Tabernacle sufficient to hold the congregation commanded by their outstanding young minister. While funds for the project were amassed, it was decided to hire the nearby Surrey Gardens Music Hall for Sunday evening services. The hall was one of the largest in London, with a capacity of ten thousand. Admission to the service was free, but advertisements pointed out a collection would be made. It was planned that the money raised would fund the hall's hiring charge, £15 per evening, and contribute towards the appeal target for the new Tabernacle.

The first service at Surrey Gardens was scheduled to start at 6:30 PM on Sunday 19 October 1856. By 5:00 PM crowds were beginning to gather. An estimated fifteen thousand men, women and children arrived to hear Spurgeon, and as soon as the hall was opened an eager mass flocked in. The Church Deacons had requested eight police officers to be present to help deal with the crowds. Two officers were stationed at the door and six were inside the hall. They were under the command of Superintendent Lund, who brought along his wife and daughter to listen to the sermon from seats near the pulpit. Just after 6:00 PM Lund ordered the doors of the hall should be closed as he considered the building was full. Many of those still outside waited on the grass, hoping to hear the preacher.

The service began on schedule at 6:30 PM and for the first twenty minutes all seemed well. Spurgeon was giving his usual electrifying performance, reading a passage from St Luke to illustrate his argument that man could not serve God and Mammon. Two hymns were sung. In inimitable style the Pastor began to pray for "backsliders from the House of God" and women who had "departed from the paths of virtue," whom, he said, he knew to be in the audience. Unfortunately, they were not the only miscreants present. As Spurgeon's prayers for the backsliders and fallen women reduced many of his congregation to tears there was a sudden cry: "The place is on fire!" The effect was immediate, and devastating. Crowds rushed for the exits, there was a severe crush on one stairway and within minutes six men and women were trampled to death and more than thirty more injured.

The exits from the Surrey Gardens Music Hall, like the exits from most theatres of the period, were woefully inadequate and ill-designed. The building had a large ground floor hall and three tiers of galleries. There were four spiral stone staircases at each corner, and these were the only means of escape from the galleries, with each stairway serving all three tiers. Had those in the galleries made equal use of all four stairways, disaster may have been averted. As so often happens in stressful circumstances, the people grouped together, and the vast bulk of the crowd headed for the staircase in the northwest corner of the building.

The crush happened at a predictable danger point—the landing of the first floor. At this landing there were two doors leading from the first floor gallery. The streams of people coming through the doors converged with the hordes pouring down from the top two floors. The stairway was about six feet wide, and each tread was about a foot wide near the outside wall, tapering to about six inches at the central balustrade. In the crush the staircase was packed, and the less fortunate were forced to make their way down the narrow section close to the balustrade.

Samuel Heard, 24, a well-built young tanner, had been standing behind a back row of seats with several members of his family. Heard was just yards from the exit on the first floor gallery, and was probably the first to topple down the staircase. Despite his strength and size—according to newspaper reports he was a broad-framed six-footer—he stood little chance against the force of the mass pressing down behind him. His brother John later told coroner Charles Carttar:

> We rushed to the staircase in the northwestern tower. I lost sight of my brother in the confusion, and never saw him again alive. When I last saw him he stood beside me in the gallery.... I fell on the stairs full five steps down, and a policeman afterwards raised me up, and I escaped, but with the loss of my boot. There was a great pressure on the stairs, occasioned by the people rushing down. When I fell on the stairs there were several people beneath me, and I particularly noticed one woman who was bent nearly double, and seemed dead.

Susannah Heard, her husband William, and young son were also in the family group jammed on the stairway. As the crush intensified Susannah grabbed the boy by the scruff of his neck and held him dangling over the balustrade to save him from suffocation. As she struggled for breath she heard cracks as a man standing close to her fractured his arm. The growing pressure forced the bannisters to give way. William caught hold of his wife to prevent her falling, and she, balancing with one leg on the stairs and one in mid-air, kept hold of their child. The little family clung together in this precarious position until the crush slackened and they were able to reach safety.

Susannah and her family were fortunate to survive. Harriet Johnson, a 20-year-old dressmaker, was at the service with her sister Louisa. Harriet fell on the stairs, and her sister was forced down on top of her. Louisa realised her sister was struggling for breath, but was unable to move and relieve the pressure. Louisa survived, but Harriet died. Money collector Albert Fullager later told the coroner: "There were 12 or 14 people fallen down upon the landing, one upon another, and the people behind could not get over them...." The death toll may well have been higher but for the hall superintendent, George Diggings, and some policemen forcing their way up the stairs to the first floor landing. They somehow persuaded the mass to move back, and prevented more people joining the crush on the stairs.

Superintendent Lund, seated on the ground floor close to Spurgeon, escorted his family to the safety of the gardens outside before returning to help tackle the chaos on the northwest stairway. By the time he arrived the worst of the crush was over. People were still crowded on the stairs, but there was space to recover the dead and injured. As people slowly cleared the stairway the tragic consequences of the panic became clear. Most of the dead and injured were sprawled on the first floor landing. More were on the stairway leading down to the ground floor. A window at the first floor gallery gave access to the roof of the refreshment room, and four of the bodies were initially taken there. The panic had started and finished within minutes. Six people died: Samuel Heard, 24; Harriet Mathew, 16; Harriet Barlow, 30; Harriet Johnson, 20; Mrs Elizabeth Mead, 48; and Mrs Grace Slipper, 40.

From his platform on the ground floor Spurgeon could see no sign of fire, and did his best to calm the people surging towards the exits. His efforts were in vain; the hall was in uproar. Those lucky enough to be on the ground floor dashed for the nearest exits; others broke through the locked glass doors along the side of the building. The *Illustrated Times* (25 October) reported:

Numbers rushed without hats or bonnets into the gardens, calling for their children, brothers, husbands or wives, as the case might be, and were met by a confused mass of people fleeing at the top of their speed. The gardens, with the exception of the patch leading from the principal entrance, were in darkness. The consequence was, that the persons who rushed out through the lower windows ran in directions the most contrary to the one they wished to reach. Some of them ran into the lake....

Spurgeon tried valiantly to resume his sermon, encouraged by his Deacons who believed he might calm the frantic congregation. All the deaths occurred in the northwest stairway, so those in the main hall had no way of knowing the scale of the disaster. All they would have seen was the mass rushing for the exits. Even so, Spurgeon feared the worst and could not continue speaking. According to the *Illustrated London News* (25 October), after a few minutes talking about the righteous and the wicked, the young pastor gave up.

> You ask me to preach, but how can I after this terrible scene? My brain is in a whirl and I scarcely know where I am, so great are my apprehensions that many people must have been injured by rushing out. I would rather that you retired gradually, and may God Almighty dismiss you with his blessing....

A last hymn was sung, and as it finished Spurgeon told those still in the hall:

> This event will, I trust, teach you the necessity of having a building of our own. We thought we had a sufficient number of police present to preserve order. But we have been disappointed....

He felt the crowd was quieter and announced he would try to resume his sermon. Under the circumstances, the text was unfortunate. "The curse of the Lord is on this house of the wicked...." Sparked by Spurgeon's tidings, or by another false alarm, the congregation made another surge towards the exits. The pastor, perhaps wisely, decided to leave the pulpit. "I am attempting an impossibility," he said. "It is impossible for me to preach to you this night. I know not how to speak to you."

Surgeon Mr C. Otway lived in Canterbury Road, Newington, close to the hall, and a police constable was sent to fetch him. He arrived to a scene of mayhem. Superintendent Lund ordered bodies to be carried from the hall and placed on a table in the grounds. Otway examined them, confirming death. He noticed Samuel Heard had a wound to his head which could have occurred when he fell down the stairs. The wound may have stunned him, but death was through suffocation. All the bodies, except for that of Mrs Grace Skipper, were taken to the workhouse at Newington. Mrs Skipper's body was taken to her own home in Kensington. Mr Feist, the workhouse master, cared for relatives arriving to identify their dead.

Otway, the surgeon, was soon joined by several other doctors, including Mr Stewer, Mr Marshall and Mr Ganon, and they did their best to treat the injured people. Four men and a six-year-old girl were taken to Guy's Hospital suffering fractures, cuts and bruising. Many more people—newspaper reports estimated around sixty—had their injuries treated in their own homes. Otway had noted one of the dead, Mrs Harriet Barlow, was in the later stages of pregnancy and asked Ganon if she could be "relieved of the child." Ganon agreed to operate and a caesarian section was performed at the workhouse. The child was stillborn.

The coroner's inquest opened two days later, on Tuesday 21 October, and concluded on Friday 24 October. Carttar took evidence from survivors, police officers and officials from the church and hall. No one knew exactly what had caused the panic. The consensus of opinion was that it had been deliberately started with a call of "Fire!" Some believed that pickpockets were to blame, others blamed enemies of Reverend Spurgeon who wished to disrupt the service and bring him into disrepute.The hall itself came in for some criticism, much to the chagrin of its director, Mr T.K. Holmes. Returning a verdict of accidental death on the six victims, the coroner's jury added a rider criticising construction of the stairways.

> Their construction is not of a character to render them safe, more especially when a large number of people are anxious to leave the galleries in haste. The treads of the stairways are much too narrow near the handrail and the descent too steep; and the jury therefore trust that the directors will give their immediate attention to the subject.

Mr Holmes, who was sitting in the court, objected to the use of the word "safe" as it "might have a meaning beyond that which the jury intended it to convey." The jury assured him they did not doubt the stability of the hall or the stairways. None of them would hesitate to enter the building no matter what degree of pressure it was subjected to.

Spurgeon was shocked to learn of the deaths at his service. His Deacons ushered him away to a retreat in the country, and he was reported to be too ill to attend the inquest. The young pastor was just 22 years old and was deeply affected by the tragedy. He remained out of the public eye for a fortnight, but then gradually resumed his normal services, including regular Sunday morning sermons at Surrey Gardens. Spurgeon came in for much criticism following the disaster. He was an unconventional preacher and the dramatic techniques and language he used to colour his services mortified many traditionalist churchgoers. The disaster, they said, was his fault. The conservative press had already criticised Spurgeon, and this incident gave them ample ammunition to drive home their point. The *Illustrated Times* (25 October) was one of the more vitriolic.

> Now, but a few weeks have passed since the press had to step out of its way to rebuke Mr Spurgeon for improper jocisty. It therefore deepens the pain of this catastrophe to reflect that a number of persons suffered death and wounds, from a crowd which must have been largely made up of those who came from curiosity—came to be vulgarly excited or impiously amused. This aggravates the misery, and checks the sympathy we might otherwise have felt for Mr Spurgeon.

He did get some support, albeit qualified by barbed criticism of his motives. The *Times* (21 October), while urging him to restrict numbers at his services, made the point:

> We have no wish to criticise his style of oratory, which severe critics affirm to be of the familiar, bold and irreverent sort. On the contrary we are delighted to hear there is one man in the metropolis who can get people to hear his sermons from any other motive than the fulfillment of a religious obligation.

The paper went on to argue Spurgeon accepted crowded gatherings because larger audiences offered the chance of bigger collections. The pastor was accused of being in bad taste, and a common public performer.

Donations had been collected at the end of the ill-fated service. These collections were normal, and proceeds funded the church's activities. Why collections were made under such tragic circumstances is unknown, but presumably those rattling the boxes knew nothing of the deaths and injuries. The £8 collected was given to the families of those killed. In the weeks that followed Spurgeon personally visited the bereaved families. The New Park Street Chapel offered a £50 reward for information that would lead to the conviction of the person responsible for raising the false alarm, but the culprits had been lost in the panic. No one ever discovered if they had been pickpockets or simply opponents of Spurgeon who wanted to disrupt proceedings.

The tragedy proved only a temporary reverse for the young pastor. However, despite his quick return to the pulpit he apparently retained a fear of crowded places. His congregation grew to unprecedented numbers, at one service exceeding twenty-three thousand. Collections made at these gatherings gave Spurgeon scope to realise his ideals. In 1866 he established the Stockwell Orphanage for 250 fatherless or destitute boys. Such children were usually consigned to institutions such as district schools run by Poor Law Unions. The schools often dealt with more than eight hundred children, and individuality was suppressed in the strictly regulated regime needed to maintain order. Spurgeon's home was different. The boys were allocated to one of eight houses, each equipped for twenty-five to thirty children under the care of a house matron. The idea was the youngsters would be brought up in a caring, homely environment where they would be encouraged to do their best and achieve their potential. The house matron was a foster mother to her young orphans and the relatively small scale of operations enabled each child to enjoy individual attention. The system was decades in advance of that seen in district schools, and a credit to Spurgeon's enlightened attitude.

Other successful projects included an innovative "sheltered housing" scheme for elderly women that was a century ahead of its time. The women lived independently in a row of terraced houses, with help at hand if it was needed. Spurgeon also established a Pastors' College. The two-year course was free to those who could not afford to pay. The Metropolitan Tabernacle, at Newington Butts, opened its doors a few years later. When Charles retired, his son, Thomas, took over his mantle.

London's next serious panic happened on Boxing Day 1858. The cause was identical—a false alarm of fire—but this time the consequences were more severe. The Royal Victoria Theatre—now better known as the Old Vic—was hardly a salubrious establishment in the 1850s. The theatre had first opened in 1818 and was initially known as the Royal Coburg, after Her Royal Highness Princess Charlotte, then heir to the throne, and her husband, His Serene Highness the Prince of Saxe Coburg, who had laid the foundation stone by proxy. The start was inauspicious. Princess Charlotte died before the theatre opened.

In 1833 the Royal Coburg was redecorated and reopened as the Royal Victoria Theatre. Again, it took its name from the heir to the throne, Princess Victoria. The name may have been luckier, but it is highly doubtful Victoria was proud of her namesake. It quickly sank to the level of a flea pit, and did not improve until J.A. Cave became manager in 1871. The panic happened during the venue's seamier period, when the clientele was strictly working class and often unruly.

The exits and entrances at the Royal Victoria Theatre were better designed than those in many theatres of the period. A main wooden staircase led from the gallery to the street, and the stairs were about five and a half feet wide. There were four landings, with a money collectors' box on the third landing and a ticket checkers' box at the top landing. A wooden bar was placed across the third landing to prevent the crowd rushing past the money takers without paying. The gallery had a second, smaller exit, but this was rarely used and would have been unfamiliar to the vast majority of the audience. Although The Royal Victoria was a licensed theatre, the qualification gave little assurance of structural soundness. Theatres were licensed by the Lord Chamberlain, more concerned with propriety and good taste at performances than with audience safety. The Royal Victoria had passed an inspection by Mr W.B. Donne, the Examiner of Plays and Inspector of Theatres to the Lord Chamberlain, in August 1858.

The promise of a Christmas pantomime made a visit to the Victoria Theatre a prime ingredient of seasonal celebration for many workers in the Lambeth district. The theatre generally hosted one show per day, but the prospect of a Boxing Day rush made matinee and evening performances worthwhile. Manager Johnson J. Towers had selected a highly-spiced production of "Harlequin True Blue" to top the bill, and the 1:30 PM show, although not expected to be as popular as the evening performance, attracted a good-sized audience. By 5:00 PM the first show was reaching its end and a large crowd was gathering for the start of the second performance at 6:00 PM. The theatre had often received complaints about the behaviour and nuisance caused by mobs waiting outside its doors and, in line with normal custom, the queue was allowed up to the money collectors' box on the gallery staircase. The stairs were packed tight with an impatient crowd eager for seats in the theatre.

Inside the theatre a member of the audience sitting near the back of the ground floor decided to flout the commonly disregarded rule banning smoking. He took a box of matches from his pocket and struck one to light his pipe. Thomas Day, a shopman of Belvedere Road, Lambeth, was standing close to the man and witnessed the start of an incident that was to cause fifteen young boys to be crushed to death. He later told coroner Carttar:

> The box took fire. He threw it down and extinguished it in a moment. Two women in the eighteen penny, or front boxes, screamed 'Fire' and upon that there was an immediate movement of the people in the boxes, and then a rush from the gallery. The people before me in the boxes conducted themselves very well. There was some smoke, but very trifling, and it did not last a minute. My belief is that the object of the person was only to light a pipe. It was the two women in the eighteen penny boxes who created the alarm. I do not think there was any criminal intention on the part of the person who struck the light. He went away immediately after the fire was put out, and I have not seen him since. I do not think he intended to create an alarm. The performance continued for about half an hour after that. I did not know what was taking place on the gallery stairs.

Theatre treasurer Henry Young was in the box lobby on the ground floor when he heard the first cry of "Fire!" The audience rose up "in a mass." Young, helped by manager Towers and other staff, managed to convince the anxious crowd that they were in no danger, and they returned to their seats. "I heard the commotion in the gallery," Young later told Carttar.

> The cry of 'Fire' went like an electric spark from the boxes to pit and from pit to gallery in a moment.... After the tumult had subsided some people, of whom I made inquiries, said they saw a boy's coat on fire, in the pocket of which there had been some fuses. No one knew who the boy was, nor whither he went.

The "electric spark" sent terror through the gallery, where about nine hundred people were sitting, and the crowd was soon in a tumult that sent people stampeding for the exit. As the gallery door was opened those waiting on the staircase below believed the performance had finished, and they edged impatiently forward, eager to be admitted. The two masses of humanity, one eager to enter the theatre and the other desperate to get out, were suddenly thrown together. Those at the front of the queue waiting to enter heard the shouts of "Fire" and turned to make their way downstairs. The people packed into the stairway formed an impenetrable barrier. The torrent reached the first landing before the inevitable happened: someone tumbled. In the mayhem that followed bodies were tangled together, crushed and broken by the relentless pressure of those behind.

Joseph Holmes of Bermondsey, 17, had gone to see the evening performance at the theatre with his friends William Cooper, 17, and Patrick Handrahan, 15. The teenagers were at the front of the queue waiting to enter the gallery. Joseph's statement at the inquest graphically depicts what happened:

> A great many people were below me on the staircase, all waiting to be admitted. William Cooper stood on the stair below me, and Handrahan on my left side on the same stair with me. At that moment the gallery door near the money-taker's box opened from the inside, and some person who came out said, 'Get out; the place is on fire.' We then all made a rush downstairs, and I was clinched on the top of some people before me.... Several people were thrown down on the landing, and I among the rest. I did not see what became of Cooper, but Pat Handrahan, who was with me, and was pressed down by the people above him so much, cried till he was black in the face. All this happened from the rush made by the people to get out.

Their friend William Cooper noticed a gas pipe on the stairway had burst. This was never verified, but could easily have happened in the frantic scramble. There was certainly no fire. Cooper had gone to the pantomime with his younger brother James, 15. James had not queued with William and his friends, but had been left alone further down the stairway. This probably saved his life. James managed to get out of the building, and when the chaos had eased he went in search of his brother. He told the inquest:

> I found him lying on the stairs with others. I called for help and a young chap came and assisted me to get my brother downstairs. I put my hand to his heart to find if it panted, but I could not feel anything. I also put my mouth to his to feel if he breathed. A doctor came, who, after feeling his pulse, said that there was a little life in him and that he was to be taken to the hospital. When he was taken there he was dead.

The struggle on the stairway was over within fifteen minutes. Fifteen lads, the oldest aged 23, the youngest just 12, lay dead or dying. Thirty others were injured.

Inspector Byron of L division heard of the disaster within a few minutes, and quickly ordered a contingent of constables to the Royal Victoria. As the *Times* reported on 28 December, Byron described the scene as:

> ...heartrending, and his exertions were made in the midst of the groans, shrieks, and the lamentations of the crowd outside, as one dead body or other was recognised by some friend or relation.

Byron had passing cabs and vans commandeered to fetch medical help and to take the injured to the nearby St Thomas' Hospital. Two of the casualties taken to the hospital were apparently dead on arrival. Surgeon Mr Gervis and the hospital dresser, a Mr Bone, tried to revive them by applying galvanism—a device remarkably like a very early and crude cardiac defibrillator—and by using the Marshall Hall method of resuscitation. The Marshall Hall method was based on the premise that movement of the chest would induce inhalation. Sadly, it was largely ineffective. The resuscitation attempts failed.

Several other medical men, including Drs Johnson, Donohoo, Dodd, Brookes and Bateson, gave immediate care at the scene. Other doctors and chemists in the district opened their premises to tend the dying and the injured. Robert Richardson, 15, was taken, apparently dead, to the home of Mr George Gill, a house surgeon at the South London Ophthalmic Hospital. Gill spent two hours trying to resuscitate the boy, and his efforts were rewarded when Richardson, although still in a "coma-like" state, stood up and walked around the room. He was taken to Lambeth Workhouse to recover.

Many of the Royal Victoria victims were clearly beyond help. Bodies were loaded into vans and taken to Lambeth Workhouse. By 8:00 PM ten lads were laid in a row awaiting identification by relatives. The master, a Mr Piercy, kept the workhouse doors open throughout the night and an estimated one thousand worried parents and relatives visited to see if their loved ones were in the temporary mortuary. The last victim was identified on Thursday, three days after the disaster. William Hammond, 19, was identified by an acquaintance. The boy was an orphan and had been taken off the streets by a shoemaker who was teaching him the trade. One lad, William Jones Jennings, 13, died from a fractured spine, but the other fourteen were suffocated. Post-mortem examinations were not made. Most people enjoying the Boxing Day pantomime in the theatre were blissfully unaware of the tragedy being played out within yards of where they sat and laughed, or stood and waited for entrance. Manager Towers decided that the evening show must go on, and the performance continued as scheduled and as if nothing had happened. The press attacked Towers for his apparently callous attitude. The *Times* (28 December) wrote:

> ...in spite of this frightful calamity, the entertainment at the theatre in the evening went on as if nothing uncommon had happened and that long before the doors opened an immense multitude congregated at all the points of entrance waiting for admission. It may be assumed, in charity towards our common humanity, that few of them could have been cognisant of the melancholy event which had happened only an hour before, but the conduct of those concerned in the management of the theatre is not susceptible of any such construction.

Towers wrote to the *Times* on 29 December to explain his decision to let the show go on.

> You say the pantomime was played in the evening as though nothing had happened. I assure you, sir, had I been able to consider my own feelings upon the matter I should certainly have closed the theatre after so dire a calamity, but I found it impossible to do so, as the gallery stairs were lined with people eager to witness the pantomime of the evening, and to attempt to force a passage through them was out of the question, and would no doubt have been attended with more serious accident than even the tragedy of the morning. By inserting these few lines you will greatly oblige and someway satisfy the public.

Towers paid the funeral expenses for all the lads killed. The dead were all from poor homes and the burial costs would have presented very serious financial problems for their families. The manager's effort at good public relations did not spare him the wrath of the coroner's jury. The inquest was opened on the day following the disaster, and concluded on Thursday 30 December, 1858. The jury was made up from some of the leading tradesmen in the district, and their criticism was blunt. They said the accident would not have happened if people had not been allowed to queue on the gallery stairway. Coroner Charles Carttar did his best to quell ill-feeling, saying he could see no reason why people should not queue on the stairs rather than in the street, especially as those already in the gallery were expected to leave by a separate exit. It was, he pointed out, normal practice for people to queue on the stairways of theatres and other public places.

The jurors retired to consider their verdict. If the panic had been caused by a deliberate act the culprit could face a charge of manslaughter; if it had been caused without malicious intent the deaths could be classed as accidental. The jury spent some time considering their options, but it appears most of their discussions focused on the theatre's management. They were keen to do whatever they could to prevent a similar tragedy, although they knew Towers was under no legal obligation to agree to any changes. At last, Carttar delivered their verdict. The deaths were accidental. In future, came their suggestion, there should be sufficient time between one performance and another to ensure the theatre was empty before crowds began to gather on the stairways. He added the jury were anxious to guard against further loss of life; if any serious casualty resulted from the continuance of current arrangements Mr Towers must feel morally, if not legally, responsible. Towers thanked the jury and promised to consider their recommendation. He did not think, he said, that he would allow further matinee performances. He would not run the risk of jeopardising human life for any consideration.

Public sympathy was tinged with a degree of reprobation. The fifteen dead were working class lads, and the working class were considered slightly degenerate, a breed apart from their more refined, well-behaved and more responsible betters. There was a definite feeling the boys had been at least partly to blame for their deaths. As the *Times* reported on 29 December, "It was in the gallery alone that the rabble refused to listen to reason and remain passive; hence the calamitous consequence that followed...."

The Surrey Gardens Music Hall and Royal Victoria Theatre panics were two among a host of similar incidents occurring throughout Britain. Captain Eyre Shaw, chief of the Metropolitan Fire Brigade, devoted much of his career to shaming the authorities into making improvements. An Irish Protestant army officer of aristocratic background, he had the confidence and personal prestige to speak his mind, even if that meant taking on the powerful theatre establishment. He was totally committed to forcing improvements. As he was quoted to the government's Select Committee on Theatres and Places of Entertainment in 1892:

> ...a theatre should not only be made safe, but it should be made in such a way that the audience would know it was safe. Indeed this knowledge would go far towards preventing a panic.

In 1876, the year a theatre fire in Brooklyn, New York killed 283 people, Shaw's book *Fire in Theatres* was published. This catalogued the lamentable safety standards in British places of entertainment and caused deep resentment among theatre owners who felt the outspoken fire chief was a threat to their livelihoods. Public opinion won the day and in 1878 the Metropolitan Board of Works was for the first time given some jurisdiction over theatres and other places of entertainment.

The Metropolis Management and Building Amendment Act applied to all "places of public resort" of not less than five hundred square feet. Two separate exits, not leading to the same thoroughfare, were to be provided for each floor; telephone communication was to be established with the nearest fire station; and basic fire equipment—hatchets, hooks, wet blankets or rugs, water buckets and other appliances—had to be kept ready for immediate use. The Board was empowered to insist on alterations, but only where they could be carried out at "moderate expense." The Act was a step in the right direction, but fell far short of what was needed to make significant progress in improving theatre safety. The new regulations were difficult, even impossible, to enforce. Most of the essential improvements required would have put theatre owners to considerable expense, and their liability was limited to moderate costs. The Act was commonly ignored, and in any case gave no powers over the proliferation of so-called "private clubs" frequently based in totally unsuitable premises.

In 1878 Act could do nothing to prevent a tragedy at such a club provided for Jewish immigrants in the East End. The incident which occurred in 1887 at the Hebrew Dramatic Club highlighted the dangers inherent in unregulated premises, and the stresses between the established Jewish community and their newer brethren.

During the early 1880s Jews in Eastern Europe were subjected to such savage persecution that many, particularly those in Russia and Poland, were left with little option but to flee for their lives. England had a long tradition as a safe asylum, and attracted many hoping for a more tolerable existence. The influx started after the systematic hounding of

Jews began in Russia during 1882, and over the next twenty years around one hundred thousand immigrants arrived and settled. As with the immigrants who came before and after them, the Jews formed their own ghetto in the poorest areas of the East End. Many had spent the last of their precious savings to reach England, and in their desperate state they were willing to accept atrocious housing conditions and to work for a pittance. The majority lived on the edge of destitution. The Jews were willing to pay a large chunk of their earnings as rent for poor accommodation, and to work for far less than most of the English poor. Many worked in notorious sweatshops, working well into the night as little more than a slave labour force.

England was in the midst of an economic slump and unemployment was rife. The result was predictable; the Jews were blamed for the economic ills suffered by the English. They became an object of resentment and their exploitation met with little sympathy. The existing Jewish population was naturally concerned. The newcomers were unpopular and they were seen as taking jobs and houses that should rightfully go to English people. The established community did not want the boat to be rocked. They had become a respected section of the population, and their numbers included highly successful businessmen, financiers and other professionals. Hordes of "co-religionist" working class labourers flocking in from Europe, they thought, could easily cause trouble and turn society against all Jews.

In the early days of the community, rich and poor Jews had lived side by side in East London and charity was administered haphazardly. The almsgivers were an integral part of the Jewish community, and were intimately aware of their poor neighbours' circumstances. As prosperous Jews moved to more salubrious districts this vital link was broken, and a system for charitable giving became essential. The Jewish Board of Guardians, formed in March 1859, was established to help needy Jews and to care for their needs outside the Poor Law system. The Jewish Board of Guardians formed various committees to take charge of different aspects of their organisation. An industrial and loan committee approved grants to help poor Jews purchase tools and equipment needed to start their own small businesses. A visiting committee investigated claims for relief, and a sanitary committee worked to improve sanitation in some of the worst East End districts.

The Jewish Board of Guardians was also in the forefront of the struggle to deal with the foreign newcomers. Its main aim was to stop the tide of hapless souls fleeing from persecution. In December 1886 the Jewish Board of Guardians resolved: "That an endeavour be made at the frontier towns of Russia to warn intending immigrants thence of the state of the labour market and dearth of employment in this country, so as to deter them at present from coming here." The next year the Jewish Board of Guardians agreed to use advertising to ward off potential immigrants. They later reported:

> Accordingly the effort was made, and the kind of requisite aid of the proprietors of many journals was obtained in editorial form, for the purpose of warning intending emigrants by the detailed account of all the sufferings experienced by new arrivals here. In addition to this, about 30 continental Jewish Congregations were addressed, asking them to disseminate the intelligence of the congested state of the labour market in this country, to point out the great difficulty which even skilled foreign artisans have to encounter in seeking employment here, and to impress that poor wanderers are utterly unable to discover here any means of support, and that therefore no tramps, pedlars or mendicants should be helped forward on their journey towards this country; and asking that relief on the continent should be strictly limited to returning such persons to their homes....

The Jewish Board of Guardians' Honorary Secretary, Lionel Alexander, and member Lawrence Isaacs visited Germany at the end of 1886 in an effort to dissuade would-be immigrants and to look at how the foreign Jews already in Britain could be repatriated. The Jewish Board of Guardians wanted the newcomers to go home, or to go on to America, and was happy to fund the costs. Many of the immigrants had no desire to stay in England; their aim was to reach America, and the promise of a new and better life. Some of those arriving at British ports had been duped into believing they were landing in America. Others planned to stay in Britain for only as long as it took them to save the fare for the next leg of their journey. But, as the Jewish Board of Guardians' officials were well aware, the homeless Jews were not welcomed with open arms, even in America. As early as August 1884 the United Hebrew Charities in New York were writing to the Jewish Board of Guardians in London asking them to check the flood of Jews coming into their country. The sentiments expressed sum up the widespread opposition to the immigrants.

> While sympathising as brethren in faith with the unfortunate residents of Roumania, Russia and other countries for so many years the victims of

cruel persecution, and ready to join with our co-religionists of other lands, in aiding them so far as lies within our power, it cannot be denied that it is in many cases misplaced sympathy to forward these people to the United States. This is emphatically a land of workers, it is not a free land for people who are unable or unwilling to earn their livelihood amid the conditions required here of all emigrants; or to assimilate with their neighbours and become American in habits, ideas and language. While many of the emigrants of late years have been welcome accessions to the population, and by their intelligence and energy are earning the goodwill of their neighbours, a large number have either returned to their old homes, disappointed and hopelessly dispirited. Others still remaining on these shores are supported as paupers by local aid societies or left to the mercies of a Poor House...."

In 1885 the United Hebrew Charities wrote again, stating New York would refuse to accept unsuitable Jewish immigrants, and in 1886 they kept to their word and returned seven to eight hundred to Europe, many of them packed in cattle ships. The Jewish Board of Guardians objected strongly, particularly as many of those arriving in England on board these ships had no means of buying a passage back to their own countries. The criticism met with a sharp response from New York:

...we fail to see in the voluntary return on cattle steamers or otherwise, with or without this Society's aid, of seven or eight hundred disappointed, friendless or diseased, dispirited or lazy and incapable European Hebrews, out of a total arrival in two years of more than 45,000 Hebrew steerage passengers, of whom half came by English steamships, an occasion for criticism...

The bickering highlighted a straightforward situation: nobody wanted the Jewish refugees landing on their doorsteps. The Jewish Board of Guardians tried to play down the problem, saying the numbers remaining in the country could give no cause for alarm, but the Guardians' attitude clearly revealed the apprehension and fear they felt themselves. In April 1887 the *Jewish Chronicle* reported the remarks of Mr F. Mocatta, a member of the Jewish Board of Guardians, concerning immigration. He said that since the influx had begun in 1882 not more than three thousand Jews had arrived and remained in London, and that the figure should be made widely known, as there was a feeling some twenty or forty thousand poor Jews had settled. A few weeks later, on 27 May, the paper lamented: "Truly, it seems that a Jew subtends a larger angle to the eye than any other human being."

In 1887 the Local Government Board decided to investigate the increase in "destitute foreigners" settling in the East End of London. They wrote to the Whitechapel Union and asked for records to show how many foreigners were in receipt of Poor Law relief and whether there had been a recent increase in the number of foreigners seeking relief. The Local Government Board wanted to ascertain whether or not the influx had caused an increase in pauperism. The answers were surprising. During the week ending 7 June 1887 just two "foreigners" were in the workhouse, compared with 275 British subjects; twenty-one foreigners were in the infirmary, compared with 528 Britons; twenty-seven foreigners were receiving outdoor medical relief, compared with thirty-two Britons. The Guardians from the Local Government Board were keen to qualify their findings:

> The figures contained in the statement above referred to cannot, however, in the opinions of the Guardians be taken as evidence of the extent to which the pauperism of the union is affected by the immigration of foreign poor, nor as a gauge of the immigration itself, since the immigrants are for the most part Jewish poor who are able and content to live upon a much smaller wage than English poor and who seldom resort to the Poor Law except for medical aid; whilst it is possible that local pauperism may be more or less augmented by the crowding out of English labour. Still, the statistics of pauperism on this Union do not go to show that any appreciable increase of burden has been imposed upon the Poor Rates of this Union by the immigration.

In 1887 the Whitechapel Union held its own investigation into the effects of immigration into the district and questioned a delegation from the Jewish Board of Guardians. It was reassured that the flow of immigrants was being monitored, and numbers of foreign Jews entering and remaining in the country was falling. The numbers of permanent immigrants was around five to six thousand per year between 1881 and 1883; and about three thousand per year after that. Numbers did not rise significantly until 1890, when they reached seven thousand. The Lord Mayor set up a special fund to help the impoverished immigrants, and established a conjoint committee with the Jewish Board of Guardians to help distribute the cash. Again, the priority was to stem immigration and to encourage new arrivals to go elsewhere.

The Jewish Board of Guardians consistently underplayed the problem. It did not want public opinion to turn against Jews and it did not welcome the publicity and ill-feeling generated by the new immigrants.

It even opposed groups set up to help the newcomers. On 25 March 1887 a "Society for the Relief of Persecuted Jews" came in for some sharp criticism in the *Jewish Chronicle*:

> ...we consider it our duty to point out that no new organisation of any kind is necessary.... The exaggeration with regard to foreign poor Jews in London although not intended to have that effect, may create a great prejudice. There are many cogent reasons why we should say in this connection 'Save Us From Our Friends.'

The Jewish Board of Guardians was clearly highly sensitive on the issue of foreign Jews. In January 1887 the last thing they wanted was a disaster that set the public spotlight upon the exact group of society the Board was desperately trying to brush under the carpet, but that is exactly what it got.

The Hebrew Dramatic Club was housed in a converted house in Prince's Street, Spitalfields. The premises belonged to a Mr Smith, a butcher of Crispin Street, and from the front looked exactly like a normal dwelling house. The sixty-foot by thirty-foot rectangular hall was at the back of the house. It could hold up to five hundred people, three hundred on the ground floor and another two hundred in the galleries constructed around three sides. The club was a focus of socialisation and entertainment for the impoverished East European Jews who lived in the cramped ghettos of London's East End. The objectives of the club were simple:

> ...to afford to its members the means of social intercourse, mutual entertainments, music, dancing, recitations, and social and intellectual improvement in general.

There was a reading room and, in an obvious effort to maintain some sense of decorum, discussions on politics and religion were banned. Membership was relatively cheap at one shilling per week, or two guineas per year. On one night each week the performance was staged in Yiddish.

The East End was home to a host of similar establishments, and as private clubs all the premises escaped the jurisdiction of the Metropolitan Board of Works. The Hebrew Dramatic Club was already known to Board of Works officials. In May 1885 a Mr Rubenstein had lodged a complaint about the condition of the building. The Board of Works investigated, but found the hall was unlicensed and not subject to even the rudimentary authority it held. The layout of the building courted disaster. The entrance, in Prince's Street, was through two doors, each about three and a half feet wide. They led into a vestibule. At the end of the vestibule a wooden pay box had been constructed by a doorway leading into the hall. Just inside the doorway a staircase three and a half feet wide led up to the gallery. This meant the audience from the gallery shared the exit with people on the ground floor, a situation that would not have been permitted in a licensed theatre.

There was some rivalry between the many small clubs, and in January 1887 the Hebrew Dramatic Club was at loggerheads with the nearby Russian National Club. Many of the National's members had joined the Hebrew Dramatic Club and ill-feelings were running high. Marks Rubenstein of Lambert Street, Whitechapel, had threatened to burn down the Hebrew Dramatic Club and do whatever damage he could, and the club had engaged a police constable to evict troublemakers. Gangs of Rubenstein's friends would gather outside the doors of the club and behave in a threatening manner.

On 18 January 1887 there were no signs of trouble. The club was staging a benefit performance—it regularly ran shows to benefit a particular club member hit by a crisis—and the bill featured a new drama, "The Spanish Gypsy." The beneficiary was Morrice King, a tailor's assistant. The show started as usual at about 8:30 PM The audience was restricted to club members and their children. Each member was permitted to bring up to two extra guests. As the show began, about four hundred men, women and children were in the theatre.

At about 11:15 PM, just as the play moved towards its climax, some lads in the gallery wanted a better view and used a gas pipe to pull themselves above the heads of the crowd. The pipe cracked, but as the gas escaped Henry Gilberg, sitting nearby with his wife and children, spotted the accident and rushed to plug the pipe with his handkerchief. His quick-thinking dealt with the danger, but could not prevent the catastrophe that was to follow. Someone in the audience smelt the escaping gas and yelled out "Fire." Almost immediately someone else turned off the gas. The terrified audience was plunged into darkness and began a frantic stampede towards the exits. People fell over chairs and benches and over each other in their single-minded determination to reach the safety of the streets outside. The crowds rushing from the ground floor hall and the gallery above converged near the pay box, and the power of the mass pushing from behind made it impossible for those at the fore to slow down. The narrow stairway from the gallery became densely packed with an immovable heap of humanity. The consequences were devastating. Within five minutes seventeen people were dead, sixteen of them crushed to death.

Henry Gilberg's son Daniel managed to scramble over the heads of those in the death trap; he dashed into the street and alerted a passing policeman, who swung his rattle to raise the alarm. A contingent of police officers entered the hall and began the difficult task of sorting out the chaos inside the theatre. The officers shouted up the gallery stairs, ordering the still struggling crowd to stand back. They then began gently easing bodies from the tangled heap, giving priority to those showing signs of life. The task was made more difficult when men with relatives in the gallery tried to fight their way over the wall of trapped bodies to find their families. Police officers forced them back.

Medical help was called for, and several doctors arrived, including Drs Dukes, Burke and Phillips. There was little they could do. Most survivors escaped unscathed, and the few that had cuts and bruises were packed into cabs and taken to the London Hospital. All were sent home after treatment. The seventeen dead were mostly women and children. Isaac Levy, 70, apparently died of a heart attack while trying to rescue his wife, Gertrude, who was 47. Gertrude was among those killed in the crush. Elizabeth Eisen, 28, Jane Goldstein, 24, and their husbands lived in the same house in Hanbury Street. The women, both pregnant, had gone together to see the performance, and died together in the panic. Sarah Renalde, 20, of Booth Street, Spitalfields, also died. She had been due to marry. The money saved for her trousseau paid for her funeral. The police found the body of a young woman clutching a child. At first they believed both had perished, then realised the child was unharmed. One of the last bodies recovered was that of little Eva Marks, 9, of Spital Street. The bodies were laid out in the club's reading room to await identification by relatives and friends.

Henry Gilberg, the man who had used his handkerchief to stem the escape of gas, and whose son had raised the alarm, was one of those to suffer most from the tragedy. He told the *Times* (20 January):

> My son Harry and I were going towards the steps when we were stopped by the crowd of people, who crushed us against the wall and hurt our

legs. We could not move one way or the other, but my younger son,
Daniel, got free and, seeing no other way out, he climbed on the heads of
the people who were jammed in the staircase and ran over them to the
street where he told a policeman, who came to the spot. When I got out
of the crush, ultimately, with Harry, I went off to hospital in a cab, where
we got our wounds dressed. We then went home, expecting to find that
my wife had got out all right; but she was not there. I then went back to
the hall and asked the police to let me in again. They would not do so for
a while, but then they did let me in, and I found that my wife was dead,
and that my boy, Isaac, was also dead.

News travelled fast around the Jewish ghetto and the Hebrew Dramatic
Club was soon besieged by throngs of distraught men and women. The
night was filled with the wailing and cries of the crowd, and the
bemused police officers decided to clear the street around the theatre,
admitting only those who believed a relative had been killed.

The disaster happened on Tuesday night. On Thursday afternoon
coroner Wynne Baxter went to the club to open the inquest. The bodies
were formally identified by a trail of distressed parents, husbands and
other close relatives. Permission was given for the burials. Late that
afternoon, after dusk, the first seven burials took place at West Ham
Cemetery. The cemetery was lit by the lamps from hearses and
mourning coaches, and by the glare from a bonfire. The remaining ten
victims were buried on Friday. The traditional Jewish burials attracted
much public and press attention. As the *East London Observer* (29
January) noted:

> Each of the ten ceremonies that were performed on Friday was painful,
> even for the mere sightseer to witness, and the demonstrative chorus of
> grief with which each body was accompanied to the graveside contrasted
> strangely with the pathetic reserve to which Christians are accustomed.

Mourners and sympathisers lined the streets in Spitalfields and filled the
graveyard burial hall where the funeral service, led by the Reverend E.
Spero, took place. "The crowd which fills the little wooden building
chants a sort of response," wrote the *East London Observer*'s reporter,

> until the hall is full of wailing, which gives a semi-barbaric air to the
> ceremonial.... The function contrasts strangely with our own service and
> jars on the unaccustomed ear.

The seventeen coffins were buried in a single row.

The fascination shown by papers such as the *East London Observer* was exactly what the more established Jewish community feared. The *Jewish Chronicle* immediately launched a disaster appeal to help the victims and their families, but their attitude suggests this was done as much to pre-empt efforts from outside the community than as a purely philanthropic exercise. The appeal was announced the day following the disaster and within twenty-four hours £200 had been collected. On 21 January, just days after the tragedy, the first flickerings of resentment were evident in the *Jewish Chronicle's* editorial.

> We hear too often from abroad of panic in a synagogue, the fall of a gallery on the Day of Atonement, or other like calamities. Our people are very gregarious and very excitable, but no such disaster has ever happened to English Jews, and the audience of the Dramatic Club had evidently not yet become nationalised or learnt the phlegm and calmness which form so valuable a feature of the English character.

On the same day the *Times* printed a letter from Chief Rabbi, the Reverend Dr Hermann Adler. The letter clearly played down the need for donations.

> The families, without exception, belong to the humble, wage-earning class, yet few are in abject want. No bread winner has happily been taken away. I am of opinion that the generous contributions which have already flowed in will suffice to meet every legitimate claim. I deem it right to state this fact, for, in the face of so much distress throughout the country, it would not be fair to divert any portion of the public bounty from other and still more urgent needs. Pecuniary gifts cannot heal the gaping wound which the sudden deaths have inflicted...

The next edition of the *Jewish Chronicle*, on 28 January, gently criticised Adler's statements.

> It has been gratifying to observe that the sympathy has been felt as strongly outside the community as within. This would have been no doubt even more widely expressed had it not been checked by Dr Adler's letter which has been absurdly taken in some quarters as refusing of outside help and sympathy as Jews are sufficient to themselves. It need scarcely be said that this could not have been Dr Adler's intention, but no step that could check the expression of goodwill on the part of our neighbours should be taken without due deliberation and foresight.

The editorial went on to comment on the inescapable bonds that linked established Jews with the unwelcome newcomers.

The disaster itself illustrates in a most striking manner the responsibility of all London Jews for one another. Whether English or foreign, the Jews are a collective whole in the eyes of the world at large and whatever befalls one section is held to apply to the whole community. We scarcely need this reminder of our common interest with all London Jews, wherever they reside or wherever their original home. If there is any tendency to repudiate this solidarity among us, this shocking disaster would be sure to show the impossibility of so doing. The reputation of the London Jews is bound up inexorably with that of the Russian Jews of the East End.

On 4 February the *Jewish Chronicle* announced the closure of the disaster fund. Donations had reached £311.13s.1d, which, considering £200 had rolled in during the first twenty-four hours, was a pitifully small total. Adler's letter had almost certainly stemmed the flow of goodwill. In closing down the fund the *Jewish Chronicle* echoed Adler's sentiments.

> It was felt that no mere pecuniary relief could assuage the grief of those who had lost relatives, and that it was due to the subscribers to the fund that no more money should be granted to each case than was absolutely needed....

The inquest into the deaths was concluded at the Vestry in Shoreditch Town Hall on 11 February. The coroner's jury returned a verdict of accidental death on all seventeen victims. Inquest over, and fund closed, on 18 February the *Jewish Chronicle* felt able to reveal its true feelings on an event that had shaken the whole community.

> We plainly tell our foreign brethren that one of the most direct causes of the recent disaster has been the persistent isolation in which they have kept themselves from their fellow Jewish workmen in all the social amenities of life. When they want aid in sickness or distress they are willing to claim their privileges as Jews living in England, but in all their social relations they keep themselves aloof from us, and thus forego the advantage of such an institution as the Jewish Working Men's Club, where every practicable precaution has been taken to avoid such a calamity as the late panic. The recent event ought to be a lesson to avoid such perform-ances of strolling minstrels acting in the jargon, and helping to keep up the alienation of the foreign contingent. In making these remarks, we are urged by a consideration of the best interests of these brethren of ours, whose chance of livelihood is largely diminished by their not helping to hasten the process of 'Anglicising.' We have felt at liberty to give this piece of advice as we have fortunately been the means of alleviating much of the

distress which has been caused by the accident that gave rise to our remarks.

The disaster drew attention not only to the immigrant Jews, but also to the lamentable fact that standards of safety in such clubs were entirely outside the jurisdiction of the Metropolitan Board of Works. The coroner's jury added riders to its verdict:

> That had the exit from the gallery been in the same direction as the exit from the body of the hall, fewer deaths would have occurred.

> With whatever intention the Club was opened, it had certainly degenerated into a place of amusement.

> That all places of this and similar kind, whether used as private clubs or other, should, to prevent a future recurrence of the calamity that had taken place, be placed under the immediate supervision of some public representative body.

The Metropolitan Board of Works sent an inspector to make a token examination of the Prince's Street premises, but was well aware that it was powerless to insist on changes. Superintending architect John Hebb reported:

> I made a survey of the premises…the day after the accident occurred and feel no hesitation in saying that they are totally unfit for the purposes for which they are used.

The Metropolitan Board of Works asked its solicitor, R. Waird, if the building could be regarded as coming under the Board's jurisdiction. His reply was unequivocal.

> I am sorry to say that I have not been…successful in solving the great difficulty of applying legislation to such buildings as the Hebrew Dramatic Club without including many buildings which the Board would not intend to include and the inclusion of which would be so oppressive that a Bill if introduced would have very little chance of any support in the House of Commons.

If it was any consolation to the frustrated officials of the Metropolitan Board of Works, facts indicated that even where regulations were applicable, they were often totally ignored. On 6 September 1887 more than 170 people were killed after a fire and panic at the Theatre Royal in Exeter. The original plans for the layout of the theatre had been altered to allow for a row of shops along one side of the building. These made the exits totally inadequate, and most of the dead were killed as they struggled and fought to reach safety. London Fire Chief Captain Shaw, who seemed to have a habit of turning up at major disasters during the Victorian period, was in the district when the fire happened, and he was made an official adviser to the coroner. The government asked him for a full report on the incident, and his conclusions were scathing.

> The saddest part of this matter is that no lesson of any kind has been taught by the event, as everyone who has studied the subject either theoretically or practically knew beyond any possibility of a doubt what the whole action of the fire and smoke would be under such circumstances; and moreover, the lessons and warning of recent years had prepared all concerned for the terrible catastrophe precisely as it actually occurred.

Changes in legislation were obviously vital, and the London County Council introduced important new regulations to tighten up safety in the capital's theatres and entertainment halls. The London Place of Entertainment Act 1889 was brought in despite strong opposition from a powerful lobby of theatre owners and managers. It gave the LCC power to carry out annual inspections and to insist on alterations considered necessary to ensure public safety. Failure to comply earned the owners a £50 fine and a £10 per day penalty for every day the offence continued. Theatres kept open without a current licence were liable to fines of £50 per day.

In 1890 a Public Health Amendment Act obliged all "places of public resort" to meet urban authority requirements. These included being of substantial construction and having ample, safe and convenient means of exit and entrance that were kept free of obstruction at all times. The premises were to be open to inspection by the authority's officers "at all reasonable times." Any unlicensed premises within the scope of the Act could be deemed a "disorderly house." The term "places of public resort" covered:

> ...a building used or constructed or adapted to be used either ordinarily or occasionally as a church, chapel, or other place of public worship or as a theatre, public hall, public concert room, public ballroom, public lecture room or public exhibition room, or as a public place of assembly for persons admitted thereto by tickets or by payment, or used, or constructed or adapted to be used, either ordinarily or occasionally for any other public purpose.

These bills were major steps forward in ensuring public safety, and were a tribute to the dedication and determination of Captain Shaw.

Inadequate exits and entrances were not the only dangers in nineteenth century buildings. The phrase "they brought the house down" rang only too true in the ears of many Victorians. Building construction often left stability in the lap of the gods, and a particularly excitable gathering might be all that was needed to send a hall or house tumbling to its foundations. Poor quality cement and other building materials, coupled with unskilled and shoddy workmanship, meant whole streets of so-called "speculative" developments were held together more by luck than design. As John Ruskin wrote in *Stones of Venice* (1851–1853):

> Some vaultless floor that drops the staggering crowd through the jagged rents of its rotten timbers, some fungous wall of nascent rottenness that a thunder shower soaks down with its workmen to a heap of slime and death. These we hear of day by day.

Building regulations did exist in London, but were almost impossible to enforce and widely ignored. The 1774 Building Act allowed for the appointment of district surveyors in Westminster and the City of London and ordered new buildings and alterations to existing buildings should meet with the surveyor's approval. It also stipulated standards of construction for classes of houses, from mansions with values above £850 to more modest abodes occupying less than 350 square feet and worth less than £150.

One of the main purposes of the Act was to prevent and restrict damage by fire. It was a step forward, but failed to deal with some key problems. There was nothing, for instance, to stipulate the width of a street. Therefore tall buildings could lawfully be constructed either side of narrow passageways, making any fire difficult to contain. Meanwhile London's rapid growth left the district surveyors with an impossible workload. When the Act was passed in 1774 the population was approximately eight hundred thousand. By 1845 it had reached two and a quarter million. A district surveyor originally appointed to steward a small and easily manageable area soon found himself in an urban ghetto where he could not hope to know of every piece of building work in progress, and in any event would lack time for proper inspections.

The London Fire service in 1845 was a haphazard assortment of parish pumps and the thirteen fire stations making up the London fire Engine Establishment, an organisation financed and run by insurance companies. Parish pumps, made compulsory in the 1774 Building Act, were often little more than "squirts," more useful for window cleaning than fighting fires. The pumps were supposed to be housed in properly maintained stations located to suit their particular parish, but in reality the system was a shambles better suited to a black comedy than a vital service on which lives depended.

Some stations were disguised to look like ordinary houses in a bid to deter would-be users. Neighbouring parishes squabbled over the use of equipment and would often refuse to attend a fire within yards of their station if it happened to fall within the official boundaries of another parish. Pumpkeepers did not always live close to their equipment and it often proved impossible to locate them to unlock the station. The numbers of pumps per parish stipulated under the Act had been made derisory by London's expansion. The City was obliged to provide 218 engines, but only seventy were required by the rest of the metropolis put together. By the mid-1850s the City was a speck on the map when compared with the sprawling mass of London, but provisions for fire equipment had not been reviewed.

The London Fire Engine Establishment came under the charge of James Braidwood, a strict disciplinarian who brought professionalism to fire-fighting and trained his eighty men to act as an efficient force. Unfortunately, the LFEE was essentially a private enterprise, existing solely to protect the interests of the insurance companies. It would sometimes tackle a blaze in an uninsured building, but only if it was a threat to nearby insured buildings. Victorian bureaucracy provided another hazard to successful fire-fighting. A policeman spotting a blaze would have to send to the nearest fire station and to the nearest turncock responsible for turning on the water supply. Rescue equipment—the so-called fire escapes—came under the auspices of yet another organisation, the voluntary-run Royal Society for the Protection of Life from Fire. The Society established and maintained escapes at strategic points across London, but worked independently from either the parish pumps or the Brigade. Opportunities for confusion and delay were manifold, and delay often proved fatal.

The London Building Act of 1844 provided the first comprehensive set of building regulations for the metropolis. Again, one of the prime objectives was to reduce the risks of fire. District surveyors were given more powers to supervise building work and authority to hoard up "dangerous" buildings and have their owners served with a notice to make them safe. Outside the City of London the Metropolitan Police was responsible for procedures to deal with dangerous structures. The force employed its own surveyors and human nature being what it is, the police surveyor and district surveyor were often in dispute and failed to agree common policies. The situation was further complicated by an 1848 Sewers Act which gave the Metropolitan Commissioners for Sewers authority to serve notice against dangerous buildings. They could also, on the agreement of two Justices, complete necessary work and pass the bill to the property's owners. The Building Act was tightened up again in 1855, but confusion remained over the responsibilities of the various authorities. This confusion, combined with the unrealistic workload of the district surveyors, meant many dangerous and severely defective buildings slipped through the net.

Buildings often remained standing against all odds, and collapsed only when structural work put extra stress on an already unstable construction. This is exactly what happened at a row of furniture showrooms in Tottenham Court Road in May 1857. Mr Hunter's showroom at number 148 had been seriously damaged in a fire earlier in the year, and in April he decided to appoint a builder to carry out refurbishments. His neighbour and trade rival, Mr Maple, thought it would be a good time to improve his own properties, numbers 146 and 147. Both men appointed respected builders and surveyors and by May work was well underway. Hunter's property was empty, but Maple's continued in use as a store and as home to more than twenty of his staff.

The first sign of impending problems came early in May. Maple's builder, a Mr Taylor, asked district surveyor Henry Baker for permission to cut back a chimney breast. Baker was against the plan, but eventually agreed subject to the surrounding wall being strengthened. Meanwhile, Hunter's builder removed an adjoining chimney breast without bothering to consult the surveyor. Baker protested, but the work was subsequently approved by a surveyor from the Metropolitan Police, so there was nothing the district surveyor could do about it.

At 6:00 AM on Saturday 9 May both sets of workmen began remedial work on the party wall where the chimney breasts had been. This involved underpinning which required holes to be cut into the wall. The extra strain this caused proved too much. Just after 7:00 AM some of the workmen noticed dust falling and seconds later there was a cracking sound, closely followed by a noise like thunder. The party wall collapsed, and the two houses and their occupants were thrown to the ground. About twenty of Maple's staff were in bed or preparing for breakfast, and they plummeted down amid the shattered timbers, bricks and plasterwork. Cook Ann Driscoll had been making breakfast in her kitchen on the second floor. As the debris and dust settled her kettle could be seen boiling merrily on the range still attached to a chimney stack. Ann was less fortunate. Her badly mutilated corpse was later dug from the ruins by police and labourers.

Rescue efforts began immediately. A contingent of police was soon on the scene and a roll call of those known to be in the premises was taken. At least twenty people were buried in the rubble, and rescuers began a careful search of the ruins. The spectacle was described by the *Times* in their report on 11 May:

> ...girders and beams are snapped or mingled together in the strangest of forms: flooring boards are wrung from their joists, and sheets of lead, torn off like paper, are rolled and curled up in the most curious shapes; lath and plaster, brick and mortar, doors and staircases, window frames and cupboards, bedsteads, chairs, tables and looking glasses, are smashed and broken and pounded up into rubbish; and, as the men work among the mass, they fall on a cup or a saucer, or some other fragile piece of crockery, still strangely preserved, secure in its weakness, amid the general wreck.

There were several extraordinary escapes. Housekeeper Mrs Christmas and two young women from the drapery department in Maple's were chatting in the second floor sitting room when their home disintegrated. They were thrown down, but managed to crawl from the rubble virtually unscathed. A young lad had been cleaning knives on the second floor, but also escaped with trivial injuries. However, Frederick Byng, the chief clerk, was in bed when the house fell, and was later found still in bed, but crushed to death by falling timbers and masonry. Byng and the cook, Ann Driscoll, were the only members of Mr Maple's staff to be killed. Three of the building workers died instantly, and a fourth, the son of Maple's builder Mr Taylor, died later in University College Hospital. The careful search through the debris went on through the night. The last body, that of bricklayer's labourer James Kivil, was recovered on Sunday morning.

West Middlesex coroner Thomas Wakley was in Brighton caring for his seriously ill wife when the disaster happened, so the inquiry was conducted by his deputy, Mr G. Brett. Architect Mr T. Marsh Nelson was instructed to investigate the causes of the accident, and his report was an indictment of building standards and existing building regulations. The Tottenham Court Road houses were in a deplorable condition, he stated, and should have been pulled down rather than refurbished. Walls were cracked in all directions and built with materials of the worst possible description." New brickwork had been of the most inferior quality and cement, although purchased from a well-known supplier, was useless. "It is much to be regretted," wrote Marsh Nelson, "that respectable houses will countenance the sale of such rubbish under the name of cement." The architect's conclusion on the condition of the houses was blunt.

> With such a state of things it is only surprising that the houses kept up as long as they did; almost the slightest disturbing cause would at any time have been sufficient to have occasioned the accident, whether it arose from the one house or the other, both were in an unsafe condition…. My belief is, from a knowledge of the buildings in the Metropolis, that not only are the houses on the eastern side of Tottenham Court Road in the state described, but that a very large proportion of the houses erected between 1774 and 1845 are, or will be in a few years, in the same condition.

District surveyor Henry Baker had come in for some harsh criticism at the inquest. He admitted he had not inspected the buildings before work began. Marsh Nelson blamed the system for Baker's failings.

> The legislature has devised the best possible means of preventing him attending to his duties. His district extends from Tottenham Court Road to Highgate Hill, a distance of about three miles, and it contains upwards of about 20,000 houses…it would take him six weeks, allowing only half an hour to each house, to visit the works going on in this district.

Marsh Nelson also criticised the system that made the district surveyor liable to superintend work ordered by surveyors employed by the police, even when the district surveyor considered the work improper. He ended his report with a call for better building laws.

> I think that the Government incur a great responsibility in continuing in force an Act of Parliament in the face of the frequently expressed opinions of all parties, from the humblest builder to the judges of the land. It is an

Act which legalises bad building; it has made London as inferior to many continental cities as it was formerly superior; and by its conflicting, and in many cases absurd and contradictory regulations, it defeats the only object that a proper Building Act should have in view, viz, the substantial construction of all houses and buildings without any exemptions whatever, the prevention of the spread of fire, and the protection of the Metropolis from such accidents as the painful one now under investigation.

The shortcomings of the Building Acts and the haphazard arrangements for fire-fighting were again brought sharply to the public eye in March 1858, when a blaze swept through a grossly over-crowded tenement.

Auctioneer Mr Taylor made his living by wheeling and dealing in the property business. One of his favourite money-making ventures was to take on the leases of old houses and rent them out at inflated prices after carrying out "improvements." In 1850 Taylor took on the lease of a coach house and stable in Gilbert Street, Bloomsbury, and set to work on extensive alterations. Using mainly old materials, and without a surveyor's advice, he constructed a house, shop and large room that extended into the yard of a house in Great Russell Street. The large room was separated from the rest of the premises by a sheet of thin, rough boarding. The shop was divided from the residential part of the house by similar rough boarding, though in this case the flimsy partition stopped short of the ceiling. Upstairs were eight small rooms, and these were let to families of lodgers. The rear of the house was windowless, so some of the rooms had no natural light. The property was part of the Duke of Bedford's estate and Taylor's work was approved by the Duke's architect, who extended the lease from twenty-one to forty-six years on the strength of it.

In March 1858 the large room was let to a mineralogist, Mr Calvert. Calvert lived in the Great Russell Street house behind the Gilbert Street premises, and built an entrance into the room direct from his own home. The shop was rented to a carpenter, and three families lived in the upstairs rooms: the Eastwoods and their three children; the Hedgers and their two children; and the Smiths. The Smiths had just two rooms with a total floorspace of 180 square feet as home for themselves and their eleven youngsters. Only one of the rooms had a window. Gilbert Street was a narrow turning, running between Museum Street and Bury Street, and at one end access was obstructed by shoring erected by a builder outside another property some eight months earlier.

The exact cause of the fire at about 2:00 AM on 29 March remains unknown, although experts of the day decided it started in the carpenter's shop. Police constable Sullivan was on patrol, and noticed smoke pouring from the front of the house. He rattled on the door and shouted, doing his best to warn the occupants of the danger. The house was already well ablaze and, as the unfortunate residents who tried to escape soon found, the narrow wooden staircase was engulfed in flames. Sullivan noticed a figure screaming from a top window. The force of the fire blew out the shop front and almost instantaneously the person leapt from the window in a desperate attempt to escape the flames, landing on Sullivan. The constable fell to the ground, momentarily stunned, but soon recovered his senses. The jumper was Richard Smith, 17, the eldest of the eleven Smith children. He suffered burns and serious fractures to his ribs, and died soon after arrival at University College Hospital.

Meanwhile the Eastwood family had woken and were screaming at their first floor window. The screams and commotion brought local people rushing to the scene. A painter named Thomas Curle, of Bury Street, found a ladder that had been left at a nearby building, and with the help of other men carried it to the burning house. Curle carefully positioned the ladder to reach the window where the Eastwoods could be seen crying for help. Curle braved the searing heat to climb up. John Eastwood, 50, handed him his daughter Elizabeth, 10, and Curle carried her to safety. Scaling the ladder again, he brought down Mrs Elizabeth Eastwood, 32, who clutched her 18-month-old daughter Mary Ann. The heat from the building was now overpowering, but John Eastwood managed to scramble down the ladder with his third child, Thomas, 3, before collapsing on the pavement. Crowds now noticed a white-sleeved arm waving from a top floor window. Curle tried to get the ladder to reach, but it fell too short to be of any use.

Elsewhere, efforts to get professional fire-fighters to the scene were thwarted by a series of problems. There were two parish engines within a minute's run of Gilbert Street and, unusually, both were in reasonable working order. The problem was no one knew who was in charge of them. The keeper had moved on, and nobody at the address given on the station had any idea where the new keeper—and the keys to the station—could be found. The message calling for the Brigade engines was somehow delayed, and they did not arrive until about half an hour after the fire had started. The fire escape, which was based at a different location to the fire engines, was delayed by the shoring that blocked the end of Gilbert Street. By the time the obstacle was passed precious time had been lost; the front of the blazing house was like an inferno. Firemen, knowing families were still trapped inside the building, tried to reach a back window, but there was none. Within minutes of the Brigade's arrival there was a thundering crash as the house collapsed, taking with it any hopes of saving more lives. The fire spread through Calvert's mineral storeroom on the ground floor and into his house in Great Russell Street. Calvert escaped, but his house was seriously damaged. The skill of the Brigade fire-fighters prevented the blaze spreading to neighbouring properties.

When the fierce flames were reduced to flickering embers, the Brigade began the grim task of recovering the dead. Mrs Harriet Smith, 41, and Mrs Eliza Hedger, 50, apparently died during their vain attempts to flee the building. One young lad in the Smith family died while putting on his trousers. The rest of the Smiths—the father, Richard, 40, and remaining nine children aged between 2 and 15 years old—died from the effects of smoke and fumes. The same fate befell William Hedger, 53, and his sons William, 20, and John, 13. The bodies were carried to St Giles' Workhouse nearby. The Eastwoods were also taken to the workhouse to be cared for until they could find a new home.

The fire killed fifteen people and incited a public outcry that provided valuable ammunition for those demanding improvements to building regulations and a statutory fire service. Coroner Wakley ensured there was a detailed inquiry into the disaster, and experts quickly decided most of the deaths had been at least partially due to the victims inhaling toxic gases emitted from minerals burning in the ground floor store room.

Wakley instructed architect T. Marsh Nelson to survey the ruins of the Gilbert Street house and to make recommendations on how management of fire escapes and fire engines could be improved. The report revealed the house was constructed in flagrant breach of building regulations, and should have been condemned. The partitions separating the store room and shop from the residential part of the property were grossly inadequate, and the general poor construction had contributed to the building's early collapse during the blaze. Marsh Nelson noted the man who had been district surveyor when the building was constructed had become so frustrated by difficulties of enforcing regulations that he, "...a gentleman of great ability, and highly respected, subsequently threw up his appointment, finding that he could no longer conscientiously hold the office". The architect criticised the number of lodgers packed into the tiny, poorly-ventilated rooms and thought landlord Taylor could have fallen foul of the Nuisances Removal Act, had it been enforced in the district.

Marsh Nelson took a broad swipe at the existing fire-fighting system, and made a strong call for the establishment of a properly run and financed statutory Metropolitan Fire Brigade. He recommended what we now all take for granted: a fire service that combined rescue and fire-fighting equipment; that operates for the good of all and without boundaries; that is housed in suitable stations; and that has access to quantities of water. While praising the Brigade superintendent James Braidwood and his managers, Marsh Nelson pointed out that the organisation was a private enterprise.

> As a financial operation, it is more profitable to them to run the risk of half-an-hour's delay, and pay the consequent loss, than to establish new stations in the suburbs of London. They have added no new stations since the force was established about twenty years ago, and fires have increased during that time in an alarming proportion, compared with population and houses.

Marsh Nelson was demanding standards ahead of his time, but his outspoken and fearless call for improvements in the fire service and building regulations helped chip away at government complacency.

Three years after the Gilbert Street fire there was a massive blaze in Tooley Street, Southwark. The fire began in a riverside warehouse and rapidly spread. Warehouse after warehouse, packed with expensive goods that had arrived in the docks from all over the world, went up in smoke. The whole Brigade was called in to bring the flames under control. James Braidwood and one of his colleagues were killed when a wall collapsed on them. The blaze was brought under control after two days, but was not completely doused for more than a fortnight. Damage amounted to several hundred thousand pounds, and the incident provided the final push needed to force the government to establish a statutory fire service at public expense. The Metropolitan Fire Brigade Act was passed in 1865 and the new brigade was launched under the command of Captain Eyre Shaw in 1866.

Effective changes to building regulations proved more difficult. Houses and other buildings continued to crumble quietly until some relatively minor disturbance sent them crashing to the ground. Usually, only those incidents resulting in multiple deaths made the headlines. Sometimes buildings collapsed when large numbers of people collected, especially when the audience decided to clap and stamp their feet in response to a performance or speech. Most incidents happened outside London, but on 26 January 1865 more than a hundred people plunged through the collapsing first floor of a school in Westminster. Around five hundred men, women and children had gathered in the Catholic Free School Rooms in Peter's Street to hear results of a lottery. The school was attached to the Church of St Mary, which was in debt, and the lottery had been organised to raise much-needed funds. Prizes were of unusually high quality, including a cabinet, gold brooches and rings, and an ivory crucifix, and interest was running high. The crowd packed into the thirty-foot by sixty-foot hall and shuffled forward as the prizes were drawn so they could see if their 6*d* tickets had been lucky. At about 8:15 PM a whole section of the floor suddenly gave way.

The screams and cries of people injured as they plunged to the playroom below mingled with the terrified screeches of those struggling to maintain a footing on the first floor. Police and firemen arrived quickly, and began sorting out the carnage on the ground floor and rescuing those trapped above. Most of the injured were taken to Westminster Hospital, and thirty were detained for treatment.

Others were taken to Guy's or to St George's Hospital. Many more went straight to their homes. As with many accidents during this period, the definitive death toll is unknown. Severely injured people would often die in the privacy of their own homes, and their deaths might not be publicised. At least two died from their injuries in the School Rooms. They were the unfortunately-named Miss Adelaide Fallen, matron of the nearby Millbank Prison, and Mary Hefferson, an elderly woman.

Number six Ely Court, in Holborn, was a four-storey dump that was home to nineteen people. It looked as though it was about to fall down for months before it took the plunge. Neighbour Mr Guanziroli noticed that a support strut placed between number six and another house had rotted, and was concerned by the number of cracks in the walls, the bulging bricks and the mortar that constantly rattled down the drainpipes. He pointed out the faults to leaseholders, Mr John Clarke and Mr William Ledger, and when they failed to take action he notified the

8 Collapsed floor of St Mary's
   Catholic Free School

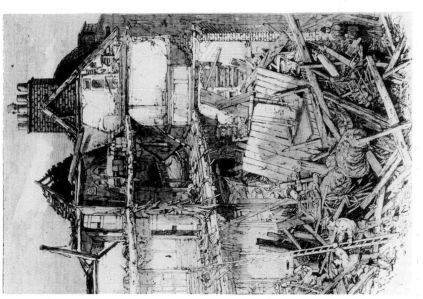

7 Ruins of Six Ely Court,
   Holborn

district surveyor's clerk. Still nothing was done, and on 16 August 1866, sixteen months after Mr Guanziroli first voiced his worries, his fears were realised: the house fell down.

Two people died in the ruins; an unemployed cook, Mrs Elizabeth Davis and, by a strange twist of fate, an employee of Mr Guanziroli, Giuseppe Carlo Casartelli. Most of the inhabitants escaped with minor injuries and shock. William Andrews, brother-in-law of the dead woman, had paid 3/9d per week to lodge at the house, and had been there for three years. He later described what had happened to coroner Dr Lankester.

> I was in bed at the time the house fell, and the first intimation I had of danger was the whole place giving way. I heard a cracking for a moment or two from the ceiling, and then the whole ceiling fell. The beams and walls all fell directly after and I was like abed in the street.

Dr Lankester asked Andrews what he did then. "Well, I put myself together and waited for death," replied Andrews. Andrews was not badly injured, and a policeman helped him to safety. Rescue work by police and labourers was slow and difficult because parts of the building were still intact, but threatening to fall at any moment. It was several hours before the bodies of Davis and Casartelli were found.

The inquest heard several fiery attacks against the landlords. Guanziroli gave a full account of his attempts to draw attention to the state of the property, and a previous tenant turned up to give his pennyworth. The coroner agreed to hear William Fox, despite strong protest from the landlords. He told how his wife had once taken a room in the house, and when the couple had moved in they found a large hole in the floor. The landlords refused to do any repairs and eventually Mrs Fox had fallen down and injured herself "for life." Fox also related how Mrs Davis, the woman who died buried in the rubble, had often remarked how they would all be buried alive when the house fell down. The jury returned a verdict of accidental death, adding the rider that there had been a lack of proper attention on the part of the landlords. Landlords Ledger and Clarke were incensed at what they considered unwarranted criticism they had suffered, and like many incensed people of the period, they wrote a letter to the *Times* on 17 August. "The house was never condemned," they insisted:

> We took a lease of this house and seven others in the year 1863, and laid out about £800 in repairing them. No main support or beam has to our

knowledge or with our sanction been cut away since we have had possession of the building.

The *Times'* editor remained sceptical.

We wonder our correspondents do not add that the house is still standing. The coroner's inquest...will, we hope, inquire how such a model lodging house was so perverse as to fall.

The majority of those who lost their lives in collapsing buildings were, at least in London, from the lower classes. They were the building labourers, or the people so impoverished they had no choice but to live in decrepit and decaying houses. Had the upper classes been more widely affected there is little doubt legislation to improve standards of building safety would have reached the statute books more rapidly. As it was, the sort of improvements called for by Marsh Nelson in 1857 were slow to materialise. The Metropolitan Police were, albeit reluctantly, responsible for taking action on dangerous structures outside the City until 1869, when the duty finally passed to the Metropolitan Board of Works. In October 1891 bye-laws were passed which gave district surveyors control over quality of walls and foundations, and materials used for supports and plastering. Three years later the london Building Act effectively brought together the various pieces of legislation that had been passed since 1844.

Buildings continued—and still continue—to slip through the supervisory net. In April 1908, for example, eight hotel workers died after their ramshackle lodging house disintegrated about their ears. The lodging house consisted of five houses next to the select Berners Hotel, Oxford Street. The houses were known to be in poor condition and were about to be demolished to make way for an extension to the hotel. In the meantime they were used to house hotel staff. At about 2:00 AM on 8 April two of the houses closest to the hotel gave up the struggle to keep standing. Twenty people were rescued alive from the rubble, but eight who had been sleeping on the ground floor were killed.

Even today the construction industry remains one of the most potentially dangerous forms of employment. Unskilled labourers continue to put themselves at risk on building sites, working long hours and often without adequate safety provisions. The Health and Safety Executive officers responsible for ensuring safety standards on building sites are arguably as hopelessly over-stretched as the district surveyors of the nineteenth century. In the 1980s and early 1990s the Isle of Dogs in London's Docklands was the largest building site in Europe and the biggest commercial construction project in the world. At the peak of the massive building programme, responsibility for overseeing safety standards fell to a single officer from the Health and Safety Executive, and the district formed just part of his territory.

CHAPTER THREE

Explosions

The Victorian era was an age of invention and innovation, and the pioneering pace of progress sometimes ran ahead of safety and common sense. This unbridled enthusiasm had its most catastrophic and lethal potential in the field of high explosives. Legislation to control manufacture of the highly volatile substances lagged well behind large-scale production.

One of the earliest and most perilous practices to warrant government action was the manufacture of the fireworks that were so much in demand for displays and celebrations in London's parks and pleasure gardens. New technology had spawned a new generation of fireworks, with multi-coloured flames and dramatic effects. The manufacture of such wonders had inherent dangers. Women and children formed the main workforce in the back-rooms of homes crammed into run-down neighbourhoods. The potential for disaster was manifest. The trade had been outlawed by an Act passed during the reign of King William III (1689-1702), which made the manufacture of fireworks a "nuisance" and ruled the manufacturer would be guilty of manslaughter if anyone was killed as a result. However, this legislation was widely ignored, and it became accepted that the authorities would turn a blind eye to the industry. In fact, the government and Queen Victoria were among the most valuable customers on the firework-makers' books. Fireworks were also popular with the multitudes and vast displays were frequent features at pleasure gardens such as Vauxhall and Cremorne, and in London's numerous theatres. Most firework factories were based in ordinary dwelling houses in the Lambeth district and, to a lesser extent, in East London. The choice of location was related to the endemic poverty of these areas and the ready availability of cheap, casual labour. From a safety viewpoint, the areas could hardly have been less suitable. Houses were tightly-packed and widespread damage and fire would be a predictable consequence of any explosion. Explosions in such premises carried the additional risk that fireworks ignited were likely to shower the neighbourhood.

Mishaps were common, and increased commensurably with the public's demand for more and better fireworks. The death toll rose as the century progressed and demands on the manufacturers and their workforce increased. In February 1842 the famous pyrotechnist Mr D'Ernst was killed after a series of explosions and a fire at his home and factory in Lambeth Butts. D'Ernst had built a small factory in the backyard of his house, and the first sign of trouble came with a deafening explosion that rocked the districts of Lambeth, Kennington and Vauxhall at about 11:40 AM. Lesser blasts followed, and thousands of spectators were soon at the scene, keen to discover what was going on. Police from the High Street station were also alerted, and sent alarms to the fire stations in the area. Rumours that a hundredweight of gunpowder was stored in the building's cellar kept the fire crews from venturing too close, and within thirty minutes the buildings had been destroyed. The firemen flooded the cellar—which contained six barrels packed with gunpowder—with hundreds of gallons of water and then made a search of the smoking ruins. Four bodies were recovered. D'Ernst had burned to death along with his sister-in-law, Mrs Hampshire, and assistants John Whiting and George Gibbets. Queen Victoria contributed £50 to a fund set up to help D'Ernst's family. In another incident, in Asylum Road, Westminster Road in October 1845, a house burned down after a squib unexpectedly exploded and ignited explosives and fireworks stored on the premises. Mrs Hengler, another well-known figure in the firework world, was burned to death. Her place as firework queen was taken by Mrs Coton, who was to share Hengler's fate at a later date.

Manufacturers farmed out much of the production to homeworkers. The job was poorly paid and the dangers grossly underestimated. High explosives were treated with frightening contempt. In January 1846 teenager William Kenyon had been sent home to King Street, Lambeth Walk to turn two hundredweight of an explosive mixture of sulphur, saltpetre and antimony into "stars." As Kenyon chatted with a group of friends in his cellar the mixture exploded. Kenyon and another youth named Holmes died instantly. Two other lads, a young woman and her child were badly burned. Kenyon had been working for pyrotechnist Mr Darby, who specialised in making fireworks for use in theatres, and whose own premises were regularly wrecked by explosions. In January

1860 two men died from burns suffered after a blast at Darby's home and factory in Regent Street, Lambeth Walk. So-called "coloured fires" burst into flames as they were drying beside a stove, and the flames quickly reached nearby stores of explosives. The three workmen present were overpowered by thick, choking fumes, but were dragged clear by neighbours who had noticed smoke billowing from the windows. The men all suffered severe burns and two died after reaching Guy's Hospital.

East London did not escape its share of explosions. As in Lambeth, the firework manufacturers lived in poor districts, with narrow streets and houses squeezed tightly together. John Clitherow ran his firework business from Weaver Street in Spitalfields. The premises were divided into different compartments for mixing, filling and storage. The chemicals used to make fireworks were highly volatile and unpredictable, and in September 1850 a minor fire in the mixing room escalated to cause extensive damage to nearly forty neighbouring houses. The sparks from a small explosion ignited other fireworks in the building and scores of rockets and flares tore through the roof in an impromptu and deadly display. Clitherow and one of his workmen were blasted into the street, but miraculously survived. One bystander was less fortunate. He was knocked down and killed by one of the fire engines rushing to the scene. Houses in Weaver Street, Spicer Street, Buxton Street and New Church Court were shaken, many suffering severe damage to their roofs and windows. Mr Clitherow's factory was burned to the ground, but the firemen managed to prevent the blaze spreading. Four years later firework manufacturer Mr Watson lost his wife and children after his home was turned into a furnace when a firework was accidentally ignited. Watson had been working overtime at his home in Coleman Street, St George's-in-the-East, in an effort to meet orders for Guy Fawkes day.

In the 1850s the Coton family were among the leading pyrotechnists in London, and they were destined to play a key role in the development of laws to control gunpowder production in Britain. In 1854 the Cotons were riding high. Mr Coton was the firework artist at the Royal Gardens at Vauxhall, scene of regular extravagant firework displays, and production must have been geared to meet incessant demand. The manufacture took place in the family home, a large three-storey house at the corner of Charles Street and Elizabeth Place in the Westminster Road. At about 6:00 PM on 6 March, Mr Coton and a young boy left Mrs

Coton, her sister and two children in the basement and went to paper some fireworks in a room on the top floor. Minutes later the house was rocked by an explosion felt by every building within a quarter of a mile. As the Coton's home began to collapse, Mrs Coton rushed into the street, screaming for help to save her husband, children and others trapped inside the crumbling building. As she spoke her home was shaken by a series of blasts, which must have been caused by stores of fireworks and explosive mixtures igniting. By this time a crowd had gathered outside, and several people were burned by Roman candles and other fireworks spat from the burning home. The fire and police services managed to lift up a grating and rescue Mrs Coton's sister and the two children from the basement. As firemen played their hoses on the flames, batches of fireworks leapt at them and into the London sky. There were eleven people in the house at the time of the first explosion. Only Mr Coton and the boy helping him to paper fireworks were killed.

The majority of people working in the firework trade were women, and Mrs Coton was perfectly capable of carrying on the family business under her own name. The house must have been rebuilt, because four years later Mrs Coton, now known as Madame Coton, was in residence and doing a roaring trade in pyrotechnics. She had secured contracts with Cremorne and Vauxhall pleasure gardens, and carried out most of the dangerous production work at her second house in Peckham. Like many large-scale manufacturers, she often used sub-contractors to help with large orders. Mrs Coton had remarried, to a William Bennett, two years after the death of Mr Coton, but she retained her name for business purposes. Madame Coton was a formidable lady. According to her foreman, Edward Tucker, she was a strong-willed woman who would not be dictated to "by anyone" and who would frequently ask his opinion and call him a fool when he gave it. Mr Bennett had little say in the day-to-day running of the business, spending most of his time on paperwork or on transporting cases made at Westminster Road for filling in Peckham, returning with the made-up fireworks before delivering them to the pleasure gardens.

Although most of the work at Westminster Road was restricted to making firework cases, some filling also took place. Small boys, aged just ten to thirteen years old, were paid about three shillings per week—a pittance even in those days—to fill cases. At about 6:30 PM on 12 July 1858, shortly after Mr Bennett had left to deliver fireworks to Cremorne Gardens, Madame Coton, her mother-in-law and some of the child workers were at the house. Three of the young lads were filling small cases with "coloured fire" when the unstable mixture suddenly caught light. The boys, brothers William and David Bray and Jack Watson, shouted a quick warning before escaping into the street with minor burns. The fire spread rapidly through the powder keg of a home. Police constable James Catell was patrolling nearby and noticed smoke pouring from the windows. On 17 July the *Times* reported how he described the terrifying moments that followed:

> I saw Mrs Bennett come out enveloped in flames, and she ran into an ironmonger's shop. I went up to the front door, and there met a young woman coming out, who said she was sure there was no-one else in the house. Several persons, who were tipsy, insisted upon getting into the house, but afterwards came out again. There was an explosion, and a second one, which set fire to the premises. The fireworks flew in all directions...

All hell broke loose as fireworks ploughed into the crowd of spectators and into other buildings. Rockets, squibs, asteroids, roman candles and other pyrotechnic devices designed to delight crowds in the pleasure gardens were transformed into deadly missiles to terrorise the district. One rocket flew through the window of Mr Gibson, a neighbouring firework manufacturer, turning his home-cum-factory into a raging inferno, igniting more rockets and explosives, and fueling the growing mayhem.

Madame Coton's house was blown to pieces. Debris cascaded down to cause further injury to spectators and innocent passers-by. One young woman ran for her life when she heard the explosion, only to be hit by a falling rocket. Her clothes were set ablaze and as she ran towards Westminster Bridge she was trampled by a horse galloping away in fear. She later died from her injuries. Little Caroline Bridges was standing in the crowd of spectators when the fury of the blast hurled her across the road. Police constable George Pike gently picked her up and placed her in water to put out the flames on her clothes. He found the skin of her back had been burned away. Caroline, 11, was placed in a cab and taken, conscious and sobbing, to Guy's Hospital where she died soon after. Another child, Sarah Ann Vaughan Williams, also 11, was returning from an errand to post a letter when she stopped to chat with her friends at Mr Gibson's house. She was burned to death after the home was set alight by one of Madame Coton's rogue rockets. Mr Dashwood was painting the outside of Mr Gibson's house when he heard the blast. He ran and dragged three children from the scene, only to discover his own four-year-old son had followed him, been knocked flying by the crowds and had suffered a fractured shoulder. A builder and his men were busy painting a house close to Mrs Coton's home when the explosion took place. They were thrown from the scaffolding but escaped with minor injuries.

Pedestrians desperately tried to dodge the fiery cascade falling across the Blackfriars, Waterloo and Westminster districts, but more than three hundred people were injured, many seriously. One of the first doctors at the scene was Dr Donahoo, who was to help at another major incident, the Victoria Theatre panic, later in the year. He treated some sixty people for burns and other injuries at his surgery in Westminster Road. Those with the worst injuries were taken by cab to the nearby Guy's Hospital or St Thomas' Hospital. At least sixteen people were detained. The known death toll reached five, including Madame Coton who died several days later from the effects of severe burns. These were days long before the advent of antibiotics, and burns were prone to infection and particularly difficult to treat successfully.

Public outcry against back-street firework manufacturers peaked with this tragedy. Madame Coton's mishap had brought terror to London's streets, and justifiable resentment against the trade reached boiling point. Property suffered greatly. At least eleven buildings were seriously damaged and several were left in ruins. On 16 July a group of influential Southwark ratepayers met in the schoolrooms at St Paul's Church in Westminster Road. Dr Donahoo was present, and lamented the fact that although the Vestry had full knowledge of firework factories in the district they had done nothing. The meeting decided to write to the Home Secretary, Mr Walpole, to demand action to stop the trade.

The full force of the long-neglected seventeenth-century Act was now turned against Madame Coton's meek husband, William Bennett. The coroner's jury investigating the deaths of two victims, Sarah Ann Vaughan Williams and Caroline Bridges, returned a verdict that the victims had died because of an accident at the Coton's firework factory, and that William Bennett was guilty of manslaughter. Bennett was remanded to appear at the Old Bailey, and granted bail on surety of £200. Bennett appeared before Mr Justice Willes on 16 August, and the jury found him not guilty of the manslaughter of Caroline Bridges. He was further remanded until the following morning, when he faced the charge of the manslaughter of Sarah Ann. This time Mr Justice Willes directed the jury to return a guilty verdict.

Bennett's conviction, although legally unequivocal, was widely regarded as unfair. The authorities were well aware of how the firework trade worked, and had chosen to ignore the illegalities for as long as could be remembered. It was hardly equitable to suddenly resurrect and apply antiquated laws passed generations earlier. It was clear the manufacture of fireworks needed to be controlled, and that new legislation was essential.

This came with the 1860 Gunpowder Act, which laid down stringent regulations to control the manufacture and storage of gunpowder and fireworks. It outlawed back-street production by stating that buildings used to manufacture fireworks had to be a minimum of fifty yards from dwelling houses or buildings where people not connected with the factory were employed. Buildings used for the process of charging or filling containers with explosive materials were to be at least twenty yards from other workshops involved in the manufacture. Fireworks containing mixtures that could easily ignite by concussion had to be thirty or more yards from other workshops on the plant, and should never hold more than ten pounds of such compositions at any one time. Firework factories were obliged to have a storage magazine located fifty yards from any other buildings. Justices of the Peace were to licence premises for the manufacture of fireworks, and they could stipulate the maximum quantities of explosives to be allowed on the site. Licences were also required by firework sellers.

The rigid requirements of the 1860 Act effectively made manufacture of fireworks in the inner city illegal, as very few of the makers had, or could afford to purchase, premises that would meet the requirements. Sadly, it did not end the trade in London, it simply drove it further underground. Many of the licensed manufacturers could not meet demand for their goods, and were constantly undercut by unlicensed operators who had low overheads and kept labour costs to a minimum by employing women and children only. Ralph Fenwick was a well-known Lambeth firework maker. In May 1843 he had lost a worker in an explosion at his home and factory in Regent Street, Lambeth Walk. In October 1873 he was still in business, albeit illegally. His mid-terrace home in Broad Street, Lambeth, housed stores of gunpowder and other explosives. At about 9:00 AM on 4 October the house was demolished by an explosion and subsequent blaze. Fenwick, his wife and six other people were killed.

In 1874 the government explosives expert, Major Majendie, told a
Select Committee on Explosive Substances that licensed manufacturers
were angry:

> They urge that people who manufacture in their private house, employing
> their children for the purpose, and observing none of the restrictions
> enjoined by law, are able to undersell people who go to the expense of
> establishing legal factories away from towns and houses, who obtain
> licences and otherwise endeavour to place themselves within the law. I
> have at this moment a long list of persons who carry on this unlicensed
> trade in unsafe and unsuitable places; and one of the leading firework
> makers assures me that the November trade in fireworks is almost entirely
> carried out in the garrets, dwelling houses and other unauthorised places.

Licensed firework manufacturer Charles Brock also gave evidence to the
Committee. Asked if the illegal manufacturers could not afford to
purchase a plot fifty yards from any dwellings to erect sheds to carry
out their business, he answered wryly: "They are so poor as to be quite
unable to erect a shed at all of any kind."

Even when licenses were applied for, there was no guarantee the
Justices would exercise common sense. In October 1869 shopkeeper Mr
Titheradge had a large store of fireworks in his confectionery store in the
narrow and crowded Moscow Road, Bayswater. Titheradge and his
family, and a family of lodgers lived in the tiny rooms above the shop
front. They were asleep in their bedroom when the firework store blew
up and the building was engulfed in flames. Titheradge, his wife and
two of his children managed to escape, but Elizabeth, nine, Emma,
seven, and Edward, three, died. The lodger, a widow named Mrs Jack,
and her three children were also killed in the fire.

The 1860 Act was a step in the right direction, but it came nowhere
near ending the dangers inherent in the manufacture and storage of high
explosives. The industry was in its infancy, and those drawing up the
Bill had insufficient knowledge to ensure that the legislation was
effective. In any case, the rapid development of powerful and dangerous
concoctions that came outside the authority of the Act, because they did
not exist when the Bill was drawn up, made a mockery of the new laws.
Restrictions on gunpowder, for example, did not apply to the stronger
and more volatile 'gun coton.' The new Act was not only widely and
habitually ignored by the illegal firework makers, but also by companies

9   *Colonel Vivian Dering Majendie*

10   *Ruins of Titheradge's confectionery store,
      Bayswater*

engaged in production of high explosives for military and industrial uses. It provided minimal real control over the industry. Premises had to be licensed, but the Justices of the Peace responsible rarely had the knowledge necessary to make considered decisions. The inadequacies of the Act became glaringly obvious when 115,300 lb of gunpowder in magazines nestled alongside the Thames embankment at Erith, just twenty yards from the sea wall, blew up on 1 October 1864.

It was an ordinary Saturday morning at the Messrs John Hall and Son gunpowder magazine at Erith Reach. Two barges, the *Harriet* and the *Good Design*, had arrived from the firm's manufacturing plant thirty miles away in Faversham, and workers were busy unloading their two hundred barrels of gunpowder. It was a peaceful site. The company had purchased eighteen acres of land surrounding the magazine and the only nearby buildings were a magazine owned by the Lowood Company located just fifty yards from Hall's, and three cottages used by employees of the two firms. At about 6:42 AM the tranquillity was destroyed by three ear-splitting explosions as the barges and both gunpowder magazines exploded with a force that removed any evidence they had ever existed. The sea wall was reduced to dust, and glass and plasterwork up to ten miles away was shattered. Every man and beast within fifty miles was startled by rumbling many presumed to be caused by an earthquake. Police Sergeant Cox was getting out of bed at his home in Erith when he heard the explosion. He guessed a magazine had blown up and, after calming his wife, he set off for the marshes, gathering other helpers as he made his way through the village. Sergeant Cox arrived at the same time as two local doctors, Mr Churton and Mr Tipple.

The dust had settled to reveal a desolate, lunar-like landscape. The two magazines had disappeared, their places taken by five-foot deep craters. The barges *Harriet* and the *Good Design* had also vanished. The three workmen's cottages were in ruins. Hall's foreman, George Rayner, 39, and John Yorke, 13, lay dead in Rayner's garden. Rayner's wife and son were rescued from the rubble of their home. Walter Silver, foreman at Lowood's magazine, had been sieving milk behind his cottage when he heard the first crack of the explosion. Seconds later his home tumbled down. Silver was found dazed and badly cut, but survived. His young niece, Eliza Osborne, 8, was staying with him and suffered terrible injuries including a fractured skull. She was tended by the medics and sent to Guy's Hospital, where she died ten days later. Two labourers,

11 Explosion of the powder magazine near Erith

John Hubbard, 53, and John Eaves, 26, had been collecting tools from Silver's outhouse when the building collapsed. Hubbard, who had buried his child a week earlier, was killed instantly. Eaves died in Guy's the following afternoon. The men were not employed by the gunpowder manufacturers, but worked for a contractor repairing part of the sea wall. Elizabeth Wright, 13, was rescued from the wreck of the third cottage, but was in a critical condition. The doctors carried out an emergency operation on the spot, but despite their efforts she died shortly after arriving at Guy's. In all the doctors sent nine casualties to Guy's Hospital, and of those three died. The trek to Guy's could not have helped their chances of survival. They were carried by makeshift stretchers, including old doors, to carts and wagons that took them to Belvedere Station. Here they were put on the train to London and then conveyed to the hospital. The injuries included severe burns, fractures and lacerations, and the journey must have been tortuous.

Exactly what triggered the disaster is unknown: the only witnesses were blown to pieces. It seems likely the initial explosion was on board a barge and that the flying debris ignited the neighbouring barge, the 750 hundred-pound kegs of gunpowder at Hall's magazine, and finally the ninety barrels in store at Lowoods. The results were devastating. The power of the explosion produced an effect bearing an uncanny resemblance to the mushroom cloud of a nuclear weapon. An immense column of smoke, topped with a vast and thick, black cloud, rose from the site and remained clearly visible for at least fifteen minutes. Bricks, wood, papers and human remains were tossed into the air and scattered over an area stretching several miles. The final known death toll reached at least twelve, but some bodies were never recovered. Remains that were thought to belong to the four bargemen and two magazine assistant storemen, were later found scattered around the neighbourhood, one head being reported as found in a garden a mile from the scene.

Engineer Mr Lewis Moore was working on the Thames embankment and staying in Erith when the explosion happened. He rushed to the marshes, and immediately realised only urgent action would save the district from an even more formidable disaster. The magazines had been located just twenty yards from the Thames, and the force of the explosion had reduced 150 yards of the river wall to rubble and caused severe damage to a further 150 yards. Luckily, it was low tide, but Moore knew the river would flood through the yawning gap within hours. He sent a message to the nearby main drainage works, asking for men with barrows, picks, spades and any other tools they could muster.

Meanwhile Mr Houghton, an engineer with the Metropolitan Board of Works, was making his way to the scene. He met Moore's messenger and instructed 450 navvies working at the Outfall works to rush and repair the breach. By 9:00 AM the men were hard at work, digging up clay and heaving barrow-loads to the sea wall. Other navvies paddled the clay to form a solid base for a replacement wall. The men worked with a will, but as the minutes ticked by Moore and Houghton knew they could not complete the marathon task within the four hours before the next high tide. A message asking for help was sent to the military barracks at Woolwich, and by 9:30 AM commandant Major General Warde had organised a detachment of 1,500 sappers and artillery troops. The soldiers brought engineering equipment and a few thousand sand bags, and their training made them an efficient workforce. There was a shortage of barrows, so the troops formed lines and passed bucket after bucket filled with freshly dug clay to the riverbank. The new wall gradually began to take shape, and the soldiers and navvies managed to keep it just above the rising water. High tide came and went, and the wall held. The Metropolitan Board of Works later awarded Mr Houghton £100 for his

> ...zealous, prompt and judicious arrangements...an act by which the whole of Plumstead level and the southern portion of the metropolis were preserved from the calamity of an inundation.

As the troops and labourers sweated to beat the tide, thousands of spectators were making their way to see exactly what was happening. A contingent from the 5th Fusiliers was drafted in to keep sightseers from disrupting work on the wall. The public's curiosity was insatiable and the railway authorities were hard pressed to keep up with the demand for trains from London Bridge to Erith and Belvedere. The rush peaked on Sunday, the day after the disaster. Between 7:00 AM and 11:00 AM several thousand people used a stream of special trains to reach Erith. London Bridge Station closed between 11:00 AM and 1:00 PM, and when the doors reopened a multitude of would-be passengers swarmed onto the platforms. In the next two hours ten extra trains were run, but many thousands were still left waiting on the platforms. Impatience overcame caution and common sense. When one train pulled into the station the mass rushed across the tracks and climbed in through windows to secure seats. The extra trains caused chaos on the line, and the railway ordered no train should leave a station before the driver had been assured the next station along the line was clear. This necessary precaution increased the normal London Bridge to Erith journey time from forty-five minutes to two hours, and added to the frustration and anger of the passengers. There was worse to come: having seen the little there was to see at the disaster spot, the crowds needed to return home. Erith and Belvedere stations were overwhelmed. As each train arrived it was besieged by mobs determined to find a place, even if it was on the roof or hanging on to a buffer or door. The police dragged people off and did their best to maintain order, but the situation was hopeless. Several people were injured and Italian Angelo Morandi was knocked under a train. His legs were crushed and he was put on board the train and taken to Guy's Hospital. Doctors advised immediate amputation, but Morandi refused to have the operation, and died shortly afterwards. The rush of spectators to Erith lasted several days. As the *Kentish Independent* commented on 15 October:

> ...there is little in the spectacle to satisfy their curiosity. Indeed the nature of the accident was such as to leave scant traces of its occurrence, the most astonishing evidence being the aspect of the ground itself, the soil having been apparently thrown up from the depth of several feet, and fallen in crumbling heaps, but this appearance was soon worn off by the thousands of feet which trampled over it, and left nothing but a few ruined walls for the eye to rest upon.... The number of persons who have visited the spot is almost incalculable but some idea may be gathered from the fact that a well-beaten road has been formed across a ploughed field which lies between the Belvedere station and the site of the magazines. The trades-people of Erith have reaped a rich harvest, which will at least compensate them for the damage they have individually sustained, an advantage in which the poorer classes of the population and those interested in the public buildings do not share.

The Erith explosion caused widespread consternation. It revealed the dramatic power of gunpowder and showed how it could put whole districts at risk. Press reports revealed an incredulity and indignation at what had happened. On 8 October the *Kentish Independent* included an almost Pythonesque summary of the effect on animal life:

> Thousands of pets have succumbed with fright, the mortality to canaries being very great. At the time of the explosion in the immediate neighbour-

12　Removing a body from the scene of the Erith explosion
13　Soldiers repairing breach in the river embankment

hood, in every instance they dropped from their perches, and in very numerous cases expired. Parrots also, dropped into the bottom of their cages refusing to move for a quarter of an hour and declining to talk for a couple of hours; whilst dogs, cats and other animals manifested symptoms of the greatest alarm.

In a letter to the *Times* on 4 October, Mr W. Boyd Dawkins of the Geological Survey of Great Britain noted:

The force of the explosion may be appreciated from the fact that loose sheets of paper were blown as far as Woolwich, and by some charred fragments of powder kegs found at Abbey Wood, at a distance of two and a half miles in a straight line.... One human head was picked up at least a mile from the spot, a leg here, a man's breast there.

When Hall and Son had opened their Erith magazine about four years earlier it had been licensed without any opposition from locals. Now they realised the danger on their doorsteps. On 22 October the *Kentish Independent* commented wryly:

We have been living for a century or more, though we ignored the danger, on the edge of a volcano almost as perilous to us as Etna is to Catania, or Vesuvius to Naples.... In our case we smoked the 'pipe of peace' in quietness and insuspicion, hardly dreaming that at any moment an explosion might spread ruin through the district...

The explosion could have been a lot worse. The magazines and barges held 115,000 lb of gunpowder at the time of the disaster. The magazines alone were capable of storing 484,000 lb. A third magazine, belonging to Messrs Curtis and Harvey and located four hundred yards from Hall's, was hit by burning debris after the explosion. Its windows were broken, but by good luck its store of ninety thousand pounds of gunpowder remained intact.

The inquest into the deaths of the Erith victims revealed an horrendous catalogue of dangerous and foolhardy behaviour that was tolerated by the gunpowder industry. Coroner Charles Carttar and his jurors heard of matches being allowed on barges carrying high explosives, of fires on board and of men smoking inside magazines. They were told the law made no limit to the amount of gunpowder that could be stored in a magazine, heard of poorly-made barrels that leaked gunpowder, and of workmen who treated the explosive with as much care as others might accord iron. One remarkable scrap of evidence was a letter written by magazine foreman George Rayner. The undated letter was part of a shower of documents that had fallen about the district after the explosion. It was picked up in Wickham Lane, Plumstead and handed to the coroner. Addressed to Mr Monk, manager of Hall and Son's manufacturing plant at Faversham, it was an indictment on the barrels used for gunpowder:

> For some time past I have witnessed the leaking of casks to a very unpleasant degree. In fact it amounts to this, that the majority of the quarters in particular are not fit to put gunpowder in... the hoops are falling off the casks as they are handled, and the heads falling in...

It was obvious the explosives industry was in dire need of regulations to ensure public safety. Carttar's jury returned verdicts of accidental death and, at the coroner's suggestion, added riders calling for legislation to impose limits on the quantity of gunpowder to be stored in one place; to control the construction of magazines, and their proximity to vulnerable places such as sea walls; to control the construction of barges and other vessels used to carry explosives; to control the shipping and discharging of gunpowder; and to stress the importance of government inspections and supervision of the storing, packing and conveyance of gunpowder. On 25 November 1864 Carttar and his jurors made a deputation to the government, depositing a list of suggestions to improve safety in the gunpowder industry. These included limiting barrels to be stored in one magazine to 250, making the government, rather than Justices of the Peace, the licensing authority for the industry and ruling magazines should not be erected near a river wall.

The government responded to a barrage of criticism by instructing explosives expert Lieutenant Colonel E. Boxer to investigate the Erith explosion and inspect conditions in other gunpowder factories and magazines. His report, published at the end of January 1865, revealed most plants were potential disaster sites. A Colonel Moody had visited the surviving magazine at Erith on 6 October 1864—just days after the explosion—and had been horrified to see a man smoking a pipe walking along a public path only yards from the store's entrance. He had been told that a young lad regularly visited the magazine to sell matches to the workmen. Tramways were covered with grit and spilled gunpowder, and the powder was carried in open trucks. Boxer's report contained a series of recommendations to improve and strengthen the 1860 Gunpowder Act. A new Bill was drawn up, but it never reached the statute books. The gunpowder industry had a powerful lobby, and was strongly opposed to legislation that would control its activities. A new Act, incorporating most of Boxer's recommendations and many of those made by Carttar's jurors, was eventually passed by Parliament in 1875. The Act was championed by the then Government Inspector of Gunpowder Works, Vivian Dering Majendie, a Major with the Royal Artillery, who was later promoted to Colonel and who was to play an important role in investigating Fenian outrages. In his Annual Report for 1874 Majendie commented on the need for the new Act, and referred to Boxer's efforts to secure changes years earlier:

> Whatever the circumstances may have been, whether pressure of public business or other causes, which led to the abandonment or postponement in 1865 and 1866 of the intention to introduce a new Gunpowder Bill, it is certain it did not include any discovered sufficiency in the existing law.

In the same report Majendie described his inspections of various gunpowder factories and magazines. He was appalled at the safety standards he encountered. Reporting one particularly hair-raising inspection he wrote:

> The sensation of walking upon a gritty, powder-coated floor of a magazine containing several tons of powder, accompanied by a farm labourer in iron shod boots, was one which I had not before experienced.

Majendie was a key witness to a government Select Committee on Explosive Substances chaired by Sir John Hay in 1874. The Select Committee preceded the 1875 Explosives Act, a piece of legislation that at long last made it possible to force the industry to adopt adequate safety standards. Licensing was now controlled by the Secretary of State, rather than local magistrates. Each application had to include detailed plans of the site and proposed operations. This ensured experts could view individual proposals and consider their safety before a licence was granted. Quantities of explosives allowed in a particular establishment were set, and had to be displayed. Tools used in such establishments were to be of soft metal or of wood. A no-smoking rule was to be strictly enforced and workmen were to wear clothing without pockets and were to be searched to ensure matches or other materials likely to cause fire were not brought in to the workplace. Children aged under 16 were not to be employed in danger buildings except under the supervision of an adult. Materials in the production process had to be sifted before use, to remove potentially combustible foreign matter such as grit. Harbour authorities, railways and canal companies were given, with some conditions, the power to make bye-laws to regulate the carriage, loading and unloading of explosives on their premises. The Secretary of State was empowered to order such bye-laws if he required them. The Act also tidied up the law concerning firework factories. Small firework manufacturers—those holding less than one hundred pounds of any explosive other than manufactured fireworks and less than five hundred pounds of manufactured fireworks at any time—were given exemption from the new licensing procedure. They were able to apply for a licence from their local authority, where their plans would be considered on an individual basis.

Shortly before the new Act came into force an explosion on the Regent's Canal in the centre of London confirmed that the new law was essential.

The *Tilbury* was a fly barge owned by the Grand Junction Canal Company used to ship merchandise ranging from nuts, coffee and sugar to high explosives. The Regent's Canal was eight and a half miles long and ran from Limehouse Dock to Paddington, where it joined the Grand Junction Canal. On 2 October 1874 the *Tilbury* was loaded with five tons of gunpowder and six barrels of petroleum at the City Road Basin. At 2:00 AM she joined four other barges in a convoy to be towed to the Midlands by the steam tug the *Ready*. It was a routine trip, and carrying high explosives was nothing unusual. The Grand Junction Canal Company charged customers extra for carrying explosives, but the loads were treated no differently from those of sugar or coffee beans. Just before 5:00 AM the little convoy passed the Zoological Gardens at Regent's Park. The three-man crew on board the *Tilbury* had a fire going in their cabin, as was their usual and accepted custom. As the seventy-foot long narrow boat passed through a deep cut and under the Macclesfield Bridge, opposite the Regent's Park Baptist College, there was a mighty explosion. The *Tilbury*'s treacherous load had ignited and blown her and the bridge to smithereens.

The massive explosion ripped through the silence of the early morning and produced panic in the neighbourhood. As the *Graphic* reported on 10 October:

Scarcely a pane of glass was left intact in the houses of the immediate neighbourhood, while those nearest the explosion were completely shattered, window frames and doors being blown in, the ceilings shaken down, and mirrors and furniture broken to atoms—in fact the whole quarter had the appearance of having undergone severe bombardment. The frightened inhabitants rushed out in the street, thinking it was an earthquake, and as far as Camden Square and Kilburn the same impression prevailed.

North Lodge was virtually demolished; North House, a mansion opposite the bridge, was wrecked and the adjacent Lancaster Terrace suffered structural damage; houses were shaken to their foundations, and hundreds of windows within a mile radius were shattered. Only one shop in Regent's Park Road escaped damage. Animals in the nearby zoo howled and screeched in terror, adding to the general commotion. Many of the zoo's enclosures were badly damaged by falling debris, and many exotic birds escaped. Superintendent keeper A.D. Bartlett later estimated repairs would cost £300. Terrified locals rushed into the street in their nightclothes, but the only member of the public to suffer serious injury was Mr Edwards, a park-keeper who lived in North Lodge. The *Tilbury's* crew was less fortunate. All three died instantly. The barge behind the *Tilbury*, the *Limehouse*, sank in the explosion but her crew escaped with minor injuries.

London fire chief Captain Eyre Shaw was soon at the scene, but there was little for him and his men to do apart from clearing the wreckage. The shock of the explosion had reached as far as Gravesend, Enfield and Woolwich, and acted as a magnet to thousands of curious Londoners. Hundreds of extra policemen were drafted in to cordon off the area. Late on Friday night the Duke of Edinburgh visited to view the damage for himself, and was taken on a tour of the district by Captain Shaw. Next morning, a Saturday, the crowds reached a peak. As the *Mail* reported on 5 October:

> ...even in the rainy morning, crowds made their way to the canal; but in the fine afternoon omnibuses ran full 'to the explosion,' traffic on the Metropolitan Railway became impeded and it was as much as 500 police constables could do to cope with the oppressive curiosity of holiday makers. The publicans and tobacconists would not be sorry to lose their windows on such terms every week.

The shopkeepers were not the only ones to benefit from the mass of spectators. Pickpockets, always attracted by a crowd, did a roaring trade.

14   *Clearing wreckage of Macclesfield Bridge, Regent's Park*

Three of the thieves were arrested on Saturday, but many more escaped detection.

Major Majendie investigated the blast and reported his findings in his Annual Report published in 1875:

> I considered that as we may hope that five tons of gunpowder will not again be exploded in London it was my duty to spare no pains to put on record all the facts relating to this disaster which it might be in my power to collect.

Majendie observed the circumstances of the explosion were ideal to create the minimum possible effects: the *Tilbury* exploded in a deep cutting beneath a strong bridge in the early hours of the morning. He found the blast was caused by vapour which had escaped from the barge's cargo of benzoline, "which, with an imprudence which is scarcely credible, was being carried in the same boat." The vapour passed through the bulkhead of the cabin and ignited on a lighted fire or lamp. The flash it produced passed back to the barrels where the vapour originated and set fire to the store of gunpowder. Majendie regarded the procedure for handling explosives on board the barges with a mixture of outrage and contempt:

> It must also be a matter for surprise that an explosion of this sort did not occur long ago. Indeed it is difficult to say which of the two circumstances—the hazardous mode of conducting their gunpowder traffic which the company adopted, or the long immunity from disaster which they enjoyed—is most calculated to excite astonishment…. It will I think be clear from what has been stated that the carriage of gunpowder has been carried on by the Grand Junction Canal Company with a degree of carelessness and with a neglect of the most elementary precautions which can hardly fail to amaze even those who have some familiarity with the recklessness which too often prevails in regard to explosives.

Majendie catalogued the damage. Buildings within four hundred yards suffered structural damage; trees in Regent's Park were blasted or blown down; railings were torn up and twisted; and the river banks forty or fifty yards either side of Macclesfield Bridge were blackened and charred. Both the bridge and barge had been destroyed and the bulk of the remains lay at the bottom of the canal. As with most explosions, the distribution of damage was often inexplicable.

> …some houses comparatively near the scene of the explosion escaped almost uninjured while others further off were structurally damaged; here

a single pane only was broken, or a window entirely escaped, while another house far more distant presented the appearance of having been wrecked by a mob well supplied with stones.

Majendie's report would probably have been far more critical of the law that permitted such dangerous transportation of gunpowder to take place had it not been for the fact the 1875 Explosives Act was already well on its way to the statute books. The incident, he commented, highlighted the necessity for the new legislation.

A temporary dam was built to stop the flow of water along the canal, and steam pumps were used to drain the section under Macclesfield Bridge. By Tuesday 6 October the debris had been removed and the canal put back into normal use. The inquest into the three dead bargemen, Charles Boxson, William Taylor and Jonathan Holloway was held by coroner Dr Hardwicke at the nearby Marylebone Workhouse. The jurors returned a verdict of accidental death, adding the rider that the Canal Company was guilty of gross negligence and that the existing laws were inadequate to secure public safety.

The majority of fire insurance companies refused to pay out for damage caused by explosions. Mr William Forsyth, Member of Parliament for Marylebone, organised a relief fund to help those who had suffered losses, and raised £6,333.8s.1d. Fund organisers gave first priority to those unable to afford the costs of repairing structural damage to their property. After these cases had been settled, the fund was distributed among those who had lost furniture, clothing and other goods. A total of 1,103 grants were made, but 945 were for sums below £10. The highest award was for £150, and there were five grants of £100 each. The majority of remaining cases were settled with sums between £10 and £20.

Macclesfield Bridge was eventually rebuilt, and acquired the nickname "Blown Up Bridge." Many locals still refer to the bridge by that title.

The location of firework factories and gunpowder magazines within and close to densely populated areas of London, and the transportation of potentially lethal loads of explosives through the capital without any real safety precautions highlighted a widespread ignorance of the dangers involved. The ambivalent attitude to safety and safety precautions was not limited to back-street pyrotechnists nor to profit-grabbing private manufacturers. One of the government's largest explosives manufacturing plants was located at Woolwich, South-East London. There were frequent explosions at the Royal Arsenal, and many workers died during the Victorian period. While safety standards tended to be more stringent in government-controlled factories, they were still lamentably inadequate to cope with the highly volatile materials and dangerous manufacturing processes that were in everyday use. On several occasions accidents at the Arsenal put the whole of London at risk, as ignited war rockets screeched through the sky like oversised fireworks, threatening the district with the destruction they were designed to bring to the battlefield. The people of Woolwich would flock to the Arsenal whenever they heard an explosion, fearful that relatives and friends employed there may have been killed.

A look at the Arsenal's history of mishaps shows how safety precautions developed in the light of painful experience. The Arsenal was formed by a series of small huts, each designated to a separate stage in the manufacturing process. This arrangement was considered the safest possible, as any fire or explosion was more likely to be contained where it originated. On Wednesday, 17 September 1845 master rocket-maker John Crake was at work with his team of men and boys in the "model room." John, 74, was highly experienced, having worked in the Arsenal for fifty-one years, and his task that morning must have seemed straightforward. The men were instructed to break up faulty fuses which had been returned from Gibraltar. Normally such fuses were discarded, but these were large ten-inch devices, and it was considered worthwhile to recover the saltpetre they contained. The construction of the fuses was simple: the cap end was covered with paper and fastened with a piece of string. John Crake removed the string with a copper knife, and took off the paper. The fuse was then passed to a boy, who shook out the meal powder before passing it on. A man then placed it on a steel chisel fixed in wood and hit it with a wooden mallet to break it up and release the explosive mixture into a pan.

The procedure was fraught with danger. The impact as the fuse was shattered against the chisel frequently produced sparks. To add to the perilous cocktail, the men wore hobnailed boots that were liable to cause sparks as they walked on the concrete floor. The doors of the hut opened inward, so hindering the chances of a speedy exit in the event of an accident. Crake and his team dealt with many thousand fuses before their luck ran out at about 10:00 AM. Precise details of what went wrong remain a mystery; all seven workers in the shed were burned to death after an explosion left the hut ablaze. The men apparently had time to make for the doors, but lacked the precious seconds needed to pull them open. Rescuers later found the scorched remains of the workers' bodies close together by the exit. Coroner Charles Carttar steered his panel of jurors through the inquest with his usual tenacity and skill. After returning a verdict of accidental death, the jury added the rider that steel chisels should be replaced by copper knives, and that men engaged in such employment should not be allowed to wear hobnailed boots. The use of copper or soft metal tools in the explosives industry was later enforced by law.

Royal Arsenal officials took little heed of the jurors' suggestions, and ten years later that complacency caused another fatal accident. Organisation at the Arsenal was in a state of flux. It was 1855 and increased output of ammunition was being demanded for troops fighting the Crimean War. Extra men were employed at the Arsenal, and more manufacturing sheds had been erected. The new arrangements meant the rocket shed was connected to a mealing shed where explosives were sifted. Men in the rocket shed were supplied with steel "rymers" to gouge out putty that had been used to temporarily plug holes at the base of rockets during the manufacturing process. The practice was treacherous, and on 3 December 1855, the friction of steel on the explosive caused one rocket to ignite. The flames caught other rockets and gunpowder that had fallen to the floor. The huts were reduced to a smouldering heap of timber. Some men dragged themselves from the ruins, but four died and four more suffered severe burns.

The inquest revealed that, despite the fact gunpowder was known to litter the floor, men working in the sheds wore hobnail boots. This time Carttar made little effort to hide his frustration at the inept practices employed at the Arsenal. His jurors found the accident had been caused by use of an improper tool, and added a scathing rider to their verdict:

> ...that due precaution has not been taken by the authorities in the supervision of the tools in use in this dangerous process and also in not providing slippers for the use of the men employed in the rocket sheds, and that a more vigilant supervision is absolutely required to prevent in future a similar catastrophe...

The Arsenal, like most Victorian manufacturing plants, made full use of child labour. Even the strict discipline of the gunpowder huts was not always enough to stifle youthful exuberance, and a boyish prank caused the next major incident to blot the Arsenal's copybook. Fifty-five lads, mostly around 13 or 14 years old, were employed making cartridges. The boys' task was to fit a shaped pellet of gunpowder into prepared shell cases, each containing percussion caps. Royal Arsenal experts believed it would be impossible for one of the caps to ignite accidentally, and so considered the process suitable for their youngest workers. As the day's work drew to an end on Saturday 5 October, 1867, young Walter Pigge decided to have some fun. He hit a percussion cap with a mallet. Nothing happened and his friend, John Lee, told him not to do it again. Pigge mischievously gave the cap another whack. His sense of fun cost him his life, and those of four of his workmates. The shell ignited and a series of explosions ripped through the little huts as more and more shell and gunpowder pellets were fired. The children rushed for the doors, but although all the plant's doors now opened outward, gas lamps had been fitted above them and made it impossible for them to open fully.

Storekeeper William Brown was working in the shed, and groped through the smoke to rescue the boys. He refused to leave the building until he was sure all the lads had been dragged out. Outside shocked workmen ripped off the children's smouldering clothes and helped them to the nearby Arsenal Infirmary. Facilities at the hospital were inadequate. There were nine beds only, and most of those were already occupied. The majority of the existing patients were packed off home. Extra bedding was brought in from Herbert Hospital, and fourteen children were admitted for treatment to severe burns. Ten more children were treated at their homes. Most of the boys lucky enough to be in hospital had to share beds, and five of them, including the wretched Pigge, died in the days that followed. At the inquest into their deaths, Carttar's jurors recommended facilities at the Arsenal Infirmary be improved, and the authorities took up the suggestion. Restrictions on the use of child labour in danger buildings were not enforced until the Explosives Act in 1875.

Even the unscheduled firework displays of Madame Coton and her colleagues were no match for the spectacular pyrotechnics the Royal Arsenal could offer—if marauding fireworks were disconcerting, rogue war rockets were downright terrifying. The cause of the explosion in an Arsenal rocket shed on Monday 24 September, 1883 must remain a mystery as the sole witnesses, Richard Stevenson and Arthur Carlick, were killed instantly. The effects were apparent to everyone within several miles. Streams of rockets, each packed with twenty-four pounds of high explosives, screeched into the sky, to plummet down both inside and outside the Arsenal's grounds with the fury of a major battle assault. They smashed through garden fences and the walls of several Woolwich homes. Journalist and author William Vincent was an eyewitness, and later recorded his impressions in his book, *The Records of the Woolwich District*:

>...the persons in the adjacent armoury, barely forty yards distant, had a narrow escape, for several of the rockets struck that building, and almost the first one went through a window at which the foreman, Mr Buchanan, was sitting at his desk, passed within a few inches of his head, and flew out straight through the opposite window.... Every two or three seconds an explosion was heard, followed perhaps by a flight of mere signal rockets, of which no-one need have any fear, but quite as frequently by the whistling overhead of a great iron Hale's rocket, sometimes at a great height, sometimes low down and close to the terrified spectators. There seemed to be hundreds of them going to all parts of the compass, but chiefly, I thought, into the town of Plumstead. One of the earliest I saw, well poised upon its axis, shoot along the course of the canal quite near to the water, break through some garden fences, and rebound from a paved road to the top of the Arsenal wall, whence it projected great blocks of masonry into the windows of Mr Parker, grocer, and fell exhausted on the tramway line in Plumstead Road.... A sergeant of artillery, with a coolness begotten of practice, was endeavouring to convince his hearers that there was perfect security in walking about provided you watched and dodged the coming shells; but, although he remained a living example of his doctrine, he made no converts.

Damage to surrounding properties was extensive. One rocket blasted through the wall of a crowded classroom in the Plumstead Road Board School; another went through two or more walls in the counting-house and shop of draper Mr Paine; a third buried itself in the grounds of the North Woolwich Hotel. Miraculously, and by sheer good chance, only the two men at the seat of the initial explosion were killed.

An explosion on 18 June 1903 holds the record of having the highest death toll at the Arsenal. Eighteen men died after an explosion in a hut where men were preparing lyddite shells. The highly-explosive lyddite was packed into shells through a hole that was then filled by ramming in a wooden plug with a lead hammer. Experts later concluded that a piece of grit had probably been sparked by the friction and caused the disaster. The blast happened just after 8:00 AM and deadly shells were flung across the Arsenal by the force of the explosion. Many of those killed worked some distance from the lyddite hut. By this time, the Arsenal's disaster management system was better organised. First Aid teams reached the scene rapidly, and within twenty minutes ambulance trains had taken all the injured to the Arsenal Hospital. Late that night, eight Royal Army Medical Corp ambulances took the remains of the dead to the Sun Street Mortuary.

The Royal Arsenal suffered many explosions, the incidents described are some of the more serious. The manufacture of explosives is dangerous even today. In the early days ignorance bred a nonchalance that made calamity an inevitable, even acceptable, part of the manufacture. A succession of working people paid the ultimate penalty for risking their lives in the pursuit of a hard-earned and meagre living. Their deaths could have forced the prompt introduction of tougher laws. Sadly, these working class labourers lacked the political muscle of their masters, and it was in their masters' interests to keep legislation at an absolute minimum. It was only when the realisation dawned that the industry put the welfare of the wider public at risk that effective action was taken to improve safety standards.

CHAPTER FOUR

The Great Freeze

The winter of 1866–1867 was one of the most severe and bitterly cold endured by the Victorians. Snowfalls were heavy and London's lakes and docks were frequently covered in thick layers of ice. The freezing conditions were a source of fun, if precarious fun, for the wealthier classes. The seasonal craze for ice skating and ice sports attracted several hundred thousand participants at every possible opportunity. But conditions that delighted the rich brought only abject misery to the poor. Many of the working class lived on the very brink of destitution and any additional strain on their limited resources could be disastrous. There was no cash to buy extra clothing or heating to ward off the cold. Survival was difficult under optimum conditions, and they had precious few resources to help them cope with the crisis.

Dockyards and associated trades were the major industry in the impoverished districts flanking the Thames. A severe economic slump was already hitting trade when the crippling effects of the great freeze of 1866–1867 forced many employers to lay off virtually all labourers. It was a vicious blow to a community that had been severely weakened by the ravages of a cholera outbreak only months earlier. The appalling weather caused suffering to the poor throughout the capital, but those living in East London, a term that included the Docklands on the South side of the river, were hit hardest. As a leader article in the *Illustrated Times*, 2 February 1867, commented:

...the greater number of what may be described as the disagreeable trades, naturally attract a large population of the least educated, the least provident, and the least thriving class, who gain a scanty and precarious livelihood by the mere use of the thews and sinews.... It is perhaps impossible to estimate, with any approach to certainty, the percentage of the community living there, not only within sight, but within reach, of pauperism, but unquestionably it is very large. The normal condition is one of hand-to-mouth subsistence; when a season of distress occurs it speedily becomes one of disorganisation. Such a season is now.

Several of the more caring employers realised that the men they could not employ were in a desperate situation, and on 8 December 1866 the *East London Observer* reported they had met and were arranging a survey to assess the scale of the problem. The shipbuilding yards, key sources of employment in better times, stood in ice-locked silence, putting around thirty thousand casual workers and men in related industries out of work.

"As a result skilled artisans who could earn their 7/– a day are without employment," reported the paper,

> and to support life have had to betake themselves to the stone yard of the Poplar Union to earn their 3*d* per day, or to join, if they could, the navvies who are engaged in preparing ground for the new dock in the Island.

> Some idea of the amount of the distress prevailing may be gathered from the fact that while this time last year only 50 men were obliged to have recourse to stone breaking and oakum picking, the number at present so employed is 550.

> Last year at this time those receiving outdoor relief from the Board of Guardians reached about 2,000, while now there are upwards of 5,000 receiving this relief. It is plain, therefore, from these figures that a hard winter is before these artisans, shipwrights and labourers...

On 5 January the *Tower Hamlets Independent* reported that the Poplar Board of Guardians was giving outdoor relief to 6,203 people, compared with 2,689 in the corresponding period of the previous year. By the following week the numbers receiving outdoor relief had rocketed to 8,319. Outdoor relief was a pittance, designed merely to ward off starvation, but it was much preferred to the alternative of the work-house. In the same edition of the paper, Mr Whitmore, a minister at St Paul's Presbyterian Church on the Isle of Dogs, reported on the distress in Millwall:

> One old man was literally perishing with hunger when we saw him. He would not declare his misery and to our gentle questioning he returned no answer; but when we gave him a little help his tears ran heavily through his worn, trembling fingers, which were clasped over his face. He had been for many years one of the chief supports of a small place of worship, but then he was starving.

Whitmore also visited a "respectable woman" who was obliged to live on a small quantity of dry toast and weak tea. The only meat tasted by her children were the ends and clippings rejected by cholera patients in the nearby hospital.

Another man had sold everything he possessed to buy bread for his family, Whitmore observed:

> There was in his one-roomed hovel no bed, nor bedstead, no linen of any kind, no clothes; two heaps of rags in a corner constituted the place of repose for himself and his family.

Deaths from starvation were not uncommon. Many poor would rather die than endure the horrors and shame of the workhouse. Outdoor relief was not given freely, and many applicants were turned away. Some managed to survive, many didn't. Richard Farrell, 46, starved to death in January 1867. His wretched end was reported in the *East London Observer* on 2 February. Farrell had been found dying in a shed and taken to die in the workhouse he feared and dreaded. His niece visited him and enquired why he had not asked for help. He answered: "Oh, pray, do not ask me. It was very cold and I crept into a shed." Farrell had no work, no home and no money to buy food or shelter. He spent the last days of his miserable life huddled in sheds and outhouses before succumbing to cold, starvation and a "disease of the lungs."

Some of the destitute turned to crime. On 19 January 1867 the *East London Observer* reported a case at Thames Police Court involving four young lads, the oldest just 14 years. They were accused of felony. The cases against Jeremiah M'Carthy and Daniel Hunt, both charged with stealing bread, were dropped. Inspector Beare, the prosecuting officer, was clearly sympathetic to the youngsters:

> A great many boys who formerly worked in the iron shipbuilding yards, and whose earnings were from 5/– to 11/– per week, were prowling about the streets of Poplar and Bromley every evening. They had no bread to eat and were in a lamentable state of distress. He had seen them in batches of five and six each, and they took everything they could lay their hands on. He had seen many of these boys who were in receipt of 9/– and 10/– per week when they was plenty of work, starving and half-naked about the streets.

Magistrate Mr Paget, invoking the true spirit of Victorian thrift, commented: "And those boys who were in receipt of such good wages save nothing?" And he went on:

It is very painful, very sad. The statement of Inspector Beare, who is an officer of great experience is not overcharged. The people in the East End are starving, and some very comprehensive plan should be adopted to save them. The numbers of paupers chargeable to the Poplar Union is very great and the rates have vastly increased.

The Poplar Board of Guardians was hard-pressed to deal with the situation, and by the end of January the Board realised that exceptional measures were needed. Pay for men in the stone-breaking yard was increased from 3d to 6d per day, despite the fact the rise meant the Guardians would make an actual loss on the enterprise. The payments were to be supplemented by a weekly ration of food. "As far as possible" the ration was to include oatmeal or rice. Relief payments were to be given immediately a man started work in the yard.

The Board became overwhelmed by applications for relief and decided to split the district into four sections to help make administration more effective. The task was massive. In the six weeks ending on 2 February 1867, 52,526 people received outdoor relief. This compared with just 18,174 during the same period of the previous year.

The Poor Law system was financed by local rates set by the elected Guardians. The Guardians realised many ratepayers were sharing the financial distress, but their only option was to levy substantial increases in the rates. The rate rose from an average 8d in the pound per quarter to an all-time high of upwards of 2/– in the pound per quarter. The extra rates burden on some traders was considerable. In the half-yearly report of the East and West India Dock Company, made in July 1867, the directors noted that, despite the fall in trade, the company would have shown increased profits had it not been

...for the sad and exceptional circumstances of the great distress in Poplar and the districts adjoining the docks, which has increased the Parochial Taxes of the company by upwards of £7,000 during the past half-year, as compared with 1866.

The situation across the Thames, particularly in the districts of Deptford and Greenwich, was no less severe. Deptford's Relieving Officer—the Board of Guardians' official responsible for assessing need and deciding on the degree of help that should be given—was besieged by applicants. This man, a Mr Patty, drafted in members of the Board of Guardians to help deal with the urgent cases. The innovation failed to avert a crisis. On 23 January a seething mass of near-starving applicants surrounded Mr Patty's home in Deptford High Street. Extraordinary action was clearly essential to prevent further trouble and normal procedures were waived. Details of a man's family and address were noted, and he was then handed a bread ticket. A similar operation took place in the nearby Vestry, where four hundred loaves were distributed during the day. The crowd clamouring outside Mr Patty's house continued to grow. It was not the first time the sheer numbers of hungry people seeking relief had caused difficulties. Mr Patty was frequently overwhelmed by hungry mobs. On 12 January the *Kentish Mercury* reported the contents of three bread shops had been handed out:

> ...the applicants being thankful for a loaf of bread, and departing like hungry wolves. But for this relief being granted an opportunity for riot might have been feared.

But on 23 January things did not go so easily. The parish officials sensed the rising tension in the mob and scrapped procedure altogether. They left the house at about 7:00 PM and mixed with the crowd, handing out the bread tickets indiscriminately. It was an ill-advised, if well-intentioned move. When the mob realised what was happening they pushed forward to grab one of the vital tickets. The officers knew they were in danger of being lynched, and they managed to force their way back into Mr Patty's house, slamming the door behind them.

The officials were probably at a loss as to the best step to take, so decided to close for the night. The bread tickets represented the only hope of food the starving crowd had for themselves and their families. Many must have been waiting in the mass for hours, and the news that no more tickets would be issued increased anxiety and resentment to breaking point. Someone in the crowd murmured that if they were not given bread, then they should take it. The murmur grew to a cry, and the bread shop opposite Mr Patty's house was a sitting target. The windows were smashed and the shelves quickly emptied of loaves. The passion of the mob took over and they stormed on to the next baker's shop, the premises of a Mr Sammon. The brave shopkeeper stood outside and begged the crowd not to destroy his premises; he would gladly give them every scrap of bread he possessed. The mob agreed, and Mr Sammon threw the loaves from his doorway. Many in the crowd had still not received any food, and moved on to a shop in the Broadway owned by a widow, Mrs Cracknell. Again, they smashed the windows and took the little bread unsold after the day's trading. By this time, about 8:00 PM, news of the riot had spread and extra police were being drafted into the district. The mob was dispersed by Superintendent Wakeford and a contingent of mounted police, and other men under the control of Inspectors King and Ebbs. Surprisingly, there were no arrests.

Thursday dawned, and once more tension rose as crowds again gathered in the streets. This time, however, there was no trouble. Hundreds of unemployed dockworkers from Greenwich and Deptford marched through the streets to demonstrate their plight, but there was no disorder. The masses behaved with dignity as they walked along Greenwich Road to the Greenwich Workhouse, where the Guardians were holding their usual weekly meeting.Wary shopkeepers were taking no chances and kept their doors locked. Police reinforcements of around two hundred men arrived at around 3:00 PM, boosting police numbers to around 320 and giving the shopkeepers the confidence to start business. The crowds dispersed quietly. Mr Patty's office was, as usual, filled with people needing bread tickets. This time five tons of bread was given out.

Press reports claimed the riots had been caused by a small band of "outsiders" who had come to the district with the sole aim of causing trouble. The Guardians, they said, were doing their best and their efforts were being supplemented by private charity. As the *Illustrated Times* commented on 2 February:

> It was a very general impression...even among working men themselves, that, when compared with Poplar and the most distressed parishes, Deptford was not so very badly off.... The police state that the really disturbing portion of the crowd was limited to a knot of twenty or thirty vagrants, not inhabitants of Deptford at all, but casuals, who may have been attracted to this parish by the hope of extra aid. On the same authority we have it that, although the distress in the neighbourhood is generally and severely felt, the privations, comparatively speaking, are not extreme. The relief agencies at work, it is said, are such and so extensive, that no honest man who finds it necessary to apply need go one day without what would be to him tolerable subsistence in 'hard times.'

Despite the apparent complacency of those better-off citizens, who refused to acknowledge the suffering in front of their noses, there is no doubt the poverty and distress in the district was genuine and severe. On 17 January, just a few days before the bread riot, the Reverend John Miller, Rural Dean and Vicar of Greenwich, had written a letter to the

15   Bread riots at Deptford: Mob storms Mrs Cracknell's bakery
16   Dragging Regent's Park lake for bodies

Times appealing for donations to ease the suffering in his parish:

> ...we shall have actual starvation in East Greenwich, a large district in my parish, unless prompt aid be forthcoming. One of my most respected parish officials has just told me that his house is beset from morning until night, and that he really fears the people will drop in the streets.

The letter ended with a prophetic postscript.

> We are not without fear of disorder and even riot, if something be not done promptly.

The letter brought in £1,000 in donations, and generated a backlash of indignation and anger from some of the leading citisens of Greenwich. They were clearly aghast that this upstart vicar, fresh from a parish in Birmingham, should dare instigate a national appeal without their approval and consent. The letter was published on 18 January and the following day a public meeting was called to discuss the plight of the poor in the area. Mr Lovibond, a prominent Greenwich dignitary, said he was aggrieved that Miller had written to the *Times* without first calling a town's meeting. The people of the district, he said, should have been given the opportunity to contribute before the population of England had been asked for donations. Lovibond was also angered by Miller's reference to the possibility of "rioting in the streets."

It was agreed, however, that something had to be done to ease the plight of the district's poor, and a relief committee was formed. John Miller, obviously feeling insulted by the criticism directed at him, refused to take part. The relief committee raised whatever funds they could and organised house-to-house visits to assess needs and give help, usually in the direct form of bread, soup and coal. The prime aim was to prevent starvation. The Greenwich Guardians employed an extra three assistants to help the beleaguered Mr Patty, and asked the police to provide ten or more constables, ostensibly to "protect regular recipients of relief," but more probably to stand bodyguard for the officials. There had been complaints about the quality and quantity of the loaves distributed by the Guardians, and it was accepted that the complaints were genuine. In one case a loaf was ten ounces short of the stipulated weight—and ten ounces represented vital nourishment to a starving family. The Guardians complained to their bread contractor and demanded improvements.

The Victorian press claimed the Deptford bread riot and the widespread petty pilfering of food throughout East London were the fault of "roughs" and had nothing to do with the "genuine poor." The sentiment may have been consoling, but is unlikely to have been accurate. The working classes were desperate, and desperation drove them to exceptional behaviour. They lived, literally, on the bread line and the bitterly cold weather forced them over the edge. At the very time they needed more money for fuel and food their incomes were abruptly cut off. Their normal wages permitted survival—just, but it was entirely unrealistic to expect them to save for "bad times." Financially, at least, their lives were one long "bad time." No one was injured during the bread riot, and the only items stolen were loaves of bread, better known as the staff of life than as the stuff of revolution.

While the cold spells were dreaded by the poor, they were welcomed by those who could afford to enjoy the sport and fun the ice and snow could offer. Daily papers carried regular "Weather Reports" summarising conditions on London's lakes in much the same way as today's papers record skiing conditions in alpine resorts. Men, women and children took to the ice on skates. Those incapable, or disinclined, to glide under their own steam were pushed around on sleighs, often travelling at breakneck speed and commonly leaving a trail of havoc in their wake. Everything that could be done on ice, was done on ice. There were ice parties, dances, hockey matches, curling matches, races, hurdle jumping, obstacle courses, skittle matches, games of quoits and even mock battles. Fireworks were a key ingredient of the fun and night-time displays were frequently organised.

London's parks witnessed some of the more riotous gatherings. Weekends regularly saw more than fifteen thousand skaters on the lake at St James's Park, ten thousand at Hyde Park, six thousand at Kensington Gardens and many thousands more at Regent's Park. A host of associated trades mushroomed around the ice. Men would hire out skates and chairs, others offered refreshments, bands provided music and firework manufacturers doubtless enjoyed soaring sales. It was a world away from the hovels where less fortunate souls shivered and starved and prayed for warmer weather, but the jollity was not without its dangers.

Accidents were frequent. People were cut by flaying skates; others suffered serious fractures and injuries from falls and collisions. Fatalities were far from uncommon and were usually caused by people falling through the ice and drowning. The main burden of ensuring safety on the ice lakes fell to a voluntary organisation, the Royal Humane Society. The Society, established in 1774 and granted its Royal Charter in 1787, was run entirely on voluntary contributions. It managed to establish more than 250 "Receiving Houses"–emergency first aid stations–close to lakes and rivers in London. The Receiving Houses were manned by "Icemen" employed by the Society and supplied with a whole range of rescue equipment. Standard kit featured a selection of hooks, ladders, boats and poles and a variety of baths, including an ingenious model that incorporated a small boiler and could be wheeled to the waterside. The Icemen posted notices whenever they considered the ice to be dangerous, but the more determined skaters ignored their warnings. The Society also set up a network of over one hundred doctors throughout the London districts, all of whom had pledged to give their services gratis and on demand. The medics were alerted to accidents by "runners" sent from the scene and would attend to give whatever help they could. At times the Society's workload became excessive. On 26 January 1861 the *Illustrated Times* reported:

> From the commencement of the frost, on 17 of December last, to the present time, the total estimated number of skaters and sliders which have ventured on the ice in the various Royal Parks and in Kensington Gardens is 170,000, of whom 160 have been immersed and rescued by the Icemen employed by this society (Royal Humane Society), and then resuscitated by the excellent methods adopted by them; in addition to which nearly 600 persons have received surgical treatment at the hands of the medical officers of the society—some suffering from the most terrible burns, the result of fireworks and torches during the mad scenes enacted of a night on the Serpentine, others from every imaginable kind of broken bone, and the majority from sickening cuts generally of the forehead and eyebrows, making it a rather difficult operation for the surgeon to dress them.

The Society's Receiving Houses were based in everything from local pubs to tents, workhouses, police stations and specially constructed mini-hospitals. The most prestigious was purpose-built on a plot of land donated by King George III beside the North bank of the Serpentine in Hyde Park. It featured offices for staff, plus two wards, a surgery and committee room. The wards were fitted with four baths and six beds, each heated through a system of hot water pipes and kept at a constant high temperature. As well as providing practical help, the Society gave awards to those who helped rescue drowning people.

On 15 January 1867 the Society's Icemen were at Regent's Park and had posted several notices warning skaters to keep off the ice. The skaters ignored the danger notices and by early afternoon several thousands were taking their chances on the ice. As the day wore on the condition of the ice deteriorated and the Icemen became more anxious, urging skaters to go home. Some took their advice, others laughed at them. By 3.30 PM there were still around three hundred skaters, watched by between two and three thousand spectators. Suddenly the ice around the edge of the lake broke away from the land. Skaters close enough to see they were in imminent danger rushed for the shore. Seconds later there was a crack as the ice heaved and the surface shattered. Around two hundred people were flung into water, clutching chunks of ice to keep themselves afloat. As the ice closed in many were trapped underneath, unable to force their way back to the surface.

The Icemen on duty were stunned. They were trained to deal with single incidents of people falling through the ice, but here hundreds needed rescue. The ice was in pieces and the Icemen's equipment could not hope to reach all those floundering far from the shore. Spectators watched, transfixed, as their helpless friends and relatives tried desperately to find a safe hold on the ice. The vast majority were wearing heavy skates and winter clothing that proved major handicaps as they struggled to keep afloat.

Mr J. Dunton of Frederick Street, Hampstead Road, was on the lake with his son and daughter and seventy yards from the shore when the ice broke. On 26 January, he wrote to the *Kentish Independent*:

> Without a second's warning the ice seemed to glide from under me, leaving us in the water quite five feet deep. The two little ones sank to the bottom, but rose again directly. I made a grasp at each of them, and was able to seise them by the shoulders, at the same time holding on to the ice with my left hand. Such a sight I hope never to see again. Quite 150 persons were struggling for life. Heads and arms were to be seen all round amongst the broken masses of ice. Two yards from me a little boy was drowning and I could not render him any help; presently nothing but his cap was visible above water. I stood in this position for nearly half an hour, sinking down in the mud deeper every minute, until the water reached my chin.

Dunton began to feel cramp in his legs but luckily William Archer, a local boat builder, saw his plight and launched his boat, edging it slowly through the ice towards Dunton and his children. Archer saved another seven people and his actions earned him a Bronze Medal from the Royal Humane Society.

Another, unnamed, eyewitness told a harrowing tale to the *Illustrated Times* (19 January):

> Women rushed about on the banks screaming out that their children, or husbands, or brothers were drowning and imploring the bystanders to save them. Boys and girls stood hysterically crying and wringing their hands, and between their sobs exclaiming, 'Oh, look at father! Oh, father, father!' and giving expression to other heartrending exclamations; and strong men convulsively appealed to those who had no means of help, and pointed out friends and relations struggling in the agonies of death...

> Only those who were on the spot, and saw with their own eyes what took place, can form an adequate idea of the calamity which in an instant placed 200 persons at the very gates of death, almost within arms' reach of those who were related to them by the closest ties, but who were yet in most cases obliged to stand helplessly by and see them fighting desperately for life, and gradually succumbing or waiting passively, clinging to pieces of ice till they became insensible and lost their hold.

James Slater described his ordeal on the ice to the *Camden and Kentish Town Gazette* (19 January):

> It can easily be imagined what ensued; the cries of 'Help' and 'Save us' were horrifying to hear, and enough to strike terror into the hearts of the most courageous. When I fell through there were 25 or 30 persons close by who fell in also; but, strange to say, when I came to the surface again I could only see my friend and one gentleman above the water. When I had waited in the water about 15 minutes I began to feel a stupor creeping, as it were, all over me, and being well aware how fatal such a symptom is, I advised my friend that we should strike out and swim for it. This we did and after a struggle of another 10 minutes, by God's help we reached the shore.

Rescue efforts were underway, but for many the situation was hopeless. There were too many people to rescue, and too few people and too little equipment to help. Many spectators rushed wildly about, grabbing sticks and branches and anything else they could find that might help rescue some of the helpless souls in the water. Others went for the park's boats, but even when they had dragged them to the lake the ice, albeit broken ice, made it practically impossible to launch and row them. One group of on-lookers frantically tied pieces of rope together to make a length sufficient to stretch across the lake. They hoped that people trapped in the lake could grab hold of the rope, which would then be pulled gently to the shore. A few people did manage to catch the rope, but they could not be pulled to safety.

There were nineteen Icemen in the park but their equipment, sufficient in normal circumstances, was totally inadequate to deal with such a large-scale emergency. They had two wicker ice boats, one pole, a sledge, three "breaker" ladders, six ordinary ladders, three folding ladders, eight drags, two boat hooks, two ice axes and eight caution boards. The horror of Regent's Park was unprecedented—a vast area of ice had shattered simultaneously. As the Royal Humane Society recalled in their annual report for 1867:

> So unheard of a circumstance took every one by surprise, and ere all the Society's men and the police could apply, over so large a space, the apparatus provided for accidents, the sad affair was over...

Some skaters thrown into the water managed to save themselves and others. Mr Abel Thomas dragged his friend, Richard Colman, from under the ice and supported him until he reached the safety of an island in the middle of the lake. Thomas then saw a young man struggling in the water "grow black in the face" before sinking. He dived in and dragged the drowning man back to the safety of the island. Thomas attempted another rescue, but was forced to give up because the bitter cold had numbed his arms and legs. The Royal Humane Society later presented him with a Silver Medal, the highest of the eighteen awards they distributed after the tragedy.

The rescued were rushed to the Society's Regent's Park Receiving House—a tent—for emergency treatment by the organisation's medical officer, Mr Obie. Other Society doctors had been sent for and worked under Mr Obie's guidance. Conditions in the tent were cramped—it boasted just one bath and two beds. Sussex Terrace overlooked the lake and its residents had a grandstand view of the disaster. They sent masses of blankets, sheets and other supplies for use by the doctors, supplementing an hopelessly inadequate supply. Despite its limitations, scores of survivors were treated at the Receiving House during the ninety minutes following the accident. Most casualties were sent home in cabs or forwarded to a local public house for a "restorative," but about forty were suffering with exhaustion after their icy ordeal and needed treatment in the infirmary of the nearby Marylebone Workhouse or at St Mary's Hospital, Paddington.

The workhouse master, Mr George Douglas, was walking in Regent's Park as the ice shattered and realised that the Receiving House would be hard-pushed to cope. He quickly made arrangements for victims to be wrapped in blankets and ferried to the Workhouse Infirmary in cabs. Messages were sent to the infirmary's medical staff and blankets, beds and equipment were quickly prepared to deal with the expected influx of casualties. The workhouse doctors treated sixteen victims, and all but one survived. This was James Crawley. He was close to death when he arrived at the Workhouse and the chief physician, Dr John Randall, immediately attempted artificial resuscitation. He used the Dr Silvester and Dr Marshall Hall methods approved by the Royal Humane Society. In the early 1800s the Society had advised mouth-to-mouth resuscitation, but this had subsequently been banned because exhaled breath was believed to be poisonous. The Silvester and Marshall Hall methods were based on the premise that movement of the chest would induce inhalation. Unfortunately they didn't work. Anyone who survived after their use, would have survived without their application. Crawley died within half an hour.

At about 4:00 PM contingents of police and extra Icemen arrived at Regent's Park. There was little for them to do. Most of those who could be rescued had already been dragged from the ice. The miserable task of recovering the bodies began. Boats were taken to the spot where most victims were believed to have perished, and the Icemen sank their drags in the hope of hooking onto a body. Dusk was already falling when work began, but nine bodies were recovered before dark.

The dead were taken to the Receiving House and at about 7:00 PM were transferred to a mortuary set up at the workhouse. By this time word of the disaster had spread and worried friends and relatives became desperate for news of loved ones they feared may have been involved. A vast crowd gathered outside the workhouse and those considered "genuine" were allowed inside to view the sick and the dead. Wherever names for the victims could be established, relatives were sent for. In all cases the initial and unusually sensitive explanation for the call was that their relative "could not return home that night, because their clothes were wet."

The next morning the work of dragging the lake for the dead began in earnest. The job was fraught with difficulties. Temperatures had plummeted overnight and the lake was again frozen solid. Ice shattered

17 *Royal Humane Society Receiving House, Hyde Park*

18 *Divers preparing to search Regent's Park lake*

the day before was welded together by thick, fresh ice, scarring the surface like a badly-healed wound. Evidence of the previous day's events—hats, scarves, gloves and other belongings discarded in the panic—were frozen into the surface. Icemen cut channels to give access to boats and allow the drag for corpses to continue, but they were hard-pressed to keep the passages clear. Police set up barriers to keep the inevitable sightseers away, but by early morning these had been breached, and thousands gathered around the lakeside. Some newspapers were clearly aghast at the dense crowds of onlookers. A reporter from the *Illustrated Times*, who had few scruples in scrutinising the scene at the lake, infirmary and mortuary himself, commented on 26 January:

> ...the vast majority unmistakably belonged to the class for which 'rough' has become the accepted designation. The air seems to carry to this class, as it does to birds of particular habits, the scent of blood. A dreadful accident happens one day, and the next there they are in thousands gazing upon the victims...there they were, following the instincts of their tribe.

The journalist from the *Kentish Independent* (26 January) was more sympathetic.

> There was far more than the gratification of curiosity and the wish to see the spot in which so many fellow beings had been lost marked in the countenances of the great balk of adult visitors to the park. A thoughtful, solemn demeanour was observable among almost all, unbroken by notes of disorder of any description.

By mid-afternoon twenty more dead had been fished from the water. The bodies were laid by the lakeside to give an opportunity for them to be identified, and were then taken to the Receiving House to await transfer to the mortuary at the Marylebone Workhouse. By the end of Friday, three days after the disaster, forty bodies had been recovered. This was to be the final death toll, but the Icemen, park-keepers and police dragging the lake had no way of knowing exactly how many bodies they were searching for. Mr Heinke, an expert in diving, offered free use of his apparatus and men to scour the lake's bottom. The following day three divers arrived. The men attracted enormous attention, and over the weekend the crowds swelled to record numbers. Despite their heavy and cumbersome equipment the divers painstakingly searched the lake, but found nothing but skates, hammers, mallets and other lost or discarded property.

On Saturday a group of the spectators decided to help. They started a collection to raise funds to pay men to clear the lake of ice. By Sunday they had £20.6s.6d and this was used to pay an army of 180 or so men 2/– each to break ice. By nightfall an estimated 110 tons of ice lay stacked around the edges of the lake. The next week the weather became milder and it was easier to keep the lake clear of ice. Meanwhile, a large trench was being dug to link the lake with a nearby sewer. This allowed the water to be drained away and a last, definitive and fruitless search for bodies was carried out.

The Regent's Park disaster caused uproar. The public was incensed that so many could lose their lives while taking such innocent and harmless pleasure. The government were blamed, the park authorities were blamed and even the Icemen—two of whom needed treatment for exhaustion after their exemplary rescue efforts—were accused of being drunk, cowardly and downright useless. The fact the victims had ignored clear warning signs was not regarded as a contributory factor. On the contrary, the recklessness of the skaters was viewed with at least some degree of admiration. A leader in the *Camden and Kentish Town Gazette* (19 January) said it all.

> The fool hardiness which ventured on the ice is so closely allied to the characteristic daring and courage of the race that they could not be separated. When they can the age of common sense will be commenced; no Grace Darlings, no volunteers to swim to wrecked and drowning seamen, none to descend into dangerous coal pits to help the suffering or succour the dying. God forbid the age of common sense!

The victims were not criticised for their failure to heed warnings, but the government was slammed for not establishing laws that could forbid people skating on dangerous ice. The park-keepers, police and Icemen had no authority to stop skating, however dangerous the conditions. They could only advise, and that advice was widely ignored. On 19 January the *Illustrated London News* lamented the lack of a Minister for London. With such an appointment, it argued, the tragedy would never have happened. A Minister for London, the paper insisted, "would have felt it his business to know whether the men, women or children of London ought to be allowed to go on the ice or not."

At the subsequent inquest, presided over by Middlesex coroner Dr Lankester at the Marylebone Workhouse, various theories about the cause of the accident were heard. Dr Lankester regretted he could not finance the cost of calling expert witnesses, but ideas were certainly not lacking. Many blamed park-keepers who had cut away ice from around two islands on the lake. This had been done, as it had for many years, for the benefit of the wildfowl and to prevent the public getting onto the islands. Witness Thomas Otley, who lost his 20-year-old son in the disaster, told the inquest he was convinced earth under the lake contained latent heat. This, he explained, had worked on the decaying vegetable matter on the lake bed and generated gas which had formed a large bubble. This had suddenly burst to the surface with a power that shattered the ice.

Exactly why the ice disintegrated on that cold January day was never discovered. The reason so many died was easier to determine—in many places the water was twelve feet deep or more and those submerged had little chance of escape. The dead were young men—all between 10 and 40 years old—and the vast majority were from the better-off classes. They included an army lieutenant, a medical student and an articled clerk. Unlike the poor, this class had a powerful voice. That voice demanded action to prevent a similar tragedy—and got it.

The inquest jury called for the police or "other authority" to be empowered to prohibit people going on to ice when it was in a dangerous condition. They also called for the depth of the lake to be reduced to prevent future fatalities. Shortly afterwards, a delegation from the Royal Humane Society had a meeting with Mr Walpole, the Home Secretary, to discuss preventive measures. The Society's secretary, Mr Lambton Young, argued strongly that the lake should have a maximum depth of no more than five feet during the winter months. Walpole promised to examine how the public could be protected with the minimum hindrance to free action and enjoyment.

The lake remained empty after being drained in January 1867, and during the hot summer that followed the stench from its rotting bed brought many complaints. Early the next year work began to reduce its depth. The bottom was levelled and covered with concrete in an attempt to keep the water free from mud and allow regular cleaning. The work took several months and while an expensive exercise, it proved provident. In 1886 there was an action replay of the disaster. Hundreds of skaters swarmed onto the ornamental lake, totalling ignoring danger warning signs and protestations from the Icemen. Suddenly there was a loud crack and a whole section of the lake's icy surface disintegrated. About one hundred people sank into the water. This time, however, the water was only three to four feet deep and most escaped with an uncomfortable dipping. No one died.

There are no records of a disaster fund for the Regent's Park disaster. Those killed were mostly young, unmarried men. However, a week after the disaster, one rescuer, bricklayer's labourer John O'Donnel, appeared before Marylebone magistrate Mr D'Eyncourt, begging for help from the poor box. He had saved eight lives at Regent's Park, but the time spent in the icy water had affected him badly. O'Donnel shook constantly as he stood in the court, and was unable to use his right arm. D'Eyncourt gave him £2 and commented the Royal Humane Society would probably give him an award. That would do him little good, retorted O'Donnel. He knew they would give him a bronze medal, but that would not feed his children. In the event the Society gave him a small sum of money instead of the medal.

Staff at the Marylebone Workhouse and Infirmary were widely praised for their efforts in caring for the victims. Their public acclaim clearly delighted their Board of Guardians, and the rewards they earned were unusually generous. The master Mr George Douglas and his wife were given an increase in salary of £50 per annum. A good wage for a workhouse master would have been around £150 per year, so the rise was substantial. The chief medical officer, Mr John Randall, whose earnings from the workhouse would have been on a par with Mr Douglas', also received an extra £50 per year. A one-off payment of £20 went to resident surgeon Mr Fuller and another £10 was distributed between another fourteen members of staff.

It is clear that attitudes towards calamity reflected in the press varied according to the class of those involved. The deaths of the Regent's Park skaters brought sympathy, even admiration, for the victims, and demands for action to prevent a recurrence. At the same time, those starving and freezing in the Docklands were expected to starve and freeze quietly, and without protest. When desperation drove the poor to civil disorder any sympathy quickly gave way to fear and suspicion. Disturbances were blamed on "roughs" who had nothing to do with the genuine poor and who were bent on making trouble. The genuine poor, reported the popular press, had enough food to get by. There seemed to be a reluctance to accept the degree of suffering taking place, and the fact that extremes of poverty and deprivation could transform a usually meek and downtrodden section of society into a potential threat. The press mirrored the majority view of their middle- and upper-class readership. There was compassion for those within their own social strata, but lack of empathy and understanding for the "other world" struggling at their feet.

CHAPTER FIVE

Fenian Campaigns

Centuries of neglect, incompetent rule and downright exploitation left Victorian Ireland discontented and desperate. The great majority of her people lived in abject poverty, struggling to eke a miserable existence from handkerchief holdings. The British government was blamed, and to a large extent rightly so, for the nation's pitiful condition. The seeds of rebellion were nurtured by decades of intense suffering and hardship. The embryo of a militant and capable resistance began to take shape. The fury of the activists turned to the mainland, where their violence could create far more sensation and publicity than they could hope for in Ireland. The Victorian era was to witness the first Irish terrorist attacks against targets on English soil.

By the early nineteenth century Ireland had been divided into vast estates, usually owned by absentee English landlords and run by agents who sub-let the property to make profits for themselves. Tenants would then sub-let their holdings, and the system proliferated until many plots were little larger than the average back garden. Land originally let at ten shillings per acre could easily be subdivided so many times that it fetched thirty shillings for a quarter of an acre. Landlords were able to evict tenants at whim, and they had many such whims. Evicted tenants received no compensation for improvements they may have made to a property and this was a strong disincentive to make any. The tiny parcels of land could not be farmed economically, and the profits were totally dependent on rents collected. Consequently, rents were pushed as high as possible and evictions because of non-payment were an everyday fact of life. A few landlords made efforts to farm their own lands, but this caused distress to the tenants they displaced. English peasants evicted during the agricultural enclosure movement could at least look for work in the mushrooming industrial towns; Ireland had little industry, so the option did not exist.

The situation was brought to a head in 1845 by an attack of potato blight that devastated Ireland's second crop. In England potato blight brought hunger to the poor; in Ireland the consequence was starvation. Potatoes were the staple diet for the bulk of Ireland's poor. It was the only viable crop sustainable on their tiny holdings and they were wholly reliant upon its successful cultivation. Peel's Cabinet realised the peasants' plight and agreed to spend £600,000 on relief measures. £160,000 was used to purchase maize from America. This "Peel's Brimstone," as it came to be known, was sold to the Irish at a penny per pound. The crisis deepened the next year. The potato crops failed completely and the poor could be found wandering and dying in the streets. A coroner's jury investigating the death from starvation of a Connaught woman returned a verdict of wilful murder against the British Prime Minister, Lord John Russell. As if to rub salt into an already grievous wound, in December 1846 a cholera epidemic broke out. The New Year brought little improvement. By March 1847, 734,000 people were employed on public works and no fewer than three million Irish were being supported by public funds. In the same month the government scrapped the public works programme in favour of a general distribution of food to the destitute. Anyone with a holding of a quarter of an acre or more was excluded from claiming, so thousands gave up their homes to keep their families alive.

Many more gave up the struggle in Ireland, and paid the £4 or £5 needed for a ticket on one of the cheapest boats to North America. The vessels available to the would-be emigrants were often appalling. Every available space on the grim ships was packed and conditions on board were often little better than those found on slave ships. Disease was rife, and spread rapidly through the ships. Of the eighty-nine thousand who left for Canada in 1847, fifteen thousand died en route. Thousands more came to England, and their transit was little better. The Irish were crammed onto unseaworthy ships and treated with less respect than the average cargo of livestock. In December 1848, seventy-two Irish migrants died on a steamboat running between Sligo and Liverpool. The ship sailed on a stormy night, and the Captain insisted passengers went below deck. The mate and crew herded the two hundred-odd men, women and children into the steerage cabin, a room about eighteen feet long, eleven feet wide and seven feet high. The last few were pushed into the room and a tarpaulin was fastened over the entrance. The cabin quickly became a charnel-house. One passenger somehow managed to escape and told a crew member what was happening. It was too late to save the crushed and suffocated victims. The ship docked at Derry and the dead were taken to the workhouse and buried in a pit.

Those who made it safely to English shores were hardly welcomed with open arms. They were looked on with suspicion and a vehement dislike bordering on hatred. The Irish, although not technically foreigners, were regarded as unwanted immigrants of a lesser race. They were prepared to take the worst jobs, work for a pittance, and be consigned to the worst slums. The English working class believed the Irish were taking their jobs and bringing wages and living conditions to unacceptably low levels.

In 1841 there were four hundred thousand Irish-born migrants living in England, and by 1867 this number had increased to some six hundred thousand. The Irish potato blight ended in 1848, but by then five hundred thousand had died and hundreds of thousands more had emigrated. Many estates lay empty and barren and landlords were keen to sell their holdings. By 1857 about a third of the land had changed hands and the majority of the eighty thousand new owners were Irish. This might appear to have heralded an improvement in the lot of the country, but instead the situation deteriorated. The new owners were keen to manage their estates efficiently, and to make the land pay. That meant enclosures, and the eviction of remaining smallholders. Approximately two hundred thousand tenants were evicted, many being left with little option but emigration or the workhouse.

Many of the Irish who emigrated did so with bitter memories of their homeland, and a growing determination to do something to remedy the situation. In 1858 a group of Irish-American militants formed an organisation dedicated to throwing off the yoke of English rule and making Ireland a self-governing Republic. They called themselves the Fenians. Exactly why they selected this name is unclear, but it is believed to originate from an Irish folk hero, Fionn. Fionn was a celebrated chieftain who lived before Ireland was converted to Christianity, and had pledged to defend the country from aggressors and to uphold the power of its king. His people—the Fenians—backed him in his illustrious campaign in support of his country. The American Fenians quickly became highly organised and gained widespread support. They collected money for arms and ammunitions, set up complex structures of command and began to train men.

The outbreak of the American Civil War in 1861 provided an ideal opportunity for the Fenians to gain military experience, and several key figures became high-ranking officers in the Federal Army. The end of hostilities in 1865 saw the Fenians at their strongest and England at its most vulnerable. The organisation had a world-wide membership, with groups established in France, Australia, Canada, South America, Europe and, of course, England and Ireland. They held large rallies in American towns, often drawing thousands of supporters. The British government was worried at the popularity and growth of the Fenian movement. It knew the rank and file of its own army was disgruntled, and was concerned America might throw its weight against Britain if the Fenians instigated a rebellion. Top figures in the Fenian leadership in England and Ireland, including the chief, James Stephens, were arrested and the movement lost a valuable opportunity for successful insurrection. Stephens was remanded in Richmond Gaol but was quickly rescued by Colonel Thomas Kelly, a veteran of the American Civil War. Stephens was whisked to safety in America, but remained a hesitant leader and was finally deposed in December 1866. Kelly took the reins and acted swiftly. He decided to stage an uprising in Ireland in February 1867 and ordered his deputy, Richard O'Sullivan Burke, to take charge of terrorist action in England. The English operation was designed to create a diversion and prevent the government concentrating its attention on Ireland.

Burke was an intelligent man who had served in the Federal Army during the Civil War, rising to the rank of Captain of Engineers. However, his first venture into terrorism against England, in February 1867, was a dismal failure. The plan was to capture the poorly defended Chester Castle, seize armaments stored there and ship them to Ireland via the port of Holyhead. Supporters from different counties were ordered to make their way to Chester to help in operations, but the hordes of Irishmen suddenly converging on the town aroused suspicions. English reinforcements were quickly put in place and the Fenian plan was aborted.

The rising planned for Ireland ended abruptly when Kelly and his aide Timothy Deasey were arrested in Manchester during the early hours of 11 September 1867. At first they were charged under the Vagrancy Act, but communication with the Irish Police made their true identities clear and the British Government realised it had a prime catch on its hands. The Fenians were determined to rescue Kelly and Deasey, and they did so later that month as the pair were brought to court in a Manchester Police van. During the struggle Sergeant Brett, a police officer travelling inside the van with the prisoners, was shot and killed. Kelly and Deasey escaped, and were never recaptured.

The furious authorities moved quickly to arrest the so-called culprits and by 13 November five men had been convicted of murder. The trial displayed British justice at its worst. The verdicts were so extraordinary that in the case of one man, Maguire, a large body of pressmen appealed to the Home Secretary for a pardon. This was granted on 21 November. Another man, an American citizen, was also reprieved. The three convicted killers, Allen, O'Brien and Larkin were publicly hanged on 23 November, and their deaths triggered national and international indignation and disgust. Support and sympathy for the Fenians reached an all-time high. A few days after the executions Richard Burke and his colleague Casey were arrested in London and kept on remand in the Clerkenwell House of Detention.

There were almost ninety-one thousand Irish-born people living in London at the time, and many lived in Clerkenwell and the surrounding districts of East London. The sympathy towards Fenians that set in after the Manchester executions was much in evidence, and in early December public meetings in support of the movement and against the hangings attracted large crowds. One gathering on Clerkenwell Green in December attracted an audience of some twenty thousand. The Government and the courts had delivered a trio of martyrs and the populace was quick to adopt them. The tide of goodwill towards the Irish militants may well have led to repercussions within the government, but a plot to rescue Burke and Casey went badly wrong and triggered a catastrophe that destroyed any chance the Fenians had of gaining political advantage in Britain.

Burke and Casey, on remand in Clerkenwell, were allowed regular visits. Burke was visited by his sister, Mrs Cathleen Barry, and Casey by Mrs Ann Justice. The women smuggled in supplies of chloride of gold, an effective form of invisible ink, which Burke used to communicate with Fenians plotting his escape. The prison wall presented a formidable obstacle. It was three feet thick at its base and some twenty-five feet high. Burke had noticed a small portion had recently been demolished to allow pipes to be laid and drew a plan, marking where the wall had been rebuilt and would be weaker. The letters were delivered to a Fenian group that met at a house in Pulteney Court. By 7 December the scheme had been finalised. A barrel of gunpowder would be ignited against the selected spot in the prison wall while the inmates were at exercise. A small white ball, thrown over the wall, would warn Burke and Casey of the imminent explosion and prepare them to dash through the debris to freedom.

The small group of activists collected money from supporters and purchased quantities of gunpowder. This was delivered to Pulteney Court but moved elsewhere to be packed into a barrel ready for the attack that had been scheduled for 12 December. Events now took a strange twist. The Fenians were plagued by informers, and on the appointed day, 12 December, news of the plot finally filtered through to the Home Office. A note, dated 11 December and apparently from police in Dublin, was received:

> ...I have just received information from a reliable source to the effect that the rescue of Richard Burke from prison in London is contemplated. The plan is to blow up the exercise wall by means of gunpowder; the hour between 3pm and 4pm and the signal for 'all right' a white ball thrown up outside when he is at exercise.

Under-Secretary Mr Adolphus Liddell immediately contacted Scotland Yard. Police Commissioner Sir Richard Mayne was not in his office, so the information was passed to his deputy, Captain Labalmondiere. Labalmondiere passed on the details of the warning to Superintendent Gernon and while he was talking to Gernon, Mayne returned. The Commissioner instructed Gernon to inform the Governor of the prison about the plot. Mayne also told Gernon to arrange for the prison walls to be examined for any signs that they had been mined, and to maintain a strict look-out. Gernon posted a double patrol of two police constables, three constables in plain clothes and their sergeants to keep observation on the prison and to notify the Inspector at King's Cross Station if anything suspicious was seen. In addition to these men there were five police constables and three constables in plain clothes already in the district.

Mr Liddell also notified Mr Henry Pownall, Chairman of the Visiting Justices at Clerkenwell House of Detention, of the potential danger. The prison took the precautionary measures of bringing in extra wardens and changing the prisoners' exercise time. The Governor, Captain Codd, was visited by Inspector Thomson. Codd and Mayne were not on the best of terms as during an earlier crisis Mayne had refused extra police support for the prison. Thomson received a stony reception. He later said:

> The Governor told me to return his thanks to Sir R. Mayne, but as regarded the internal arrangements of the prison he was quite competent to provide for them, and did not want any suggestion. The Governor then walked away. He afterwards called me into his office, and in the presence of Chief Warden Moore again told me to return his thanks to Sir R. Mayne, but as for any suggestions to the interior of the prison, to tell Sir R. Mayne to mind his own business. He did not believe the prison would be attacked. He hoped he might live until it was, and he would be pretty sure to live to a ripe old age.

Inspector Thomson had arrived at the prison at about 3:00 PM. At 3:30 PM, probably during Thomson's talk with the Governor, Fenians Captain Murphy and two lower-ranking associates were trundling a thirty-six-gallon beer barrel, packed with gunpowder and covered with tarpaulin, to the weak spot of the prison wall. As usual at this time of the day, the prisoners, including Burke and Casey, were walking around the exercise yard bordering the wall. The Fenians gave the signal to warn Burke of the impending explosion—the small white ball was thrown over the prison wall. Warden James Tait later told how he picked up the india-rubber ball and took it home for one of his children. Burke recognised the sign, and left the exercise line. He stood by the wall, slowly taking off his shoe and brushing his stocking. Meanwhile the hapless Murphy was having immense difficulty in lighting the fuse to set off the explosion. He lit the fuse three times, each time darting off to await the explosion from a safe distance...and each time the fuse fizzled out before it could have any effect. After the third attempt the fuse was dangerously close to the gunpowder, and although police had not seemed to notice the activity, some bystanders were showing interest in the proceedings. Murphy decided to give up the attempt, and the barrel was wheeled off.

That night the Fenians met to discuss their bungled efforts, and it was decided to stage a second attack the following day, Friday 13 December. This time Michael Barrett would light the fuse. Anne Justice and Cathleen Barry visited Burke and Casey early in the afternoon, presumably to let them know about the revised plans. Neither men could have known the Governor had decided to scrap the afternoon exercise session, a move that would make the destruction of the prison wall pointless. The extra policemen were now on duty outside the jail, but Barrett and his two colleagues had no difficulty in wheeling the truck holding the barrel of gunpowder up to the prison wall and unloading it into position. It was about 3:45 PM when Barrett took a match to light the fuse. As had happened the previous day, the fuse wouldn't light. John Abbott, 13, had a clear view of proceedings from the doorstep of his home in Corporation Lane, directly opposite the prison wall. The *Times* reported his account on 21 December:

> ...I saw a man cross the road from St James' Court and go over to the barrel.... He had two squibs in his hand, one of which he put on the pavement. There were two little boys playing. One of them picked the squib up. The man put the other squib in the front of the barrel. The boys offered the man some paper to light. The man lighted a Lucifer and put it to the squib in the head of the barrel. The man stood there for one minute; he had one foot on the kerb and the other in the gutter. When he saw the squib begin to flare he moved away, and when the squib had burnt half way down he ran...

John Abbott wasn't the only one to notice the strange goings on. Milkman John Bird watched as the Fenians positioned the barrel against the wall. The *Times* recorded his story on 18 December:

> They took either a tarpaulin or mackintosh from the truck and put it across the barrel.... He put the light to the end of the barrel before he drew the tarpaulin over the end. He put the light to the end next the wall. Mrs Parr, a woman whom I was serving with milk, observed the man as well as I did, and when she saw him apply the light to the barrel she said, 'Good God, Mr Bird, what is the man doing! We shall all be blown up.'

Mr Bird was obviously not a man to panic easily. He stated he served other customers, and then went to look for a policeman. Police constables Ambrose Sutton, George Ranger and John Goldsmith had grown suspicious of Jeremiah Allen, Anne Justice and Timothy Desmond as they seemed to be loitering in the area. Sutton had been on special duty outside the prison since Burke's arrest, so must have observed Justice on her many visits. He later told how he watched as Desmond walked from a barrel on the pavement near the prison wall. He lost sight of him just as the temperamental fuse finally triggered the gunpowder packed into the barrel, and the whole district was rocked by a massive and devastating explosion.

The Fenians had vastly over-estimated the amount of gunpowder needed to blow a hole in the wall. The thick choking dust cleared to

Suspects in the Clerkenwell bombing
19   Top left: Anne Justice
20   Top right: Timothy Desmond
21   Bottom right: Jeremiah Allen

reveal a section of wall some twenty feet wide at the base and sixty feet at the top had been blasted away. Most of the three-storey homes in Corporation Lane lay in ruins, and houses in fourteen other streets suffered structural or superficial damage. One woman had been killed instantly and three others died as they arrived at hospital. Another two succumbed in the days that followed, and the eventual death toll crept up to fifteen. Forty men, women and children were injured severely enough to be detained in hospital. The prison exercise yard resembled a battlefield littered with fallen bricks, masonry and shattered glass. Flying bricks and debris had bitten deep indentations into the wall of the main prison building opposite the seat of the explosion. There is little doubt the death toll would have been far higher had the prisoners been at exercise. Burke and Casey may well have been killed by the over-enthusiasm and terrifying lack of expertise displayed by their supporters.

As the dust and shock subsided there was a flurry of activity. Pc Sutton grabbed the fleeing Anne Justice and Timothy Desmond, and Pc Ranger arrested Allen. Inspector Thomson—the officer who had visited the prison the day before to notify the Governor of the potential danger—had just left the jail after taking someone to identify Burke and Casey. His cab was a few yards from Corporation Lane when it was rocked by the explosion. He leapt out and quickly made arrangements for police reinforcements. Inside the Clerkenwell House of Detention, frightened prisoners banged at their doors, believing the place was on fire. Doors of some cells had been sprung by the force of the blast and prisoners wandered in the corridors, but order was soon restored. During the fracas Casey repeatedly shouted offers of money to anyone who would rescue him, but no one came forward. At the height of the tension a crowd of on-lookers walked through the gaping breach in the prison wall and into the prison yard. Governor Captain Codd, probably stunned and fearful of another assault, ordered them to leave. When they failed to obey he ordered a volley of blank musketry to be fired over their heads. This had the desired effect, and the curious spectators beat a hasty retreat.

News of the disaster quickly reached Scotland Yard, and five hundred policemen were ordered to the prison to keep sightseers at bay and maintain order. Captain Eyre Shaw, chief of the newly-formed Metropolitan Fire Brigade, commanded his men at what must have been their first major incident. The Captain could be seen directing operations from the top of a pile of rubble. The firemen worked quickly to release those trapped in the debris of their homes in Corporation Lane. It was a poor district, but most of the residents were craftsmen and many worked from home. The Brigade commandeered cabs to take the wounded to the nearest hospitals; thirty-six were detained in St Bartholomew's and another six in the Royal Free. As soon as they heard of the explosion, staff at St Bartholomew's prepared to deal with up to a hundred casualties. In the event, all the victims received were in beds and under treatment of senior surgeon Mr Luther Holden, house surgeon Edward M'Clean and other medical staff within thirty minutes of arrival. Later that evening hospital treasurer Mr Foster White telegrammed the Prince of Wales, the hospital's President, to tell him how the hospital had coped with the crisis.

The damage to human life was appalling. Casualties had been crushed in the rubble of their homes, hit by debris hurled at force by the explosion and cut by flying glass. Injuries included multiple fractures, deep lacerations, amputated limbs, damaged and destroyed eyes, concussion and deep shock. The Thompson family, of 3a Corporation Lane, suffered particularly badly. They lived directly opposite the explosion and their home caught the full force of the blast. Brass finisher Frederick Thompson was in the workshop at the back of his home when he saw a flash and heard what he thought was a thunderclap. The noise continued, and his house began to tumble down. As the shuddering subsided he managed to escape into the yard through a casement window, and saw his wife, Elizabeth, crawling in the rubble. He watched as she clutched the mangled and barely recognisable form of their daughter, 11-year-old Martha. Frederick took the child and placed her in the corner of the yard while he searched for his other children. Lizzie, 17, had lost an eye and suffered facial injuries; Harriet, 13, was also blinded in one eye and had cuts to her face and arm. Emma, eight, had severe cuts to her neck and hands. Martha had lost both eyes and most of her face in the explosion. Surgeons at the Royal Free realised her condition was hopeless. She died after two days. Other casualties included Maria Abbott, 34, who lost an eye and suffered severe cuts to her head and face. Her young daughter Minnie, 7, died shortly after arriving at St Bartholomew's. John, 13, had cuts to his face; Frederick also suffered severe cuts to his face and body, and lost part of his nose; Annie, 2, suffered slight concussion; and Arthur, 5, was blinded.

Captain Shaw and his men worked quickly and efficiently, sending victims to hospital in cabs as soon as they had been freed. Several houses in Corporation Lane were in a precarious state, and Shaw supervised their demolition to make the area safe. Thousands of sightseers arrived and threatened to hinder operations. A police cordon kept them at distance while large barricades were secured at both ends of Corporation Lane. The breach in the prison wall was temporarily sealed with a thirty-foot-high wooden barricade topped with iron hooks. Security inside the prison was bolstered with the arrival of one hundred Fusilier Guards under the command of Colonel Moncrieff, Captain Goaling, Lieutenant Moray and Lieutenant Inigo-Jones.

The Clerkenwell explosion was the first Irish terrorist bomb in England, and the public and political outcry which followed was of an intensity unparalleled in other disasters. Any sympathy drummed up by the Fenians after the executions at Manchester vanished. A widespread hatred for the movement—and for the Irish—became rapidly evident, and sympathy for the sufferers was universal. Early the next morning the Chancellor of the Exchequer, C. Ward Hunt, sent his private secretary Mr Montagu Corry to Clerkenwell to give immediate financial relief to those in need. Corry carried a leather bag filled with money and walked the district with Mr John Lambert of the Poor Law Board. Later that day Queen Victoria ordered telegrams expressing her sympathy to be sent to St Bartholomew's and the Royal Free hospitals. She also instructed her physician, Dr Jenner, to visit patients and to send them a large quantity of hot-house grapes and fresh fruit. A long list of VIPs attended the hospitals to visit the injured. The Duke of Cambridge, Lord Colville, Lord Barrington, Lord Bingham, Lord Henry Lennox and Lord George Lennox were among those visiting St Bartholomew's. The Home Secretary, Mr Gathorne Hardy, and his Under-Secretary Mr Liddell visited the prison to discuss security arrangements while the wall was being repaired. Police outside the prison were under the command of Deputy Commissioner Captain Labalmondiere. Their number was increased to fifteen hundred, and the men were armed with cutlasses. Later that same Saturday the government announced a £300 reward for information leading to the arrest and conviction of the person who had caused the explosion, plus another £100 for information leading to the conviction of accomplices.

Saturday also saw Allen, Desmond and Justice brought before magistrates at Bow Street Court and formally charged with

22   Clerkenwell House of Detention after the bombing. Courtesy Islington Libraries.

23   Same view as depicted in the Illustrated Times

...being concerned with others not in custody in the wilful murder of Sarah Hodgkinson, William Clutton and Minnie Abbott, by wilfully and maliciously firing an explosive substance, supposed to be gunpowder, at Corporation Lane, Clerkenwell.

They were remanded in custody. Burke and Casey also appeared at Bow Street Court that day, still facing charges of treason. Their solicitor, Dr Kenealy, refused to appear for them, stating that although he believed the two men had nothing to do with the outrage, he believed it was probably orchestrated by their friends whom had instructed him to represent them. In the circumstances he was unwilling to continue defending Burke and Casey. In turn, Burke and Casey declared they had had no knowledge of the plot, and that they regarded it with abhorrence. Both men were again remanded in custody.

The inquest into the deaths of the first to die from the effects of the explosion opened the following Tuesday, 17 December, and was adjourned until the following Friday. Two witnesses identified Allen as having thrown "something" to the man who lit the barrel. Several police officers noted Allen, Desmond and Justice had been talking to each other outside the prison. The ill-feeling between prison Governor Captain Codd and Police Commissioner Sir Richard Mayne was also brought to light. It emerged that some of the policemen on duty at Clerkenwell were unaware of the suspected plot. Constable Edward Moriarty testified he was on his "normal beat" when he was called to look at the barrel placed against the prison wall. "Fire was streaming out from the end facing the road; it was a blue jet, as thick as my wrist...." Moriarty stepped back to see what would happen. He added: "I had heard nothing about an attack on the prison." Inspector Potter told coroner Mr Serjeant Payne that he had heard several "intimations" that an attempt to rescue the Fenians would be made, but he had heard nothing of any specific plot. Payne commented that "Wolf" had been cried so often that at last the police did not believe it.

Payne made it clear he believed the prison should have been better defended, and that the Governor and Police Commissioner should have discussed the best arrangements. He went on:

> The consequence of this neglect has been that the houses in Corporation Lane have been blown down, and great loss of life and injury to persons have ensued. ... If more precautions had been taken, in all probability these sad occurrences would not have taken place.

Codd was quick to defend himself:

> I beg you not to lose sight of the fact that I did give intimation originally
> that protection would be required, and the clerk also gave intimation,
> while Sir R. Mayne was the man who sent me information that an attack
> would be made on the prison walls. I told him that I would take care of
> the kernel if he would take care of the shell.

The jurors took just twenty minutes to return their verdict. The deaths
had been caused by the explosion, and they found Desmond, Allen and
Justice guilty of wilful murder.

The government issued an appeal for volunteers to act as Special
Constables and in London more than twenty thousand men were sworn
in. The "Specials" were under the control of Lieutenant-Colonel C. Ewart
and were instructed to meet at designated rallying points whenever an
alarm was raised. The government promised to increase the regular
police force by a thousand men. These steps may well have been in
response to the public outrage against a force whose complacency and
inaction had allowed the catastrophe to happen. There were widespread
calls for Sir Richard Mayne's resignation. Shortly after the explosion the
Middlesex magistrates only narrowly avoided passing a resolution
demanding a full investigation into Mayne's "passive" behaviour. The
nation's press were less inhibited. One of the most blistering attacks
appeared as a leader in the *Illustrated Times* of 4 January 1868:

> There is no use in mincing the matter any longer. It is high time that Sir
> Richard Mayne were relegated to private life—in other words the Chief
> Commissioner of the Metropolitan Police must be 'allowed to resign.'
> (That, we believe, is the proper official phraseology in which to couch such
> an opinion). Under his command the force is rapidly becoming a scandal
> and a by-word...They seldom seek to hinder the criminal from carrying out
> his nefarious designs; they devote their energies mainly to catching him
> afterwards—if they can. But even in that line they are not over-successful,
> for cases of detection are about as rare as roses in December - at least that
> is so whenever the affair in hand is of special importance.... Whatever may
> have been Sir Richard Mayne's original recommendations for the post he
> occupies, it is plain that years of routine and irresponsibility have spoilt a
> naturally not very brilliant intellect, and induced habits of domineering in
> small matters and of wrong-headed official conceit that make him unfit to
> cope with special emergencies...upon him we do not hesitate to charge the
> whole responsibility of permitting that outrage to be perpetrated.

Questions about the debacle were asked in the House of Commons. Home Secretary Mr Gathorne Hardy carefully explained the police had been caught out because they had expected the prison wall to be blown *up*, whereas it was in fact blown *down*.

> What their attention was apparently directed to was the undermining of the wall; they thought it would probably be blown up from underneath, and had no conception that it would be blown down in the way it really was.

Sir Richard Mayne was in his 70s, and had served as Commissioner since 1829. He died within a year of the explosion.

The Clerkenwell Explosion was unique among nineteenth-century disasters in the attitude it provoked. People had lost their lives, homes, health and workplaces by a terrorist act that should never have been allowed to happen. There was a general desire to ensure the victims were cared for and suffered as little hardship as possible. The disaster fund that was established was one of the most thoughtfully and carefully managed of the century. The first appeal for contributions to the fund came from the Reverend Styleman Herring, a man who would later play an important role in organising the *Princess Alice* Disaster Fund. On 14 December, the day after the explosion, the *Times* carried a letter from Herring:

> Sir, I have just visited several poor families in the locality of the explosion. Never have I witnessed such desolation, misery and woe. Neighbours tell of terrible heart-rending scenes of poor innocent babes, children and people lacerated in a most horrible manner. Fifty eight are reported as dead or wounded. Not a window has a pane of glass in it for many yards around. It is to plead for these poor desolate folks that I write and any money entrusted to me and my friends will personally administer to their relief.

Clerkenwell was nowhere near Herring's parish. It lay firmly on the doorstep of the Reverend Robert Maguire, who was none too pleased at the interference. The next day the *Times* recorded a long list of donations sent in response to the appeal, and also published a letter from Maguire:

> ...All the locality affected is within my parish, and within the district of the parish church of Clerkenwell. It is far from Mr Herring's district, and he is in no respect called upon to act while the parochial staff are actively engaged in the matter. Mr Herring says he has been to the scene of the outrage; but I have gone far beyond it, having visited my suffering

parishioners in the two hospitals that have so generously received them. I hastened down immediately to the scene of the explosion and thence to the hospitals where I spent the whole of the evening and until past midnight, with a brief interval between. I know all the sufferers, and they know me...

Herring wrote to Maguire and apologised for having acted "on the spur of the moment." The apology was accepted and, despite the inauspicious start, the two men went on to work together on the Clerkenwell Explosion Relief Fund Committee. The committee staged its first meeting at the Parochial School Rooms in Amwell Street on 16 December. Donations were flooding in and most national newspapers encouraged their readers to support the appeal. Comments made in a leader in the *Times* on 14 December were typical:

> ...it is probable that several families have not only to mourn the loss or disablement of a member, but will be plunged into deep distress. They have a claim on the public, for they may be said to have suffered in a public cause...if the country, however, can do nothing else, it can take care that those who actually suffer at the hands of these public enemies shall not want care in their sufferings and compensation for their losses.

Maguire tapped the same sentiment in an appeal letter sent to the press, and printed in papers including the *Standard* of 28 December:

> This is a matter that we desire to conduct to its completion by the loyal bounty of the nation. This would be as well the most gracious as also the most simple method of dealing with the wrong. Here no conflicting interest would clash; the sympathy of the nation would cover all claims; and a loyal protest would be borne, by Englishmen and Irishmen alike, against the cowardly and wicked deed that has been done. Every contribution large or small, is a testimony for law and order against the outrage...

By early January more than £7,000 had been collected. By the end of the month the total had reached £9,500 and the appeal was wound up. Other well-wishers sent clothing, boots and bedding, and these were distributed according to requirements.

The committee worked methodically and with compassion. In most cases their judgement was sound, and compensation was carefully matched with genuine need. One of their first acts was to write to St Bartholomew's and the Royal Free and give instructions for the victims to be reassured their homes would be restored and that everything possible would be done to mitigate their suffering and losses. The affected district was divided into eight zones, each of which was allocated to a sub-committee consisting of between two and four committee members. These sub-committees were responsible for visiting sufferers, examining claims and giving appropriate assistance and relief. They were authorised to draw up to £100 to meet urgent needs. Special sub-committees were set up to deal with larger claims, including those from Corporation Lane, and to visit casualties still in the hospitals. The organisers announced all claims for assistance must be received by 11 January 1868. By 20 December some twenty-six hundred claims had been registered and arranged in an alphabetical list. There were seven hundred individual cases and nearly six hundred eventually received compensation. Nearly all the claimants settled for a lesser sum than they had asked for. Mr Joseph Brown, of Rosoman Street, asked for £10 and received £4; Mr William Green, of Rosoman Street, put in a request for £55 and received £20; and Mr George Squire, also of Rosoman Street, gave up his claim for more than £200 to settle for £5 cash. The bulk of the available money—£5,500—was earmarked for those who had suffered serious injury.

The Reverend Maguire and Messrs Dix and Wortley visited the hospitals and received medical reports on the blast victims. The reports listed details of injuries, the prospects of recovery and the likelihood of patients being able to make their own living. Maguire, Dix and Wortley went back to the Relief Fund committee with recommendations for payments, and these were largely accepted. Few lump sum payments were made. Instead, money was invested on behalf of the sufferer, who then received a regular annuity. This innovative scheme ensured that many who may have been left destitute could rely on a regular, if small, annual income. Mrs Clutton lost her husband, William, in the explosion, and was left to cope with her imbecile son. The Fund purchased her an annuity for £270, and this guaranteed her the annual sum of £20. Teenager Lizzie Thompson, 17, had lost an eye and suffered severe facial injuries in the disaster. She was awarded an annuity of £15. Her sister Harriet, 13, also lost an eye and was given an annuity of £12.10s.0d. Payments to children were generally made through trusts, which became payable when they reached the age of 21. The committee put £300 in trust for the three surviving Abbott children. Ann Cross, eight, had suffered a severe compound fracture to her leg in the explosion, and had not been expected to live. She survived, and the Fund invested £300 in a trust for her. When she reached 21, and gained access to the money, it had reached the maturity value of £413.8s.6d, a very tidy sum in the 1880s. Henry Hodgkinson, 22, lost his wife Sarah, 23, in the disaster, and suffered disabling injuries to his right arm. While he was in hospital the fund paid a Mrs Bright ten shillings per week to care for his son Harry. When Henry had recovered the Fund paid £50 to purchase tools to set him up in business, and another £40 to purchase stock. The family received a total of £187.10s.3d from the Relief Fund.

Local doctors were instructed to give necessary medical treatment free of charge to the patient, and claimed their expenses from the Fund. Dr Dyes received £39.16s.0d, Dr Berry had £33.18s.0d and smaller sums went to Drs Brown, Cackie, March, Barringer and Taylor. Some of the doctors' expenses went on caring for pregnant women who had suffered the effects of the explosion. The Relief Fund Committee glumly noted that of twenty-six maternity cases in the district in December, three had resulted in live births; three children had been stillborn; one mother had been seriously injured and was in hospital; and sixteen cases were of "doubtful issue." The *Times* reported on 29 April 1868:

> Forty mothers were prematurely confined and 20 of their babes died from the effects of the explosion on the women; others of the children are dwarfed and unhealthy. One mother is now a raving maniac...

More than 90% of money raised went directly to victims, the remaining amounts covering advertising, printing costs and general expenses. Soon after the explosion the Government agreed to meet the costs of rebuilding and repairing the shattered homes. The bill came to £7,500. On 4 May 1888 there was still £89.19s.9d remaining in the Clerkenwell Explosion Fund Relief Committee account at Finsbury Savings Bank. The Royal Free Hospital was given £10, another £10 went to the Clerkenwell District Visiting Society, £5 went to the Clock and Watchmakers' Asylum and another £5 to the Goldsmiths' and Jewellers' Annuity and Asylum Institute. The Fund's hard-working clerk, Robert Paget, was asked to accept the remaining £59.19s.9d in recognition of his services. No cash from this distribution went to St Bartholomew's Hospital. This was probably because that hospital had already received donations from the Fund, including a gift of six beds.

While efforts were in hand to care for the victims of the blast, the wheels of British justice were grinding into place to deal with the suspected culprits. The police were naturally sensitive to the heavy criticism directed at them, and the need to make arrests and make them quickly became paramount. Desmond, Justice and Allen had already been charged and were being held on remand in prison. Press reports stàted Allen appeared to be in a state of shock during his court appearances. They were probably right. Things had gone badly for the 36-year-old bootmaker. He was, in fact, a police informer posted outside the gaol by his contact, Inspector Brennan. After the explosion he had instinctively ran for his life. His flight, and the fact that several police officers had been viewing his continual presence with some suspicion, made him an obvious target for arrest. His piteous claims of innocence were ignored, and his insistence on being a police informer was probably regarded with hilarity. One known informer, John Davaney, had been taken to see him in prison and promptly identified him as a member of the Fenian Brotherhood. Poor Allen no doubt thought his unfortunate venture into the world of coppers' narks would end with a trip to the gallows. However, shortly after the coroner's jury had found him guilty of wilful murder, Allen was identified and released.

Meanwhile army deserter and drunkard James Vaughan had come to the police to turn informer and claim the advertised reward. One of those he named as a Fenian, Patrick Mullaney, turned Queen's evidence and became the key prosecution witness in the trials that were to follow. By the end of January 1868, six "Fenians" had been charged with wilful murder. In April 1868 Anne Justice, 22; William Desmond, a 28-year-old bootmaker; Timothy Desmond (no relation), a 46-year-old tailor; Nicholas English, 46, a tailor; John O'Keefe, 25, a bootmaker and Michael Barrett, a 27-year-old stevedore, stood trial at the Old Bailey.

The cream of the country's legal profession was ranked against the six. The prosecution was led by Attorney General Sir J. Karslake, and he was assisted by Solicitor General Sir B. Brett, Mr Gifford QC, Mr Poland and Mr Archibald. There was no system of legal aid and the Fenians had only managed to raise funds to appoint their defence counsel on the Saturday before the case began. The defending lawyers, Mr Warner Sleigh, Mr Straight, Mr Keogh, Mr Montagu Williams, Mr J. Clarke and Mr Baker Greene had been given just forty-eight hours to prepare themselves, and Old Bailey judges Lord Chief Justice Sir A. Cockburn and Mr Baron Bramwell refused an adjournment. The prosecution evidence was sparse, contradictory and inconclusive. Much relied on identification, and descriptions differed from witness to witness. The

Crown may have been certain it had the right culprits, but it certainly could not prove it. Its whole case rested on evidence from the informers Vaughan and Mullaney. Vaughan admitted in court that he was an army deserter and had a drink problem. One doctor, he said, had told him to stop drinking, but another had told him to carry on. Mullaney was giving evidence to save his own skin, and cut a contemptible figure in court. As the *Daily News* commented on 23 April:

> While pressed home by the various counsel Mullaney's long, nervous fingers close half convulsively round the brass knobs of the rail before him; he moves restlessly from foot to foot; his voice is so low and husky that he is frequently reproved for not 'speaking up,' while his tongue rolls and lips quiver as if the one clove to his mouth and the other were parched and dry to a degree which makes free speech impossible. Every eye is on him, and as he stammers out his answers and explanations in a broad Irish accent, he strives to avoid looking at the dock, as if the sight of his late comrades and victims were unbearable; yet now and again he glances there as if fascination overcame and conquered self-contempt.

The trial began on 20 April and by the third day the prosecution had completed their case. The Lord Chief Justice immediately threw out the charge against Anne Justice. The sole evidence against her was from Vaughan, who said she had gone to the prison on the day of the explosion and gained information about the exercise times. This, said the Lord Chief Justice, must be a lie as an attempt to blow up the wall had been made the previous day, so information about exercise periods must have already been available. O'Keefe's counsel asked for the case against his client to be dropped because of lack of sufficient evidence. The Attorney General agreed, declaring the evidence of identification and complicity was "much too weak" to warrant seeking a conviction.

Lawyers defending Timothy Desmond, William Desmond and Nicholas English based their defences on lack of evidence, and the inconsistent and circumstantial nature of the evidence brought. Mr Baker Greene, for Michael Barrett, produced an alibi. He called six witnesses to prove Barrett had not been in Clerkenwell at the time of the explosion. He had been having his boots repaired in Glasgow. Barrett had been arrested in Glasgow in mid-January, and brought to London to face the Clerkenwell charges. The alibi tactic was unfortunate. In his summing up the Lord Chief Justice described it as the "most extraordinary" he had ever heard. The Lord Chief Justice's comments on evidence against the two Desmonds and English swung heavily in favour of the prisoners. He stated bluntly that William Desmond had not been identified as having even been in Clerkenwell on the day of the explosion. Timothy Desmond, he said, had been there, but witnesses had stated he was drunk. Inspector Thomson had seen him standing outside a public house, drunk, and a good distance from where the explosion had taken place. Evidence against English did not indicate he had been an active participant in the scheme.

The jurors considered their verdict for two hours. They found William Desmond, Timothy Desmond and Nicholas English not guilty. Barrett, they declared, was guilty. Barrett then took the opportunity to make a speech to the court, and his oratory displayed an intelligence and ability that shocked the establishment. Without benefit of notes, he accurately summed up the evidence against him, and skillfully shot it to pieces, highlighting inaccuracies and contradictions, and pointing out where he believed witnesses had been coerced. The speech ended with a simple protestation of his love for Ireland.

> I am far from denying, nor will the force of circumstances compel me to deny my love of my native land. I love my country, and if it is murderous to love Ireland dearer than I love my life, then it is true I am a murderer. If my life were ten times dearer than it is, and if I could by any means redress the wrongs of that persecuted land by the sacrifice of my life, I would willingly and gladly do so. As your Lordship has said, I will now turn my attention to that other land where the injustice of selfish mortals cannot follow me, where man has no longer the power to persecute his fellow men, and where might no longer triumphs over right.

Barrett was the last man to suffer a public execution in Britain. He was hanged on 26 May, and his body was left dangling from the scaffold for an hour. It was then buried in unconsecrated ground in Newgate prison. When the prison was demolished Barrett's remains were re-interned at a plot at the City of London Cemetery, Manor Park.

The charges against Burke and Casey were heard immediately the Clerkenwell trial finished. After Burke had been found guilty of treason, and sentenced to fifteen years' imprisonment, he began a speech. Mr Baron Bramwell, obviously still flinching from Barrett's spectacular oration, quickly snapped:

> Silence! I have made up my mind that it is a most inconvenient thing that a man who has been condemned by the lawful proceedings of the tribunal of the country, which has gained what one may call the victory in the

contest, should afterward assail that tribunal, making a speech and having apparently all the honours of the contest remaining with him.

Burke was led away. He suffered greatly in custody. Like many of the Fenian prisoners he was badly treated. He came close to death at the end of 1868 and received last sacraments. He recovered, and was released under an amnesty in 1872. He went to live in America, and became the assistant city engineer of Chicago.

The brutality of the Clerkenwell bombing sent shock waves throughout the country. The Fenians may well have intended to blow a small hole in the prison wall. The devastation caused was probably unintentional and caused more by lack of skill than lack of compassion for fellow human beings. But the episode set an important precedent in English law. The Fenians had been charged with premeditated murder, even though it was accepted they may not have intended to kill anyone. It became embodied in law that those taking part in a terrorist acts where someone's death was foreseeable would be liable to be convicted of murder, even when murder was not part of the perpetrator's plan.

The Clerkenwell Explosion was an unmitigated disaster for all concerned. The bungling Metropolitan Police force and their Chief Commissioner were humiliated and lost public credibility; the Fenians succeeded only in transforming a groundswell of support and goodwill into deep-rooted hatred; and the innocent people of Clerkenwell endured terrible suffering. Public opinion could easily have sanctioned another long period of governmental indifference to the plight of Ireland and her people. Fortunately for the Irish, William Gladstone became Prime Minister in February 1868 and he took office with a determination to solve the seemingly interminable Irish Question once and for all. He viewed the Fenians as a danger. He knew they had support abroad, particularly in America, and he aimed to remove any vestige of respect they might demand by negating their grievances against the British government and removing any justification their cause might hold.

Gladstone's first step was to steer the Irish Church Act through parliament in 1869. The 1861 census revealed there were fewer than seven hundred thousand Anglicans in Ireland, and about four and a half million Roman Catholics. Despite this the Anglican church, the so-called Church of Ireland, commanded far more wealth and power. Gladstone's Act vested the property of the Church of Ireland in a Temporalities

Commission. The state creamed off £16 million, but paid back £10 million in "compensation." The surplus was carefully invested and yielded £13 million. This was used over the next fifty years in various relief measures, including the encouragement of agriculture and fisheries. The Church Act was quickly followed by the 1st Irish Land Act in 1870. This Act was considerably less successful than Gladstone had hoped, mainly because its many loopholes allowed easy evasion. In theory, tenants' rights in Ulster were made enforceable by law. In cases of eviction—except for non-payment of rent—the landlord was forced to pay compensation, and a land purchase scheme was established to allow tenants to borrow two thirds of the sale price from the state in a loan repayable over thirty-five years. In practice, Ulster tenants' rights were tortuously difficult to define, landlords avoided paying compensation by raising rents to impossible levels, and land prices were so high no tenant could afford to buy.

Evictions and suffering continued and resentment among the Irish continued to grow. The clamour for Home Rule grew ever more intense and violence within Ireland reached new depths. Cattle-maiming, arson and "Boycotting" of those who took over the holdings of evicted tenants were commonplace. Again, the troubles spread to English soil. Irish Members of Parliament disrupted proceedings in the Commons by using the technique of filibustering: making long and time-consuming speeches with the sole intent of causing as much obstruction as possible. Arson attacks around the country were frequently blamed on Fenian terrorists. In February 1881 a massive blaze that caused £500,000 damage in the Royal Victoria Dock, East London, was widely believed to have been started by Fenians.

Gladstone's 2nd Irish Land Act became law in 1881. This promised the "three F's"; fair rent, free sale and fixity of tenure. The Irish were not satisfied: Home Rule was now the only solution they considered acceptable. Disturbances increased, and in May 1882 the Chief Secretary for Ireland, Lord Frederick Cavendish, and his Under-Secretary, Mr Burke, were stabbed to death as they took an evening walk in Phoenix Park, Dublin.

Luckily, the Fenian's exploits in London after Clerkenwell caused relatively superficial injuries to people and buildings. They generally used nitro-glycerine, and attacks were often co-ordinated for maximum effect. There were many incidents, and government and other so-called "establishment" buildings were prime targets. In March 1883 a 15–20 lb bomb was planted on a window ledge of the Local Government Board offices in Whitehall. The device exploded, causing little structural damage but shattering windows. Shortly afterwards a second bomb exploded at the offices of the *Times* in Play House Yard, again causing only slight damage. Both devices were in tin bonnet boxes that had slits in their lids. In May 1884 four bombs were set to explode almost simultaneously in Central London. The first two were in St James's Square. A blast at the Junior Carlton Club was followed just fifteen seconds later by an explosion at the home of MP Sir Watkin Williams-Wynn. Two seconds later a bomb exploded in a public urinal located beneath the CID department of Scotland Yard. Shortly after that a young boy picked up a black bag left in Trafalgar Square and took it to Scotland Yard. Police found it was packed with dynamite. Nearly thirty people were hurt in the three explosions, but fortunately most injuries were minor. Thirteen of the sufferers were taken for treatment at Charing Cross and Westminster Hospitals, but only five were detained. At the end of the year a device containing 20 lb of dynamite exploded, killing the bomber, on the Surrey side of London Bridge. The "Dynamite War" against key English landmarks reached its peak in January 1885, with simultaneous attacks at the House of Commons, Westminster Hall and the Tower of London. All three bombs exploded, causing widespread terror but surprisingly little damage to either people or property.

Railways were another favourite target for the terrorists. At the end of October 1883 the terrorists caused chaos on London's Underground system. At about 8:00 PM one bomb exploded in a tunnel near Praed Street Station on the Metropolitan Line, and another in a tunnel between Charing Cross and Westminster Stations. The Praed Street device exploded just as a train passed, and the last three carriages were badly damaged. More than sixty passengers were injured by flying glass and debris, and five were detained at nearby St Mary's Hospital, Paddington. The bomb on the District Line between Charing Cross and Westminster stations had apparently been thrown into the tunnel through a ventilation shaft. The blast sent clouds of soot and dust gusting through both stations, but miraculously there were no injuries and the tunnel escaped serious damage. In February 1884 the terrorists attempted another ambitious onslaught, designed to cause maximum disruption. Bombs were planted in the cloakrooms of Victoria, Paddington, Charing Cross and Ludgate Hill stations. Two of the devices were set to explode at midnight, and two to detonate at 1:00 AM The plan, had it been successful, would almost certainly have stretched the emergency services beyond their limits. Fortunately the ignition system adopted by the terrorists was anything but reliable, and three bombs failed to go off and were removed by police. The alarm was raised by an explosion that wrecked the booking hall, waiting room and cloakroom of Victoria Station at 1:04 AM The station was virtually empty at the time, and the only injuries were to the night porter and a tinsmith who had rushed to help. Both men were cut and bruised by flying debris. The police immediately organised a search of other stations, and the three remaining bombs were discovered.

The finds gave explosives expert Colonel Majendie a perfect opportunity to see how the bombs were constructed. All the explosives were packed into black American cloth portmanteaus fastened with straps. The ignition devices were made using American-style alarm clocks known as "Peep of Day" clocks and available in London for around ten shillings each. The alarms were removed and small, nickel-plated vest pocket pistols were fastened to the movement of the clock, so that the alarm action would cause them to fire. Majendie found two of the pistols had misfired. The third, at Paddington, had jammed but would probably have exploded if the case had received the slightest jolt. Colonel Majendie investigated most of the bomb outrages and must have become an expert on the style of explosive devices in use at the time. Captain Shaw, commander of the Metropolitan Fire Brigade and a veteran of the Clerkenwell Explosion, was also a familiar figure among those attending the incidents. The general public was outraged by the increasing violence, and there was a general ill-feeling against anyone who happened to be Irish. A leader in the *Times* on 16 March 1883, after the attack on the Local Government Board Offices and at the *Times'* own buildings, made the Editor's attitude very clear.

> The English people, the most lenient and the most easy-going in the world, is always too much inclined to be sceptical about political outrages till they are proved, and to forgive and forget within a short time afterwards. It was not till the tragedy of the Phoenix Park that the mass of Englishmen realised the tremendous nature of the struggle that was going on in Ireland; and it is only by outrages like those of yesterday that it is likely to be convinced of what the authorities have known all along—that there are in London men as desperate, as determined, and as uncompromising enemies to England as any of the invincibles of Dublin. Now, however, it is to be hoped that the public will come to know with whom it has to deal.

24 *Damage from the explosion at Scotland Yard*
25 *Ruins of the cloakroom at Victoria Station*

It has to deal with men who hesitate at nothing; with men to whom human life and the works of human hands, and the fabric of society itself, are as nothing in comparison with the satisfaction of their own wild demands. These men can be met in only one way—by a resistance as stern and as uncompromising as their own attack.... In Manchester, in Leeds, in Liverpool, in London, the feeling of the English workman towards his Irish companions, which once was sympathetic, has become cold; it only depends on a few more cases of dynamite to turn it into a feeling of angry hostility that authority will find very difficult to control.

The paper's tone on 26 January 1885, after the bombs at the House of Commons, Tower of London and Westminster Hall was unchanged.

We are convinced...that a policy of terrorism is not one to which Englishmen will succumb, unless their nature has undergone a complete and unsuspected change. Their traditional and inbred spirit will save them from submission to the insolent dictation of murderers, and their common sense will warn them that if they begin to pay blackmail to one gang of terrorists they will have to go on paying it to others.

Prime Minister Gladstone, however, adopted a more prosaic attitude and the violence at home did not deter him from becoming increasingly convinced that Home Rule was the only real answer to the Irish problem. On 8 April 1886 the veteran statesman introduced a Bill that would give Ireland a separate legislature and executive. Two months later it was defeated by 341 votes to 311. Gladstone called an immediate election and lost to the Tories. He was back in power in 1892 and early the next year made another bid to secure Home Rule. This time the Bill was defeated by a 419–41 vote in the Lords. Gladstone retired in March 1894. The main aim in his political life, to settle the Irish problem, remained beyond reach. His frustration was to be shared by generations to follow. The Irish problem remains as difficult and seemingly insoluble as ever, and Irish terrorism on mainland Britain has continued to generate outrage, bitterness and resentment. To the majority of people on the mainland the essence of the Irish problem is as obscure and confusing as it was to the people of Clerkenwell more than a century ago.

CHAPTER SIX

Forest Gate School

The Victorians viewed pauperism as an infectious disease. Paupers were an underclass of degenerates, best restrained from contaminating more worthy members of society by being confined in workhouses set up under the 1830 Poor Law Amendment Act. Pauper children were a slightly different matter, and even the early Victorians felt uneasy at seeing such youngsters condemned to a hopeless existence in bleak and cheerless workhouses.

In 1844 the Poor Law was again amended. Now parish unions were authorised to form "school districts." Boards of Guardians could pool resources with neighbouring authorities to build and administer large boarding schools to educate and maintain orphans and the children of workhouse paupers. Many schools were vast institutions caring for a thousand or more children under the age of 16. They were controlled by Boards of Managers elected by the Poor Law Unions involved. The idea was considered excellent. The schools were viewed as a means of stemming the ever-increasing tide of pauperism. As the *Illustrated Times* commented on 16 February 1867:

> Nothing destroys the independence of character and engenders the pauper spirit so effectively as associating with paupers. The race of workhouse children if reared away from workhouses, may be so trained as to cease to be in their turn, as they have hitherto generally been, the propagators of pauperism.

Reality was less rosy. Many of the district schools were little more than junior workhouses. The children lived regimented lives of drudgery and boredom that gave them precious little chance to develop as independent individuals. They were cogs in a gigantic machine, ill-equipped to cope with the outside world. Children were packed into the schools and disease spread rapidly. Ophthalmia—infectious eye disease—was endemic and countless youngsters suffered permanent damage to their sight and even blindness. Teachers in the district schools were paid less than their counterparts in Board Schools and the jobs tended to attract less able individuals. In any event, many of the children spent at least half their time in "industrial training." This was meant to prepare them for employment in fields such as tailoring and carpentry for the boys and domestic service and needlework for the girls. In many cases, however, the "training" was simply doing the drudge jobs necessary within the institution—scrubbing floors, mending linen, doing the laundry.

Forest Gate School was typical of the district school system, but its children endured more suffering and tragedy than most. It had been built by the Whitechapel Guardians in 1854. In 1868 the Whitechapel Guardians joined those of Poplar and Hackney to form the Forest Gate School District. The school premises were purchased for £34,000, plus £5,380 for fixtures and fittings. The school was initially given a certificate to take 859 children, but this was later reduced to 720. It was soon clear that more space was needed and, as an alternative to extending the buildings, the Board of Managers decided to establish a training ship.

The training ship system was a brighter side of Poor Law provision for pauper children. Ships, usually old men of war, were converted to take several hundred boys and train them for a career in the army, navy or merchant navy. These were among the few fields that could offer ample employment opportunities to suitable strong, healthy and well-trained lads. While pauper girls could usually be found employment in domestic service after leaving Poor Law school, placing the boys had proved more difficult. The training ships helped solve two problems; they provided extra places for pauper children at a relatively low cost, and gave training that could offer the youngsters at least the chance of a reasonable future. Parents of boys admitted to the ship had to agree to their sons completing their training on board and signing up afterwards for twelve years' service in the navy or mercantile marine. There's little doubt these children fared better than their peers in the district schools. The regime was harsh, but the environment offered plenty of fresh air, exercise and stimulation, and many children showed an almost instant improvement in health.

The *Goliath* was purchased in 1870 and moored off Gravesend, under the command of Captain Superintendent William Bourchier, a retired naval staff commander. It was soon packed with more than five hundred boys from the Forest Gate School and from other Unions in London. The youngsters received a basic formal education as well as training in seamanship and swimming. A leader in the *Times* on 11 October 1871 commented on the ship's value:

> We are told, and we can well believe, that the training supplied on board the *Goliath*—education not only in books, but in work—transforms with astonishing rapidity and completeness even the facial and bodily characteristics of the street arabs who have the good fortune to be drafted to the school ship at Gravesend. Dull eyes brighten, narrow chests expand, stunted figures erect themselves, and the mental and moral nature partakes of the health change. In this metamorphosis we have a promise for the future...

The first boys boarded the ship in October 1870. An infirmary was established on shore at Sherfield House and a brigantine, the *Steadfast*, was purchased for sail training and fetching supplies of fresh water to the *Goliath* from Sheerness dockyard. All continued peacefully and well until about ten minutes to eight on the morning of 22 December 1875.

Lads on board took responsibility for the routine tasks associated with life at sea. Picking up skills in the various jobs was seen as an important part of their training, and doubtless enabled considerable savings on the ship's running costs. Robert Loeber, a 13-year-old orphan, had been on the *Goliath* for nearly three years. A week earlier he had taken over the role of lamp trimmer. He had to light and hang oil lamps about the ship at night and collect them again in the morning. That December morning was particularly dark, bitterly cold and very windy. As Loeber collected the lamps he turned them down rather than off, as he needed light to help him find his way. Back in the lamp room he burned his hand as he went to hang up one of the lamps which was still burning. He dropped it, and instantly set fire to the oil-soaked wooden floor. The young lad desperately tried to stifle the blaze with his serge frock and blue Guernsey jacket. When that didn't work he sat on the flames, but the fire spread rapidly and he was forced back from the room.

By this time, only seconds after the lamp had fallen, others were aware of the impending catastrophe. Mr Hall, the ship's chief officer, raised the fire alarm and all boys, officers and staff members rushed to their emergency posts. Everyone knew exactly what they should do—fire drill was a priority on board the *Goliath*. Fate, however, was against them. There were heavy winds and each of the wooden ship's eighty-four port holes was open. The fire bell was designed to ring for three minutes. Before it stopped the whole of the main deck was ablaze. Many officers didn't have time to reach their designated posts and the hoses brought into play were rapidly burned through. It quickly became clear that the ship was doomed; the main task was to save the lives of the 456 youngsters on board. Panic would have been disastrous, but the boys were strictly disciplined and well-drilled, and despite the terrifying circumstances the children remained calm and obedient.

Mr R. Fenn, head schoolmaster on the ship, later described the rescue efforts in a small booklet published in February 1876. This account is based on his observations.

Mr Thompson, the *Goliath*'s carpenter, made a brave attempt to reach the storeroom on a lower deck, where he aimed to break a large pipe that connected with the sea-cock. Breaking the pipe would have flooded that section of the ship with water, and possibly stopped the rapid progress of the fire. Sadly, thick smoke forced him to abandon the plan. As he struggled back Thompson found some boys trapped beside portholes blocked with iron bars. He forced the bars apart, and the children climbed out. The carpenter then fractured pipes serving the hot water system. But the ship was fast becoming an inferno, and the water pouring into the lower decks had little effect. Thompson managed to reach a lifeboat on the starboard side of the ship. He cut through the single davit holding it in place, and the craft plunged into the water. Thompson and ten boys scrambled on board but the boat immediately began to let in water. The carpenter and lads used their boots to bale out and keep her afloat until they drifted ashore.

Mr Hurley, an officer, escaped through a porthole and managed to reach the forecastle of the ship along with a small group of boys. The smoke and flames threatened to overpower them, so Hurley ordered them to drop down onto the mooring cable. They clung to this cable until a boat sent from a nearby barge came and plucked them to safety.

Young, a little fellow who was one of the smallest boys on ship, clung to the forecastle, obviously petrified. "It was a pitiful sight to see the poor child," wrote Fenn.

> With flames every minute approaching nearer and nearer to him, looking down on the master of a steam tug, whose open arms were ready to receive him, and to observe the terror with which the boy regarded the fearful gulf between him and his deliverer.

26   *Fire on board the training ship Goliath*

At the last minute, just as the tug, the *Milton*, began to steam away, the boy jumped to safety.

The situation on board was becoming dire—flames were spreading with alarming speed, and the ship was burning fiercely. The *Goliath* had fourteen lifeboats, but four were being used for trips ashore, and the blaze spread so rapidly that most of those at hand could not be launched. Able swimmers were ordered to take their chances in the water, and head to the Essex shore one hundred yards away. Captain Bourchier threw some wooden bread crates into the water to help the lads making the attempt, but there was a gale force wind and conditions in the water were treacherous. The "water tank," a small barge used solely for carrying water supplies, was moored by the side of the *Goliath* and offered one means of escape. Twenty boys clambered on board and were about to set off when a 13-year-old "petty officer," William Bolton, threatened to knock them down if they didn't rescue more. In the end the barge left for shore with 120 youngsters squeezed on board. Many feared they would capsize before reaching land, and quietly said their prayers.

Meanwhile around forty boys were standing in a gangway with Captain Bourchier. Bourchier realised they were all in mortal danger. A launch capable of carrying 150 children was moored between the *Goliath* and the shore, and the Captain sent two volunteers to fetch her. Unfortunately they were unable to climb aboard, and carried on swimming to the shore. The fire crackled around Bourchier and his young followers, and flames were soon bursting through from the decks beneath them. About fifteen boys opted to swim for it; the rest huddled closer to their captain. In a ploy to prevent panic Bourchier ordered them to shout out "Bring the launch." Four of the ship's officers, Messrs White, Murphy, Wastell and Kingdom, were returning from shore leave when the fire broke out. As they drew close to the old warship they heard the shouts of Bourchier and the children, and manoeuvred their boat to reach them. The boys quickly climbed aboard, but the blaze made it a precarious operation. A boy named Mudkin asked Bourchier to get to safety first. The captain refused with the words: "No, my boy, I must be last, that's the way at sea." As Mudkin climbed to the rescue ship a red hot funnel fell from the *Goliath*, giving a glancing blow to Mudkin's head; he survived. The funnel settled on the ship and the crew had to douse it with water to prevent it burning through the deck.

Captain Bourchier's wife and two daughters lived with him on board the *Goliath*, and were rescued in one of the few lifeboats to be successfully launched. Head schoolmaster Mr Fenn was with them:

On reaching the upper deck, after the alarm of fire, I met Miss Ethel, the captain's youngest daughter, and persuaded her to make for a pinnace which was still hanging by the davits. I then met Messrs. Gunton and Norris...and we made an attempt to lower the galley. The flames however on the upper deck prevented the possibility of our doing so.

Mr Gunton then cut the galleys' falls, and I was precipitated into the water, the friction of one of the ropes lacerating my hands; the galley was swamped and floated away.

Norris joined Ethel in the pinnace, a small boat attached to the *Goliath*, and Gunton managed to cut the falls to launch it. It plunged into the water, narrowly missing Fenn as he struggled to keep afloat. He was dragged on board. Mrs Bourchier was persuaded to jump the twenty-five feet from her window into the water, and was also pulled into the little boat. Florence Bourchier was dangling on a rope. Gunton and Norris tried to reach her in the pinnace. "This was no easy task," wrote Fenn,

as the wind freshened, and we could, with difficulty, keep the boat clear of the cables of the after moorings. Quite exhausted, Miss Florence at last dropped just clear of the cable, and we dragged her into the boat. Her hands were much injured from the friction of the rope.

Other ships came to help the *Goliath*, the huge flames leaping from its carcass alerting all within several miles to its plight. But most ships, boats and barges were constructed in wood and the flaming debris, falling and blowing from the stricken *Goliath*, made it hazardous to move within close range of the ship. Despite these problems, crews of several ships ignored their own safety and went to the rescue of the boys. Mr Coppen navigated his barge *Forest* to within yards of the *Goliath*, where he anchored and picked up many boys struggling in the water. A small boat sent from the barge was rowed even closer to the blaze and picked up more survivors. Increasing gales made it impossible for Coppen to leave his anchorage, but the tug *Milton* arrived on the scene and towed him to safety. Coppen rescued sixty-five lads. The *Arethusa*, another training ship, was moored at Greenhithe and her Captain, Walters, first saw the flames of the *Goliath* at exactly 8:00 AM He quickly launched a flotilla of small boats and, aided by the high winds, reached the scene within twenty minutes. As Walters' boat drew close a small boy, named Naylor, was spotted clinging to a timber fender hanging under the *Goliath*'s starboard bow. Ignoring the flames engulfing the foremast, which was threatening to fall at any moment, Walters and his crew plucked Naylor to safety, singeing their shirts and beards in the process.

Not all the struggles had happy endings. Assistant schoolmaster Mr Wheeler had joined the *Goliath* only ten days before the blaze. He couldn't swim, and had taken to a lifeboat with Mr Hall, the chief officer. Sadly, the tackling holding the boat had been damaged by flames and it hit the water badly after it was launched, and was immediately swamped with water. Wheeler, Hall and two boys clung to the sides as the useless boat was tossed about by the swell of passing steamers. Hall and one of the youngsters managed to keep their hold, but Wheeler and the other lad perished.

The villagers of Grays gathered along the foreshore as the bedraggled survivors were brought to land. Women took off their petticoats to clothe the naked children, and others were wrapped in blankets and spare clothing that had been hastily gathered together. Some of the generous folk offered medicinal swigs of brandy, but just a few weeks previously the *Goliath* had been visited by a clergyman of the Church of England Temperance Society, and the children dutifully declined the alcohol.

At first Bourchier believed all the boys had been saved, but his hopes proved sadly mistaken. The fire spread so rapidly that no one had the time to salvage important records and papers. This made a roll call impossible, because nobody had a list of who should have been on board. Instead the children were arranged in the order they sat for meals, and the grim truth became evident. Eighteen boys and Mr Wheeler, the assistant master, were missing. All had died in the blaze or drowned as they tried to escape. Most of the bodies were eventually washed ashore, but several were never recovered. The *Goliath* had been home to more than 450 children when the fire broke out, and the ship was now beyond repair. Many boys were housed in the ship's infirmary, Sherfield House, while others were billeted in nearby schools, churches and chapels.

By afternoon officialdom had ground into action and most of the youngsters were on their way back to Forest Gate School or their respective workhouses. The London, Tilbury and Southend Railway provided free transport and the children were escorted by officers. These children had been sent to the training ship from their Poor Law Unions, and they knew only too well the conditions they were returning to. It says much for the *Goliath*, and little for Forest Gate School and the workhouses, that several boys absconded when they heard of the transfer plans. They were all brought back the same day.

The *Goliath* continued to blaze. It was feared she could drift down the Thames, destroying shipping in her wake. Efforts to scuttle her failed, but in the end she became wedged on a mudbank and burned harmlessly, until all that remained was a hideous and unrecognisable heap of charred timber.

News of the disaster spread quickly throughout the country. During the day Bourchier received sixty-three telegrams offering sympathy and help, and there were many visits from local dignitaries and Poor Law officials. A Relief Fund was started. Henry Cook, at that time one of the Managers of the Forest Gate School District, wrote an appeal letter to the *Times* on 23 December:

> Now, Sire, surely some of your readers, before enjoying their 'Merry Christmas' at home would feel a pleasure in sending a trifle to ameliorate the suffering of those who, yesterday morning, were looking forward to their comparatively simple, though none the less merry festival, and who are now destitute, and thankful only that they have not shared the fate of the poor fellows who have perished...

Cook was referring to the personal losses suffered by Bourchier and his twenty-four staff members, who had all lost clothing, furniture and other personal belongings in the fire. The pauper children had very few belongings and their losses were deemed trinkets of nominal value. The *Goliath* Appeal, started by the good villagers of Grays the day after the disaster, was taken over by the Lord Mayor of London and quickly raised the target of £1,500. Donations came from across the country, and included £10 from Florence Nightingale.

The managers of the Forest Gate School District met the day after the fire and agreed to take immediate steps to replace the *Goliath* with another suitable ship. They also appointed a sub-committee to look into the cause of the tragedy. This reported back on 5 January 1876, deciding the blaze had been caused by the boy Loeber upsetting a lamp and that no blame was attributable to any of the ship's officers.

The same conclusion was reached by the Coroner's jury after an inquest into the deaths of four boys whose bodies were the first to be washed ashore. The usual flurry of rumours and speculation that are part and parcel of any disaster—Loeber had thrown a pail of oil over the initial fire...oil used on the ship was highly inflammable—added spice to the proceedings. None of the accusations could be substantiated, though the Forest Gate Managers instructed Bourchier that the type of oil used on board the *Goliath* should not be used in the Sherfield House infirmary. The fact was that the fire was started by the fumbling of a child given sole responsibility for a dangerous task. Fire appliances on board were inadequate to deal with the blaze when the wooden ship ignited like a well-designed bonfire.

During the *Goliath's* five years moored off Grays, 1,160 of its young "graduates" joined the Merchant or Royal Navies or the army. The people of Grays had fostered strong links with the ship, and they were determined to see it replaced. At the beginning of January 1876 more than fifty villagers signed a letter sent to the Forest Gate Managers.

> We have been gratified to see waifs and strays from London, especially the Eastern portion of it, improving from day to day, both physically and morally.... Let us be permitted to hope that good may be brought out of apparent evil, that the calamity may be a means of attracting the attention of the nation to the success of your past labours, and that whilst you are yourselves encouraged to redouble your attempt to stem the tide of pauperism and to cut off the supplies which are recruiting the ranks of our criminals, your example may be imitated in other localities and that many another vessel built in readiness for external war may be utilised for an object bearing so largely upon our domestic economy and internal peace...

The stories of heroism on board the *Goliath* filled the national press and caused a sensation among the public. Here were good-for-nothing pauper brats behaving with the courage and intelligence more commonly associated with those of a higher class. The youngsters were applauded the length and breadth of the nation.

Bourchier set about searching for a ship to replace the *Goliath*. In the meantime he was keen to keep as many of his children together as possible. He had the full support of the Local Government Board. On 30 December the Board wrote to the Forest Gate Managers:

> It is heart-rending to think of the relegation of so many boys to the workhouses and District Schools, who under your wise beneficent treatment were casting off in a manner the most satisfactory, the stigma of pauperism.

It was decided to rescue at least some lads from the horrors of the District School and workhouses. The *Goliath*'s infirmary, Sherfield House, was used as a temporary "on land" training school, and 107 training-ship lads were brought back. Conditions were cramped. The dining hall doubled as a dormitory and twenty-two children slept in a cold and cheerless loft over some stable buildings. A visiting committee from the Hackney Union was appalled at what confronted them when they called on 27 January 1876. They advised the Hackney Board of Guardians that the Union's children should be removed

> ...with the least possible delay to more comfortable quarters, believing as they do that with every possible desire on the part of the management it is utterly impossible to make the boys even moderately comfortable.

The outrage these comments probably generated are not recorded. The attitude of the Hackney Guardians certainly went against the grain of unbridled praise and support for Bourchier and his staff. Suffice to note, the following year Hackney broke all ties with the Forest Gate School District, switching its allegiance to Shoreditch to establish the Brentwood School District.

Many won recognition for bravery shown at the fire. A special awards ceremony took place at Mansion House early in August 1876. By this time little William Bolton, the boy who refused to allow the water tank barge to head for shore until she was packed with children, was working as an apprentice on an emigrants' ship. Bolton, along with Captain Bourchier, and another thirty-one ship's officers and boys, received certificates for their work in saving lives. Bolton also received the Silver Medal of the Liverpool Royal Humane Society, a silver watch from the President of the Local Government Board, £10, and a book from Mrs Bourchier.

An Indian Prince, the Maharajah of Burdwan, read of the disaster in the *Times* and sent the newspaper a letter and cash to cover the purchase of silver medals to be presented to those who had distinguished themselves. He offered to top up the donation if it was insufficient to meet the needs. He wrote that his awards, coming from India,

> ...will prove to the boys that deeds like theirs have not merely a local force but a marked and appreciated one by their fellow subjects in the most distant parts of Her Majesty's Empire.

The Lord Mayor presented these medals at Mansion House. Bolton, hero of the episode, received one of the Maharajah's medals, as did Captain

Bourchier and several officers and boys.

Captain Bourchier eventually found a ship to succeed the *Goliath*. This was the *Exmouth*, and the vessel was managed by the Metropolitan Asylums Board as it was agreed it benefitted children not only from the Forest Gate District but from throughout London. The ship was ready to take its first pupils soon after Christmas in 1876. Bourchier worked as its Captain Superintendent until his retirement in 1902. The *Exmouth* remained a training ship until it was condemned in 1905, when it was replaced by a ship with the same name. The second *Exmouth* was used until the start of World War II, when the boys were evacuated.

On 2 January 1876, just eleven days after the *Goliath* had been destroyed, the *Warspite*, a ship run by the Marine Society, caught fire soon after midnight. Flames quickly engulfed the vessel. Again, the 180 or so children on board were well-drilled and disciplined. This time the fire took longer to reach the rigging and the lifeboats could be launched. All left the ship safely and there were no casualties.

A few years after the destruction of the *Goliath*, a bandmaster at the Forest Gate School won a spectacular career advancement. Charles Duncan was promoted to school Superintendent, a position that gave him authority over the daily lives of more than seven hundred children and seventy or so staff members. It was an extraordinary achievement. Duncan would have been earning about £50 per year as a bandmaster, and the new appointment trebled his salary to £150 per annum. The Board of Mangers must have been deeply impressed with his character and confident in his ability to run the school. Duncan undoubtedly wielded fearsome power and influence over those around him. During two major incidents that rocked the school in the early 1890s he maintained the unstinting faith of the managers and somehow manipulated the local press to ensure their lapdog-like support. Others were not so understanding, and the school's mismanagement—or misfortunes—made a major contribution to a damning investigation into the District School system by a government Select Committee in 1896.

Forest Gate School epitomised some of the worst faults of the system. Its four blocks stood in twelve acres of land in Forest Lane, Forest Gate. The main building had three floors and housed four schoolrooms, two recreation rooms, a dining hall, kitchen, sewing and needlework rooms and eighteen dormitories. There were another five dormitories in the infants' block, which also had two schoolrooms and two day rooms. The third block, an infirmary, had six wards to cater for up to sixty-six children. The fourth building, a probation or "reception" lodge, took thirty-six youngsters during the thirteen-day "quarantine period" before they were allowed to join the main school. The quarantine was intended to cut down on the spread of infectious diseases.

On 1 January 1890 the school housed 542 children. Forty-six of these had been deserted by their parents, fifty-nine were orphans and fifteen were illegitimate. The remaining 422 youngsters were paupers, with parents who could not afford to keep them or who were in the workhouse.

The children, aged between 3 and 16 years, were given numbers when they entered the school and this number was marked on the uniform allocated to them. Main school boys wore dark brown knickerbocker suits, brown cloth Inverness cloaks, dark blue knitted socks, white collars and fawn woollen caps. Girls were dressed in blue serge frocks with white pinafores, brown leather belts, dark blue knitted stockings, brown Gypsy cloth cloaks and black straw hats. There was some variation in uniform for children in the infirmary or receiving wards.

The day started at 6:00 AM and breakfast, a meal of bread and butter with milk and water, was an hour later. Dinner was at noon and the type and amount of food served was strictly regulated by the Local Government Board. A typical meal for a 12-year-old would be four ounces of meat, eight ounces of vegetables and three ounces of bread. Supper came at 6:00 PM and usually consisted of dry bread and a drink of milk and water.

Children were taught in large groups—there were only four class-rooms in the main building designed for well over three hundred children—and the curriculum included reading, writing, arithmetic, scripture and composition. Older children spent some time in "industrial workshops." These were supposed to give them essential training for future employment, such as sewing, carpentry, laundry and shoe repairs. In reality the children were all too often used as a captive labour force to keep the institution ticking over. The school laundered between thirty-two and thirty-five thousand items per week, and teams of girls were doubtless useful in ensuring the job was done. The sheer scale of the system meant the "skills" picked up bore little relation to the everyday laundry required in an average household. A similar problem arose in the kitchens. The girls were accustomed to dealing with large amounts of food—more than fifty pounds of meat would be used at one sitting—and they had no idea how to prepare individual dinners or meals for an ordinary family. As early as 1867 Florence Davenport-Hill wrote in her book *Children of the State*:

> The children...are herded together, are taught, fed, tended, trained, and cared for wholesale. Under these circumstances it is not surprising to find many of the worst defects of workhouse life cropping up in the schools, in spite of their large staffs and costly organisation.
>
> Changes which, in a family or other household of natural size cause neither difficulty nor discomfort become really stupendous in their consequences when vast numbers have to be dealt with, and they are instinctively avoided.
>
> Thus the events of daily life are stereotyped for the inmates of our big schools, each day sharing the dull likeness of the day before in the monotonous grind of a machine-like existence.

Davenport-Hill commented that District schoolchildren became dull and apathetic. Their narrow range of experience made them ill-equipped to cope with everyday problems they encountered in the outside world. One servant girl, she wrote, was sent to bed and given a candle to light her way. She came back to ask the mistress how to turn the candle off.

At about 5:00 PM on New Year's Eve, 31 December 1889, chimney sweep James Tillet, of Broadway, Stratford, arrived at the Forest Gate School to clear an iron pipe that led from the stove in the centre of the ground floor needlework room and through a wooden partition into a chimney in the wardrobe room next door. Tillet lit a fire in the stove, to check it burned properly. All seemed well, but sadly it wasn't. Just after midnight, burning soot fell from the chimney and started a fire that was to kill twenty-six helpless children.

It was a Tuesday, bath night, and the children followed their normal routine. At 8:00 PM, eighty-four boys filed into their beds in dormitories nine and ten. The dormitories, both "doubles," were on the first and second floors in a back wing of the main block, directly above the needlework room. As usual, doors leading from the dormitories to the main staircase were locked. There was an additional door at the end of each dormitory and this led to an enclosed staircase. The section leading from dormitory ten, on the second floor, down to dormitory nine was wooden. The flight from dormitory nine to the yard was in stone. The door at the bottom of the staircase to the yard outside was kept locked.

At about 12:20 AM wardrobe mistress Maria Bloomfield, in bed in her room on the first floor, next to dormitory nine, thought she could smell smoke. The gas had been turned off at 8:00 PM and the school was in pitch darkness. Maria peered into the needlework room and saw a small fire near the wooden partition dividing it from the wardrobe room. She dashed back upstairs, woke needle-mistress Laura Terry and told her to fetch Mr Duncan from his apartment in another wing of the block.

Meanwhile dense smoke was rapidly seeping into the dormitories above the needlework room, and boys began to wake, coughing and choking. The children knew their doors were locked, and several of them ran to the windows and screamed for help.

At the same time as Maria Bloomfield was investigating the smell of smoke, people living in homes surrounding the school were becoming aware something was wrong. Perhaps because it was New Year's Eve, many people were awake and reacted quickly to the screams of the youngsters and the sight of sparks pouring from the school chimney. Samuel Roberts and his son, of Forest Lane, noticed sparks rising from a chimney at the school, and thoughtfully brought a long ladder to the smoke-filled building. Thomas Oakley, an iron moulder of Tower Hamlets Road, was another local soon on the scene.

Watchmaker Herbert Roe was sitting in the back kitchen of his home in Tower Hamlets Road when he heard children screaming "Fire!" He climbed over a fence to get into the school grounds, and saw sparks coming from a chimney in the main block. He rushed to the quarters of Henry Elliott, the school's reception block officer, and battered on the door to get his attention. Elliott was destined to play a key role in the rescue attempts and subsequent scandals at the school.

In the meantime Roe's neighbour, Walter Crisp, was also on his way to the school. His wife had heard the children shouting and had gone into the garden to wish them a Happy New Year. "No, not a Happy New Year," they answered, "but fire; call Mr Elliott!" Crisp quickly joined Roe, and Elliott led them to where ladders were stored.

Railway guard James Larter was walking along Forest Lane when he noticed one of the school's chimneys seemed to be on fire. The flames seemed fierce, and were threatening the roof, so he blew his whistle to attract police, scaled a boundary fence and rushed to the main block.

The situation in dormitories nine and ten was becoming desperate.

The needlework and wardrobe rooms were filled with clothes and spare linen which produced vast volumes of dense, black smoke as they smouldered and burned. The boys in dormitory nine were alone. The officer who usually slept in a cubicle at the end of the room, a schoolmaster named Mr Way, was on leave. Alfred Flack woke coughing. "I was sleeping beside my brother Herbert," he told the *Stratford Express* on 4 January,

> and I wakened up coughing. Herbert said 'Stop that coughing,' but he began coughing himself. There were a lot of the boys coughing, and Hipkins, the monitor sung out to them to stop.

Charles Hipkins, 12, had been woken by a "knocking noise," and realised the room was "full of something." Some of the lads were already awake, and Hipkins tried to rouse the others. He then ran down the back stone staircase but found the door at the bottom was locked. He clambered back upstairs and opened windows to let in some air. His initiative didn't help much. "When I put my hand out of the window the smoke was worse there than inside," he later told the coroner. Flames were beginning to break through the floor as Hipkins and the other boys rounded up as many children as they could. Some lads were already suffering from smoke inhalation, others were too terrified to save themselves. As Alfred Flack told the *Stratford Express*:

> There was a little boy of seven named Searle. We had made him get up out of bed, and we had brought him to the door, but he ran back. Another little boy named Taylor got in a corner of the room and crouched down. We couldn't get him away.

Searle and Taylor, aged 6, both died. Hipkins told the boys to hold hands, and led the line down the room to the stairway leading to the yard.

The situation in dormitory ten was tense. Yardsman George Hare was asleep in a cubicle inside the room and held keys to both doors, but he was a heavy sleeper and difficult to rouse. After Miss Terry had left to fetch the Superintendent, Miss Bloomfield and pantry maid Ellen Davey had hammered at the dormitory door in a futile attempt to wake Hare. Bloomfield went downstairs and Davey, apparently oblivious to her imminent danger, went back to her bedroom. She shared the room with scullery maid Mrs Hill. When the pair opened their door the smoke was so thick they could not breathe. They went back into their bedroom,

27 *Forest Gate School*

28 *Fire damage in the school dormitory*

shutting the door and throwing open a window. They could hear the boys screaming for help, and their own cries were drowned in the hubbub. Hill slid to safety down a water pipe. Davey leapt onto the roof of the dining hall twelve feet below, dislocating her ankle in the process.

After two or three precious minutes the peace of Hare's slumbers was finally broken by the screams and shrieks from the terrified boys he was charged with caring for. At first he told them to go to sleep—the smell was merely that of puddings baking. Reality slowly dawned on him and, after dressing and lighting a candle, he used his key to open the dormitory door leading to the main staircase. Smoke belched in and he slammed the door shut, realising escape in that direction was impossible. He then made his way through the dormitory to the back staircase, calling for the children to follow him. Some did, but many were incapable. The boys had tried to wake as many of their sleeping comrades as they could. Charles Jones, 11, had gone to his younger brother, 7-year-old John. John started to put his socks on, but was overcome by the smoke and fell back on his bed, where he died. Hare, and the trail of boys following him, made their way down the wooden section of the stairway.

Elliott had wedged ladders against dormitory nine's windows, and climbed up to call to the youngsters inside. Four boys, led by Herbert Flack, made their way down the ladder. Elliott noticed a carpenter's sawing stall lying on the ground and used it to force down the door at the base of the stone staircase. He made his way up to the dormitories and met Hipkins and a line of boys making their way from dormitory nine. He then passed Hare, followed by a few youngsters from the top floor dormitory.

Efforts to rescue boys still in the building began in earnest, but the smoke was fast becoming impenetrable. Elliott, Hare, the local residents who had rushed to the scene and others alerted by the commotion, did their best. It was pitch dark and rescuers had no chance of seeing how many boys—if any—remained in the dormitories. Thomas Oakley helped rescue some youngsters with the help of a single candle. Smoke had filled dormitory nine, but it was noticed the eighteen inches above the floor were less congested. The candle was lowered to light the precious opening, and several children followed its flicker to safety. Elliott and Hare made several brave forays up the stairs and managed to drag out several more boys, but the dormitories were rapidly becoming impenetrable tombs.

While the drama within and outside the dormitories unfolded, school superintendent Charles Duncan was busy fighting the fire. As soon as Miss Terry had alerted him he had sent messengers to the local fire station and made his way to the needlework room, armed with a "Fire Queen" extinguisher. He later explained to coroner Charles Lewis:

> The door of the needle room was open, and I saw a fire at the top left hand corner of the wooden partition. At first I saw nothing but smoke. The fire burst into a blaze while I stood there. I was there about three minutes before it broke into a blaze, and then I turned the extinguisher on to it.... I used the extinguisher for about five minutes, and then took the hydrant.

Chief Superintendent Edward Smith of West Ham Fire Brigade received the alarm call at 12:49 AM and arrived nine minutes later. The brigade sent three steamers, a hose cart and an escape ladder. Smith made his way to where Duncan mistakenly believed he had the blaze well under control. The superintendent asked Smith to take his hose, stating: "But I think I have it all out." The fireman went into the needlework room, saw the wardrobe room next door was "well alight" and ordered extra hoses to be attached to hydrants in Forest Lane, to avoid the risk of reducing pressure from the school's own water supply.

At first it was thought all had been saved, but the scale of the tragedy soon became apparent. Those rescued had been taken to Elliott's quarters, and when the stream of boys from the building ceased, he went to count survivors. There were fifty-six, all wrapped in blankets. There should have been eighty-two, and Elliott told a disbelieving Duncan that twenty-six children were missing. Charles Duncan, Chief Superintendent Smith, several policemen, many school officers and civilians, and even firemen on an escape, made valiant efforts to reach the dormitories, but smoke made the task impossible. The few boys dragged out were dead.

It took the brigade forty minutes to put the fire out, and it was even longer before the dense, choking smoke had cleared. The smoke slowly lifted to reveal the horrific death toll. Most of the children were slumped on their beds. Others, probably in a futile effort to escape, had crawled beneath them. A few lads had died trapped in other parts of the dormitory. Twelve bodies were recovered from dormitory nine, and another fourteen from dormitory ten. The dead were aged between six and twelve.

Outside the school Dr Robert Millar of Forest Lane made desperate efforts to revive the children. He selected the bodies that were "still limp and warm," and attempted artificial respiration. For reasons best known to the good doctor he applied mustard to some of the corpses. Ether was injected under the skin of a few bodies, and Millar tried to administer brandy to others. Three of the lads were placed in warm baths. Dr Millar's efforts were in vain. None of the twenty-six boys was revived.

The bodies were taken to a room in the infirmary and laid in two rows to await identification. As morning dawned anxious parents gathered around the gates of the school, worried in case their youngsters were among the dead. Duncan made a roll call to check names of missing children. By noon, only fourteen bodies had been identified by school staff, a fact that says much about the lack of individual attention received by the children. Parents were allowed to enter and scan the rows of little corpses, each wrapped in a blanket with only the face exposed. William Flowers, a pupil at the school, identified the bodies of his two brothers Augustus, 10, and Theophilus, 9. The children had been placed in the school after the death of their father.

The Board of Managers was summoned to an emergency meeting later that day and an immediate investigation into the tragedy began. Managers questioned staff and children to give themselves a clearer picture of what had taken place. The coroner's inquest opened in a girls' classroom at the school on 2 January.

The children were buried the following Monday, 6 January. The service took place at the nearby St James's Church and burial was at the West Ham Cemetery. Five deep graves, side by side, had been prepared. Hearses arrived at the school early in the afternoon. When the bereaved parents and relatives arrived they were invited to eat sandwiches and cakes provided by the Matron, Miss Perfect. Few took advantage of the offer. The twenty-six coffins, draped in sombre grey cloths, were gently loaded into five horse-drawn hearses. These were followed to the church by eight carriages filled with mourners. The school Managers had allocated a carriage seat for one relative of each dead child, except in cases where a surviving brother or sister was at the school. School officers and other officials followed on foot. Forty children from the school, dressed in black, also joined the cortége. The route to St James's was lined with people. Press reports estimated their numbers reached several thousands. After a funeral service led by the Reverend Dr Nicholson, the cortége re-formed and moved on to West Ham Cemetery. Again, the road was lined with thousands of respectful on-lookers.

Public sympathy was widespread and the school managers received messages of condolence from across the globe, including one from Queen Victoria and others from King Leopold of Belgium and the Lord and Lady Mayoress of London.

Essex coroner Charles Lewis took evidence from anyone he believed might shed light on the disaster. Witnesses included school officers, surviving boys, police and fire service officers and the doctor who had tried to resuscitate some of the dead boys. Not surprisingly, there had been excitement and confusion at the incident and some accounts were slightly contradictory. But at the resumed hearing on Wednesday 8 January Henry Elliott caused a sensation by beginning his evidence with the words:

> I am now a ruined man. I have sworn to give my evidence and I will give it. I am a ruined man.

Elliott told his story to a doubtless riveted audience. He described how he had been called to the fire, and how he had helped to rescue the boys. He then came to what he obviously regarded as the most important part of his story. After saving as many boys as he could he went into the school by the front door, and knocked against Mrs Hill, who had earlier escaped from her bedroom, onto a roof and been helped down to safety. "She was then carrying a pail of water to the Superintendent," Elliott told the coroner.

> He was shouting 'Water, water.' I replied 'Where?' He says 'Run to the lodge and get it turned on.'

Elliott described how he got to the Porter's Lodge, where the stop-cock controlling the school's water supply was located, and was told the water was already on "and had been for some time." The coroner and Mr Nairn, a lawyer representing the school, questioned Elliott on why he thought he was a "ruined man." The only explanation he could give was:

> After having given the evidence I had to give, it would be impossible for me to serve under the present superintendent.

He had not been threatened, by Duncan or anyone else. Henry Cook, now chairman of the Board of Managers, told the inquest he and his colleagues were "pained" by Elliott's remarks. They managed the school, not Duncan. If Elliott had been intimidated they wanted to know about it. Elliott was assured that if he had been truthful he had nothing to fear. The Managers would not dismiss him.

John Birch, the gate porter, told the inquest the water supply was routinely turned down every evening. On the night of the fire no one had instructed him to do anything, but he had turned the water on to full power after someone knocking had woken him at about 12:35 PM. Elliott had arrived two or three minutes later. Elliott believed the school's water supply had not been turned on, that Duncan was well aware of the fact, and that his disclosure would mean trouble. However, the coroner clearly considered Elliott was an over-excitable character, probably affected by the trauma of the fire. Elliott later apologised to the Managers for his outburst and was told they had no wish to censure him.

There was no appeal to help or compensate the families of the dead children. This is in stark contrast to the appeal launched after the burning of the *Goliath* to compensate officers for their losses. On 9 January Francis Fether and John Gunn from the Gurney Lodge of the Son of the Phoenix Total Abstinence Society attended a Managers' meeting to ask permission to start a public appeal to raise money for a memorial. The Managers refused. Churchwardens at St James's, however, felt little need for protocol, and launched an appeal to place a stained glass memorial window in the church. The school Managers refused to support the project, but the money was raised and the window installed. The Managers contributed the £36 needed to set a memorial headstone on the boys' graves.

Mr Robert Hedley, the Local Government Board Inspector, visited parents or closest relatives of the dead children. It was later reported to the Managers:

> It would be gratifying to the Managers, as it had been to himself, to find that the mothers of the unfortunate children, without exception, expressed their warm sense of the treatment and care which their children received at the Forest Gate School.

Criticism of the school was limited, despite the fact that most children had died because of the delays in giving them a means of exit from their locked and lightless dormitories, and that it was glaringly obvious there was no set fire drill. Coroner Lewis recommended the jury consider adding riders to their verdict, in the hope their suggestions might prevent similar suffering. He told them his view of what the riders should be, and they obliged him.

The jury returned a verdict of accidental death, recording the children had suffocated because of a fire caused by burning soot that fell from the newly-swept chimney. The riders were:

● Dormitory doors should be unlocked at night. A night-watchman should check the boys' wards at night, and a wards' woman should do the same in the girls' quarters. The watchman should also check the outside of the building, completing inspection logs to prove he had done his duty.

● There should be staff sleeping on the premises to work fire appliances, and fire drills at frequent intervals; water should be kept on full power at night and the Superintendent should be in direct communication with the Fire Brigade. The jury considered the use of candles dangerous.

● Facilities to prevent loss of life by fire in buildings such as the school should be as liable to inspection as they were in places of entertainment; the dormitories, staircases and passages in the school should be lit at night; inflammable stores should be kept well away from the main school building; when any official in charge of a dormitory was on leave their post should be covered by another person.

● Stairways should be erected outside all buildings of two of more storeys; all doors should be hung with double-action spring hinges; iron plates should replace wooden boards covering fireplaces; no smoking to be allowed in dormitories.

The jury praised those who helped in the rescue efforts and made a final criticism of the school:

The jury deeply regret that the Board of Management did not provide a substitute in the place of Mr Way, absent on leave, as in all probability more lives might have been saved.

The Managers decided to act on all the jury's recommendations, and had taken the initiative in making some changes before the verdict was given. The wooden staircase linking dormitories nine and ten was replaced in iron. Locks on dormitory doors "not in practice used" were removed. The door at the foot of the external staircase was to be locked, but with a key hung on either side. It was agreed to appoint a night-watchman at a maximum wage of £1.4s.0d per week and a fire drill was quickly drawn up. The Managers wanted the drill to be inspected "by a competent person" at least four times per year, and Chief Superintendent Edward Smith, who commanded firemen at the tragedy, agreed to do the honours for the fee of four guineas per year. The Managers also recommended the payment of two shillings to officers showing the "required smartness" at fire drill, and West Ham Council was asked to erect a fire alarm close to the school.

Despite the loss of twenty-six lives, some of the Managers' proposals were thwarted. West Ham Council would not agree to Chief Superintendent Smith doing the drill inspections and the Local Government Board refused to pay two shillings to officers behaving well at the drills. West Ham Council would not put up an alarm close to the school, and the Managers decided they could not afford their own line.

The school's insurers, Sun Fire Office, paid £2,050 in compensation for damage to the building and loss of contents. The company also donated £10 for distribution among those who had helped at the fire. More awards came from the Royal Society for the Protection of Life from Fire. They gave thirteen certificates, testimonials and medals, as well as several monetary awards. Charles Hipkins, the 12-year-old dormitory monitor, was presented with a silver medal and three guineas, a sum that must have seemed a fortune. Henry Elliott also received a silver medal and three guineas. Charles Duncan was awarded an illuminated testimonial on vellum.

Great emphasis was put on the presumption the dead children had not suffered, but had died quietly and peacefully in their sleep. A leader published in the *Times* on 2 January stated:

> It is some consolation to feel that the sufferings of the victims were less than they might have been. In only a single case, as it appears, was death directly caused by burning...

A letter to the Managers expressing the condolences of Queen Victoria commented:

> It is a blessing to think the poor children cannot have suffered or even have been aware of what happened...

And the Reverend Dr Nicholson, in a service at St James's Church on the Sunday following the disaster, told his congregation:

> For the manner of their dying we have cause to be thankful. Experts have told us it is well nigh certain that the little children were suffocated by the smoke before the fire reached them. Can we not hope that many of these little children passed away unconsciously in their sleep...

In fact we don't know how the children died. As Dr Nicholson went on to say, the bodies were "scarred" and "disfigured." As Hipkins, the dormitory nine monitor, was rounding up lads to get them to safety he noticed flames were licking through the floor. Whatever the actual cause of death, there's little doubt many of the children suffered a terrifying ordeal before they succumbed. They were trapped in locked dormitories, with no lights and no obvious means of escape. Those in the lower room had no adult to help them, and those above were obliged to spend vital minutes trying to wake their heavy-sleeping guardian. The school had no fire drill. Duncan opted to fight the blaze, knowing nothing of what was happening to the children. Elliott and others concentrated on getting the youngsters to safety, without knowing if anything was being done to control the fire. Actions were left to the initiative of those at the scene. The School District and its Managers knew only too well about the dangers of fire. The appalling death toll at Forest Gate School would have undoubtedly been reduced by adequate management and planning.

Any doubts or misgivings generated by the circumstances of the fire, or by Elliott's strange outburst, would have probably been forgotten if the school had not plunged into another crisis just three years later. In June 1893 more than 140 of the school's children suffered a severe attack of food poisoning. The first children became ill early on Friday, 23 June. Edward Puttick, 14, died during the early hours of the following morning and Hannah Fish, 13, died early on Tuesday morning.

The deaths made an inquest essential, and coroner Lewis opened the hearing at the school premises on the Tuesday, 27 June. Normally inquests were attended by journalists from all local papers. This was something different. There was just one reporter, from the *Stratford Express*. The paper's leader later commented: "It so happened that the information reached the public only through our columns, and only reached us somewhat late."

At first the story that unfolded at the inquest threw little light on the cause of the illness. On the day before the children became ill, the Thursday, they had apparently enjoyed a meal of bread and butter for breakfast, soup for dinner and dry bread for supper. The soup had been made from the stock of fourteen stones of salt beef boiled on Tuesday, two days earlier. Bones had been added on the Wednesday, and the mixture boiled up again for several hours. On Thursday morning soaked peas, other vegetables, pieces of meat left from joints and some raw meat were added, and the soup was simmered from 8:30 AM until it was served at noon. School cook Annie Evans told the coroner she had tasted the soup herself and found it was "perfectly sweet."

Early on Friday morning yardsman James Bennett noticed boys were "continually going to the w.c." The inquest heard Duncan was told of the sickness and sent a message to the school's medical officer, Dr George Bell, at 9:00 AM. The doctor arrived at 11:00 AM and examined Puttick and the other twenty-nine children taken ill. He told the coroner Puttick had been "vomiting freely" and had complained of pains in his head and stomach. By the time Dr Bell saw him he was sitting up in bed and feeling better. The doctor prescribed hydrocyanic acid, bicarbonate of soda and aromatic spirits of ammonia for Puttick, and instructed the children should receive only water, or milk and water, until their vomiting stopped. Bell did not call at the school again that day, despite the fact that by evening ninety-three boys and girls in the school were ill.

No one stayed up through the night to watch the sick youngsters. Yardsman Bennett told the inquest he offered drinks of water at 11:00 PM, and Puttick had told him he felt better. At 5:10 AM another boy, Robert Butchford, called Bennett to Puttick's bed. The child was dead.

On Saturday another forty-one children became ill. These included Hannah Fish, whose condition rapidly became serious. Dr Bell first saw her at 12:00 noon, and had her transferred from her dormitory to the infirmary. Hannah received rather more attention than the unfortunate Puttick. She had two special attendants, and Dr Bell saw her three times on Saturday, three times on Sunday and four times on Monday. His treatment included injections of brandy, ether, strychnine, morphia and atropine. Hannah died during the early hours of Tuesday morning.

Dr Bell performed post-mortem examinations on both children. Puttick, he said, died from acute inflammation of the stomach and intestine. Fish had died from exhaustion, caused by sub-acute inflammation. Bell could not determine the cause of the inflammation, and specimens from both children were sent for analysis by Dr Stephenson at Guy's Hospital. The inquest was adjourned to await his findings.

The hearing resumed on 10 August. Dr Stephenson reported the children had died from ptomaine poisoning. Such poisoning, he said, could only result from eating unwholesome food. Ptomaine was an animal poison, usually found in food such as bones and pork pies. He stated the poisons could not have been generated in the soup unless the meat used had been unwholesome in the first place. The doctor would not swear the meat used in the soup had caused the poisoning as he had not seen it, but said he thought it was "probably the meat." Puttick had been working in the gatehouse on the Thursday when the soup was served for dinner. He had a different meal—some of the salt beef from which the soup had been made. This pointed the finger of blame firmly at the salt beef. Annie Evans, the cook, was recalled and stated the salt beef she had used in the soup had not been as good as it usually was. It looked blackish, but tasted sweet so she presumed too much saltpetre had been used in its preparation.

The evidence would have ended at that point. Just as Lewis was beginning his summing up for the jury, Henry Elliott, the same man who had generated shock waves at the inquest after the fire, walked towards him and said he wished to speak. Lewis agreed, and the testimony sparked a bitter controversy that put the school under national scrutiny and was to dog it until the district was disbanded in 1897.

Elliott said that during the week prior to the outbreak of sickness, children had been fed meat infested with maggots. He had been called to the dining room by his wife, Mary Jane, who worked in the school's Reception wards. He said Mary Jane had told him the meat being cut up was "running away with maggots." Asked why he had not complained to either Duncan or the Managers he replied, "I have made hundreds of complaints as to the state of the meat and other things." He said meat had been buried in trenches alongside the school because it was bad, and there was too much of it for the school's pigs to eat.

Caroline Hart and Emily Judd, two serving hall maids Elliott said had witnessed the maggots, were called. Both denied seeing maggots in the meat. Charles Duncan was given the chance to reply to the allegations, and he vehemently denied them. He had heard nothing about the meat containing maggots; Elliott had complained to him about the quality of bread, and the Managers had been informed; food had been buried because the school did not have sufficient pigs to eat all the table refuse. The matron, Harriett Parkiss, gave evidence that she made daily inspections of the meat in the kitchen, and had never seen any maggots.

Coroner Lewis decided to end the discussion. It was a matter for the Managers, he said, and not for him. Duncan seemed distraught at the accusations. He told Lewis:

But it is so easy to sow things of this sort broadcast. It is a shame! Why, everybody who knows me, knows that for 42 years it has been the whole scheme of my life to make these children happy.

The coroner replied:

I have known you, Mr Duncan, so long, that I am perfectly certain you have the interests of the children at heart.

The jury returned the verdict that Edward Puttick and Hannah Fish had died from inflammation of the stomach and intestines, the result of ptomaine poisoning. They placed on record their confidence in Mr Duncan.

Duncan may have won the day at the inquest, but he was destined for considerable problems in the months and years to follow. The man seemed able to manipulate those around him. The *Stratford Express* was the first paper to report the deaths and sickness at the school. They covered the first inquest hearing and, as they commented themselves, were "late" in receiving the news. Inquests were part of the bread and butter of newspaper reporting at the time, and the paper should have been well aware of cases being heard. Why the *Stratford Express* journalist was the only press reporter present remains a mystery.

The way in which the case was reported raises questions about possible outside influence on the reporters or the newspaper's bosses. The first report published on Wednesday, 28 June, the day after the opening of the inquest, carried the headlines: "Forest Gate District School—Supposed Wholesale Poisoning—132 Children Affected." A report of the inquest opening followed. Duncan was not best pleased and next day one of the paper's journalists visited him at the school. The report of the visit appeared in the next edition of the paper, on Saturday 1 July. It represents a grovelling sop to the Superintendent. It quotes him as saying the report was accurate, but that the headlines had caused needless anxiety among parents with children at the school. "Wholesale poisoning," he said, "and the statement that the remainder of the 132 children are very ill are both incorrect and needlessly alarming." Amidst a plethora of apologies the reporter managed one retort:

It is a great pity the press were not informed of the inquest beforehand. If they had been, then the reporters could have made inquiries and have got to know more than actually came out in evidence.

The piece then details Duncan's view of the story:

Well, to say 132 were poisoned and were seriously ill is not correct. Some of them were really not ill at all—they were frightened—but the safest course was to treat them as ill...

The great majority of the cases—although of course they had to be attended to, and were attended to, immediately—have not been what you would call cases of 'poisoning,' but cases of diarrhoea, such as might naturally occur at this season of the year.

Asked what he thought had caused the outbreak, Duncan replied:

I cannot form an opinion. Every inquiry—except of course the analysis—has been made and nothing whatever has been discovered. All provisions are carefully examined as they come—in fact officers and children all live alike here—have the same bread, the same meat, the same milk and the same potatoes...

The reporter described the Utopian scene of the school's children at play.

It gladdens one—and evidently gladdens Mr Duncan more even than anybody else—to see how full of life and vigour all are now.

The article ends:

As we leave Mr Duncan we feel that this time at any rate we have to tell not what will cause unnecessary pain, but what will allay any alarm that may still exist in connection with this sad and mysterious outbreak.

The "Interview With Mr Duncan" ran alongside the report on the inquest opening, a repeat of the piece that had caused Duncan offence. The headlines had been changed to read: "Forest Gate School District. Supposed Food Poisoning. 100 Children Affected." It is interesting to note the inquest report includes Duncan's figures for the numbers of affected children. He detailed how many boys and girls were affected each morning, afternoon and evening, and gave a final total of 132. In fact, his addition was faulty. The total was 143.

The *Stratford Express'* support for the school continued through future editions. In the paper of 12 August, that also carried a report of the inquest hearing where Elliott told of the maggot-ridden meat, a leader article gave short shrift to the allegations.

We attach no weight to the extraordinary statement of the witness Henry Elliott. This man declared he saw maggots in the gravy from meat a day or two before the salt meat came, and that two of the maids also saw them. Both maids denied this point blank...

The leader commented a man named Elliott had startled those at the inquest into the deaths of children killed in the school fire in 1890 with his statement: "I am a ruined man."

> There was nothing in this man's statement to account for his ridiculous outcry. What he said corroborated the Superintendent's statement in every particular but one; and in that one Elliott was shown to be mistaken and the Superintendent accurate. Is the Henry Elliott of this inquest the Henry Elliott of that? If so, he was clearly not 'ruined' by his former evidence, but the Managers will now have to consider whether they ought to retain him any longer in their service. We have received an abominable anonymous letter upon this matter. If the writer do not at once communicate with us, we shall forward it to the Managers, who will have little difficulty, we apprehend, in tracing the writer and dealing with him as he deserves.

Elliott's allegations left the school Managers with little option but to investigate, if only to defend the "good name" of the school. The Managers' school visiting committee interviewed Elliott and in a report to a Managers' meeting on 17 August the committee claimed he had "practically contradicted" the evidence he had given to the coroner. They concluded Elliott's actions had been designed to get rid of Duncan:

> Your committee are of the opinion that the statement made to them by Mr Keating, third schoolmaster, that in the course of a general conversation which he had with Elliott on the 8th he (Elliott) suddenly stated, with no apparent connection with the subject of conversation: 'I'll tell you what! I am ready to bet money that that man Duncan will not sleep in the school on Thursday; he will be summarily dismissed,' has an important bearing upon the evidence given by Henry Elliott at the inquest.

The Managers immediately suspended Elliott from duty, without pay, and asked the Local Government Board to institute an inquiry. Elliott lost both his £32 per year salary and his accommodation. His wife, Mary Jane, continued working at the school, so the couple suffered an enforced separation.

Mr Hedley, Local Government Board Inspector, started his inquiry on 22 September. He looked at the school's record books and uncovered startling irregularities. The children did indeed eat the same food as the school's officers. The catch was they ate the officer's left-overs.

Hedley studied the school's Provision Receipt and Consumption Account book and soon realised it represented a web of lies, or at the very least gross and irreconcilable inaccuracies. Duncan had entered that fifty-two pounds of meat had been taken out of store on 22 June to make soup for all children in the school. In fact, as Medical Officer Dr Bell's report proved, the soup had been made with only ten pounds of fresh meat. The rest of the meat was left-overs from the dinners school officers had eaten on previous days. Dr Bell's report also highlighted how the infant children had not even had soup for dinner, they'd been served with bread pudding.

Dr. Bell's conduct also worried Hedley. He felt the doctor had not realised the severity of the outbreak. Someone should have watched over the dying Puttick during the night. Also, at the inquest Bell had sworn under oath that he had arrived at the school at "about 11 AM" after Duncan sent for him at 9:00 AM, but the Porter's Book, which recorded all comings and goings at the school, showed the doctor had not arrived until 12:10 PM, and left at 1:15 PM. In those sixty-five minutes Dr Bell apparently had time to examine and assess sixty or more sick children. Despite the severity and spread of the illness Dr Bell did not return to the school until summoned after Puttick's death. Dr Bell argued the school's record of timings was wrong; the lodgekeeper had been ill at the time and his tasks were being performed by a boy. He insisted he had arrived at the school at 11:00 AM.

Hedley took evidence from the school's staff and children on the question of the maggot-infested meat served on 17 June. Not surprisingly, the witnesses were hesitant. Only Elliott's wife insisted the meat did contain maggots. Mary Jane said: "I saw a good quantity of maggots. They were white. They were crawling on the table, nearly half an inch long." Hedley decided Henry Elliott had grossly exaggerated the situation. The meat was not maggoty, only flyblown.

Duncan tried to explain the inaccuracies in stock-keeping. He had made an error, he said, when he recorded fifty-two pounds of meat had been taken from the store for the soup, but he had forgotten to record meat taken to make beef tea for eighty-five children. He also claimed the decision to give the infants bread pudding instead of soup had been reached after the soup had been prepared.

Hedley made his report on 1 March 1894. Clearly angered by the discrepancies revealed in the Provisions book, the Local Government Board sent a strongly-worded letter to the school Managers.

> It is clear that these occurrences seriously affect the reliability of the entries throughout the Provision Receipt and Consumption Account as a true

record of actual facts.... They lead the Board to fear that the entries, instead of being always made from the statements by the responsible officers as to the provisions weighted out from the stores day by day and distributed to the children, have been sometimes made from a computation of the quantity that should have been consumed, regard being had to the numbers in the school and the prescribed Dietary and Ingredients Tables.

The Dietary and Ingredients Tables, issued by the Local Government Board, stipulated the amounts of food to be fed to children, and they suspected that Duncan used these tables to work out how much meat could be taken from the stores for a particular meal. He then entered that amount in the records, whether or not it had in fact been served. The Local Government Board said it trusted Duncan would take steps to ensure no such errors could be repeated in future. There was also the question of what to do with Henry Elliott, still on suspension. The Board told the Managers:

> ...though certain of his allegations are apparently without justification while others much overstate the facts, certain of those made in regard to the provisions are not altogether without foundation. Moreover it is not clear that he has not been actuated in the matter by a misdirected zeal for the interests of the children.

The Board suggested Elliott's suspension be removed "...upon the understanding that he forthwith places his resignation...." Elliott had little choice, and agreed to resign. The resignation took effect on 3 May, and Elliott then requested back pay and residency allowance for the period of his suspension. The Local Government Board instructed this sum, totalling £63.6s.6d, should be paid. Henry's wife, Mary Jane resigned from the school in June 1894.

Duncan suffered no disciplinary action for his "inaccuracies." No one questioned what had become of the meat allegedly taken from the stores when the children had in fact made do with officers' waste, even though the cumulative amounts must have been enormous and represented considerable sums of money. The Managers said they were satisfied Duncan had acted for the benefit of the children.

The school Managers may have hoped that, with the removal of the recalcitrant Elliott and the conclusion of the Local Government Board inquiry, their traumas would be at an end. But their problems were just beginning. Staff morale was badly affected by the scandal. Records show that between August and December 1893 at least fourteen of the school's seventy-four employees left. The credibility of the school Managers was damaged. The Whitechapel Board of Guardians criticised the school's management. At a meeting of the Board on 10 April 1894, chairman James Brown and two other Board members, Mr Harris and Mr Johnson, put on record their opinion that the school Managers had dealt "flippantly with a matter of much gravity."

Doubts on the value of the District School system were growing, and in September 1894 the government appointed a Departmental Committee to report on the existing District School system and to advise on any changes that were desirable. The committee, chaired by the Rt. Hon. Anthony John Mundella, MP, had fifty meetings and interviewed seventy-three witnesses. Its report, in 1896, signalled the end of District Schools, and, largely because of testimony from Elliott, delivered a resounding broadside damning the management at Forest Gate.

Elliott had won some influential friends. During the Local Government Board inquiry he had been represented by Mr B. Costelloe, a barrister and chairman of the London County Council's Local Government Committee. Costelloe was acquainted with Ernest Hart, editor of the *British Medical Journal* and chairman of the British Medical Association's parliamentary committee.

Hart was one of the first witnesses called by the Departmental Committee. He was clearly opposed to the District School system, and used incidents at Forest Gate School to illustrate his arguments. He said the large number of deaths in the 1890 fire had been caused by disorganisation brought about by an epidemic of ophthalmia. The main thrust of his criticism was aimed at the poisoning episode and the subsequent inquiry. "Nothing happened to the Superintendent," he said.

> The unhappy man who made the complaint, who brought out all the facts, and whose statement at the inquest led to the investigation—he was turned out into the world, as his wife was turned out into the world.

Hart said Duncan was "altogether the Guardians' man." Elliott, he said, had given excellent service and saved the lives of many children in the fire.

> ...when this man comes to give evidence his facts are evidently corroborated as far as they go; there is nothing to be said against them; but the inquiry is held as though he were the criminal, and the other persons—the Guardians and the Superintendent—were the plaintiffs, and he is throughout treated accordingly.

Hart said Elliott's counsel, Mr Costelloe, had been refused access to the school's record books.

> The question is, was this place properly supervised? How did this fire take place? How did these poisonings take place?

The committee called Mr Costelloe as a witness and questioned him closely on the Forest Gate poisoning. His evidence was devastating to the school. The barrister said the Local Government Board inquiry had been "very unsatisfactory." It was not an unbiased investigation. Hedley had taken on the role of defender of the school against objectionable charges. Costelloe said the children called to the inquiry had been painfully anxious and nervous.

> ...the Superintendent of such a school has such supreme autocratic power in his hand that it must be excessively difficult even to find out grave irregularities. It seemed to me quite obvious that it was very unlikely that any officer, or still more unlikely that any child, would be willing to give evidence.

He said the Managers' faith in Duncan had been "almost sublime." He added: "I think they believed a great deal too implicitly that nothing could be wrong in their institution."

Costelloe wanted to check on discrepancies in the Provisions book at the school. On 22 June, the day the soup causing the sickness was served, fifty-two pounds of meat had been shown as being taken from the stores, whereas it was now known the vast bulk of meat used had been waste from meals eaten by officers on previous days. After 22 June the practice of using officers' waste had been stopped. Costelloe wanted to know if there had been a subsequent change in the amount of meat logged as being taken from stores for soup. Committee chairman Anthony Mundella asked what would be signified if amounts recorded as taken were the same.

> As a lawyer, the first conclusion I would draw would be that there had been a grave irregularity in the keeping of the accounts.... And the next conclusion I would draw would be that it is the business of the Managers of the school to see what became of the difference in the alleged quantities of meat.

Henry Cook, chairman of the Forest Gate Managers, was also called as a witness. He was obviously taken aback at being questioned on the poisoning episode. "I had no idea this question was to be re-opened," he told the committee. "I thought the Local Government Board had had their inquiry and as far as that was concerned it was settled." Cook said he believed a single joint of unwholesome meat had caused the problems. His own sister had died in her own home after eating unwholesome meat. Medical men agreed that, even with the greatest of care, such meat might not be spotted. Cook told the committee he had not been involved in suspending Elliott as he had been away at the time. But he added: "I think it was a necessity that either Elliott or Mr Duncan should have been suspended." Cook denied maggots had been found in the meat. He said the joints had been "fly blown."

The Committee must have demanded sight of the school record books. Committee member the Rt. Hon. John Gorst MP prepared a Memorandum on the incidents at Forest Gate, and this appeared as an appendix to the Committee's Report, published in 1896. It was a damning indictment and gave Elliott a belated but comprehensive victory. Gorst said the Local Government Board inquiry had been:

> ...an inquiry into Elliott's veracity only. No inquiry as to how the children came to be poisoned has ever been made either by the Managers or the Local Government Board.

Gorst stated Elliott's claims had been "completely proved," the only debate being over how many flies had laid eggs on the meat, and to what degree those eggs had developed. The Provisions book showed that the amounts of meat taken from the stores for soup were practically the same before and after 22 June, although it was admitted officers' waste was used before 22 June but not afterwards. "What became of the fresh meat," wrote Gorst,

> thus charged as served to the children, but not, in fact, served, has not been the subject of any inquiry either by the Managers or by the Local Government Board.

The Forest Gate Managers were incensed. At a meeting on 13 August 1896 they minuted their anger:

> It would appear that in framing the memorandum the writer has discarded the sworn evidence of the witnesses at the inquiry as well as the evidence given before the Departmental Committee by the Chairman of the Board of Management, while giving implicit credence to statements emanating from the least reliable source.

Was Charles Duncan a scoundrel, or a careless but caring master? The discrepancies in the Provisions books were irrefutable. He was the only one to make entries in the book and must have been responsible for the "inaccuracies." The missing meat must have gone somewhere. Even today it seems incredible Duncan escaped prosecution for theft or fraud.

The lowly Elliott seems to have established a unique rapport with the children. He worked in the Reception wards and as every child entering the school spent a fortnight in this "quarantine block," Elliott would have met them all. On New Year's Day in 1890 when the locked dormitories filled with smoke and desperate children yelled from their windows, it was Elliott they called for. At the hearings of the Departmental Committee there had been a discussion on bed-wetting. Ernest Hart, a top member of the BMA, had discussed the problem with Henry Elliott. Elliott had kept a notebook showing five thousand beds were wetted in the boys' department during a twelve-month period. Elliott and his wife were in charge of the Receiving wards and were emphatic that not one in a hundred children had the habit on admission. Elliott blamed bed-wetting on lack of attention. The fact that this man, a lowly employee earning just £32 per year, had bothered to keep a notebook and to think carefully about the problem reveals an extraordinary degree of concern.

In 1897, the year after the Departmental Committee published its report, the Whitechapel Union pulled out of the partnership with colleagues in Poplar and the Forest Gate School District was dissolved. The Poplar Guardians used the school for their pauper children until 1908, when the premises became a temporary workhouse.

In 1911 the premises were purchased by the West Ham Union, and re-opened as a workhouse infirmary in 1913. By 1931 the hospital, Forest Gate Hospital, had been extended and had seven hundred beds. The hospital was well-known for its maternity unit and nurses' training school. It closed in the mid-1980s and the site is now being used for housing.

CHAPTER SEVEN

The Silvertown Blast

Silvertown, in the borough of West Ham, has had a long history as an industrial dustbin. Ron Leighton, Member of Parliament for Newham North East, described the era during a parliamentary debate on the London Underground Bill in June 1991 as "the backside of London." It is an area which, he said,

> ...has always been the poor relation.... It has always had the sticky end of the stick. Whether in housing, health, educational achievement, leisure facilities, employment, income, life opportunities or transport, the East End has always had the worst end of the deal.

The district owed its nineteenth-century boom to the Metropolitan Buildings Act of 1844, which imposed tight restrictions on noxious trades inside the boundaries of London. West Ham lay just outside these boundaries and, with its rapidly developing docks and the North Woolwich Railway, offered a prime site for industrial development. The district was mentioned in Dickens' *Household Words* (1857) as

> ...a place of refuge for offensive trade establishments turned out of town,—those of oil-boilers, gut-spinners, varnish-makers, printers' ink-makers and the like.

The population of the area grew rapidly and row upon row of tightly-packed houses were built to accommodate the new workforce. In 1800 there were just 6,485 residents; by 1900 there were 289,030.

Silvertown, densely populated and already crammed with highly volatile chemical, oil refining and manufacturing industries, was not an ideal location for a trinitrotoluene—TNT—factory. But it was precisely here that the government decided to establish such a factory in 1915, during the early years of the First World War. The consequences ought to have been predicted.

The First World War presented logistical problems unlike any previous warfare. The new weaponry showing its paces in the endless and usually fruitless battles at the front consumed vast quantities of ammunition. Militarists feared stocks were becoming perilously low. It became clear the war would not be "over by Christmas" and was likely to drag on far into the foreseeable future. There were complaints, sometimes made public in the press, that shortages in ammunition were putting troops at a disadvantage in battle. In January 1915 an Explosives Supply Department was established. Its newly-appointed Director-General, Lord Moulton, came under immediate and increasing pressure to boost production, and to do so quickly.

TNT, the army's favoured ammunition, was thought to be a "safe" explosive and its manufacturers did not have to comply with the regulations of the 1875 Explosives Act. It was recognised that the purification process was more dangerous than that required to produce the raw TNT and, in order to protect supplies, it was considered essential that the two operations should be carried out in separate plants. Moulton quickly set about building government-owned explosive plants, and looked around for private manufacturers able to supplement production.

In 1894 Brunner Mond and Company had built a chemical factory on a rectangular site stretching the four hundred yards between the North Woolwich Railway and the Thames. At first the factory produced soda crystals and then expanded output to include caustic soda. The company abandoned the caustic soda plant in 1912. The unused factory attracted Ministry of Munitions officials in 1915 when they were searching for sites to purify TNT. The men from the ministry were undeterred by the knowledge that TNT and caustic soda was a volatile and potentially lethal cocktail.

In an account to a government committee of inquiry in 1917, Moulton explained how he came to the dubious conclusion that the abandoned caustic soda plant at Brunner Mond should be adapted to purify TNT:

> We had established a place at Rainham which was well removed from any habitation and was very suitable in every way for the purpose of purifying crude TNT, but that was obviously insufficient, and the other supplies were clearly too small if the artillerists insisted on having purified TNT for their charges...the consequence was we had to look about for some method of promptly meeting this deficiency.

I heard, I think from a member of the firm Mssrs Chance and Hunt, that these works at Silvertown were standing idle, and that they were the only works which he knew of which were capable of being adapted to a method of purification which was not recrystallisation but was a method of washing in hot alcohol. Accordingly we communicated with Mssrs Brunner Mond and Co and although there was no formal commandeering of the works—because Mssrs Brunner Mond and Co have always met our wishes so willingly and so energetically—yet practically we requisitioned these works and put them in the hands of Brunner Mond and Co as our agents to adapt them to this process of purification.

Brunner Mond directors, as their official company history relates, were strongly opposed to converting their plant for TNT purification as it was in such a densely populated area. They relented because of the urgent need for the explosive to support the war effort, and the plant was "practically requisitioned" in June 1915. The necessary modifications were minor. The plant was scrubbed to remove all traces of caustic soda and an extra floor was added to house the necessary melt pot. By September production was underway, with Silvertown turning out around nine tons of purified TNT per day. The enterprise was no money-spinner for Brunner Mond. The government footed the production bill and paid the company 5/– per ton of purified TNT, amounting to some £750 per year. Dr Andrea Angel, an Oxford lecturer, was employed at a salary of £400 per year to supervise the process, so Brunner Mond's profit margin on the deal was minimal.

The TNT plant employed sixty-three staff, split into three shifts to ensure twenty-four-hour production. Security was obviously important, and the plant was surrounded by a corrugated iron fence topped with barbed wire. So far as was possible, workers were selected from employees known and trusted by the company, or at least known to existing workers. The purification process, and its workers, were kept entirely separate from the firm's main plant, which continued to manufacture soda crystals from ammonia soda.

Production techniques were relatively simple. Crude TNT was delivered to the plant in sacks and barrels and hoisted to a room above the melt pot. Here about five tons at a time were poured through lead-lined funnels into the pot. The melt pot was heated by steam coils, and the molten TNT ran through an open steam-heated iron gutter into one of four vertical cylinders, where it was dissolved in warm alcohol. When the solution was cooled TNT was left behind as crystals. The alcohol solution, containing most of the crude TNT's impurities was then run off. Crystallised TNT was dug out and put back into the melt pot and the process repeated. The end product was the purified TNT so sought after by the military. This was packed into fifty-pound cotton bags and stored until collected. At any one time, therefore, the building could house crude, part purified and purified TNT.

Exactly what caused the Silvertown factory to explode at about 6:50 PM on Friday, 19 January 1917 will never be known; the two people who must have witnessed the start of the small fire that sparked the disaster inevitably lost their lives. But we can piece together the sequence of events by using witness statements collected by police for the government inquiry set up a few days after the explosion.

At about 6:40 PM on 19 January hoist workers Betty Sands and Ada Randall decided to take their tea-break. Betty went up to the melt pot room to see if Walter Mauger and Catherine Hodge had sufficient crude TNT to keep them going. Betty saw Catherine was busy opening bags with her knife, and Walter said they had plenty of crude for the moment. Betty and Ada left the building and made their way to the toilets. Betty reported: "Whilst there we heard a noise like the shaking of a door, shortly after there was another similar noise." Betty sent Ada out to investigate and the terrified girl rushed back, screaming: "Good, God, it's all afire!"

The pair darted towards a field between the munitions factory and the Venesta Works next door, but couldn't scale the iron fence. They were joined at the fence by Alice Davis, another Brunner Mond worker. Alice had left the still room to see the time, and noted it was 6:48 PM. As she walked back into the still room she had seen the reflection of fire on an open flight of stairs. She rushed for safety, and was the last woman to leave the building alive. As the three girls debated how to climb the boundary fence to safety a gigantic explosion knocked them unconscious.

Young James Arnell was sweeping up spilt TNT as Betty and Ada were making their way to the toilets. He stopped in his tracks when he looked around and saw "some spirit dropping down through the roof, it was like red hot glass." The lad rushed to the ground floor, stood against the door and yelled "Fire!" As he reached the door he heard foreman Edgar Wenborn shouting for everyone to come down and

EXPLOSION
AT A
MUNITION FACTORY
NEAR LONDON.

CONSIDERABLE LOSS
OF LIFE.

DAMAGE TO PROPERTY.

At a quarter to twelve o'clock last night the
Press Bureau issued the following statement:

The Ministry of Munitions regrets to
announce that an explosion occurred this
evening at a munition factory in the neighbourhood of London.

It is feared that the explosion was attended
by considerable loss of life and damage to
property.

29   Headline in the Daily Telegraph

30   Explosion damage at the Silvertown
     munitions factory. Courtesy Museum
     in Docklands Project

calling for Dr Angel, the superintendent chemist. As Arnell ran for his life, he noticed that firemen were already on site, playing a hose at the top floor of the building. He scaled the boundary fence and ran down to the fire station in North Woolwich Road, where he watched the blaze. A few minutes later the force of the explosion threw him to the ground.

Frederick Blevins, assistant chemist, was in his cubicle above the works laboratory when the alarm was called. He rushed out and saw the melt pot room ablaze, although the fire was "confined to one spot." He must have realised the terrible danger, but decided to hurry back for his coat and hat before dashing for the main gate, warning everyone he passed to run for their lives. Blevins passed firemen getting their hoses ready to fight the flames. He was aware that Dr Angel was still in the works and ran back to find him. He met the doctor coming back from the plant to his office and begged him to come away. Angel was obviously determined to return to the office, and Blevins ran off alone. When he reached North Woolwich Road he heard a loud rumble and explosion. When he regained consciousness he found the blast had propelled him some three to four hundred feet.

The fire station which had been built three years previously stood opposite the factory. It is clear the Silvertown firemen reached the scene before many of the workers realised there was any problem. A small boy had run into the station and rang the fire bell, shouting that the munitions factory was on fire. At the same time Station Officer Samuel Betts heard a small explosion and looked out of the window to see Brunner Mond burning. His ordered the "duty man," his son Thomas, to call for more help and then immediately set off with two engines. The fire-fighters were warned to leave, as there was nothing they could do, but the men bravely began to set up their equipment. Samuel went to find another water hydrant. As he walked, the fire must have reached the TNT and triggered the major explosion. Samuel was knocked unconscious, but suffered relatively minor injuries.

There were around eighty-three tons of TNT at the Brunner Mond plant, comprising twenty-eight tons in crude form, twenty-seven tons in process and twenty-eight tons which had already been purified. In addition, there were nine tons of TNT oil stored in barrels. Experts later estimated about fifty-four tons of TNT exploded and a further thirty tons of TNT and four tons of oil burned in the resulting fire. Amazingly, five

31 *Another view of the blast damage. Courtesy Museum in Docklands Project.*

tons of the TNT oil was later recovered intact from the ruins.

The Brunner Mond munitions factory turned into a gigantic bomb. Molten metal, bricks, mortar and hundreds of tons of earth and debris rained down on the district, bringing death to hapless residents and workers with no chance of escape. The fountain of destruction started fires that were to rage for nearly forty-eight hours and cause almost as much damage as the blast itself. It was, as a reporter from the East Ham Echo and Mail later commented, "as though the pent-up forces of the earth's consuming centre had suddenly cracked the crust on which we live."

Within minutes, the landscape had changed beyond recognition. Brunner Mond and the neighbouring Venesta plywood and packaging case works were obliterated. The Silvertown Lubricants works, which also shared the munitions factory's site at Crescent Wharf, was devastated. Two of its vast oil tanks were torn open and were ablaze. Several streets packed with small houses were flattened, the fire station was reduced to a heap of rubble and the St Barnabas Church and Hall as well as the nearby Girls' and Infants' schools were little more than ruins. A gas holder on the Greenwich peninsula—across the river—was destroyed, shooting its eight million cubic feet of lighting gas into the night sky in one furious and spectacular fireball. A boiler weighing fifteen tons was tossed a quarter of a mile before landing in the middle of North Woolwich Road. The Port of London Authority estimated some seventeen acres of warehouses and other buildings in the docks were destroyed or seriously damaged. The customs barrier was breached and goods worth thousands of pounds were left exposed and at risk. Silvertown, with its oil refineries, warehouses, flour mills, chemical and paintworks was an industrial tinder box. Fires quickly began to blaze out of control, and high winds rocketed flaming debris into the air on a capricious course to set more buildings alight. Two flour mills began to burn, and soon fueled a furnace that proved one of the toughest blazes to control.

The shock was not confined to Silvertown. Almost everyone in London must have been aware that something of catastrophic proportions had occurred. Across the capital around seventy thousand homes were damaged in some way, most suffering shattered windows. Electricity lines to Silvertown were cut, and except for the glare of the fires the district was in darkness. One of the main water pipes was blasted, leaving the area with half its normal supplies at a time when millions of gallons were needed to quench the fires. The blast was heard as far distant as Norfolk and Cambridge, and the glow of the blaze was clearly visible for at least twenty-five miles. All communication lines had been destroyed, and contact with outside districts was not restored for thirty minutes. During that terrifying half-hour the people of Silvertown recovered from the initial shock to find themselves engulfed in a fiery nightmare where many lost their homes, livelihoods and loved ones. At least the very scale of the disaster acted as a beacon to alert emergency services and summons desperately needed aid to the East End. The *Stratford Express* reported:

> It seemed as if some vast volcanic eruption had burst out in the locality in question. The whole heavens were lit in awful splendour. A fiery glow seemed to have come over the dark and miserable January evening, and objects which a few minutes before had been blotted out in the intense darkness were silhouetted against the sky. The awful illumination lasted only a few seconds. Gradually it died away, but down by the river roared a huge column of flame which told thousands that the explosion had been followed by fire and havoc, the like of which has never been known in these parts.

Considering the scale of the damage—the explosion remains the largest ever recorded in London—it is surprising the casualty list was relatively low. Sixty-nine people died instantly and four more later succumbed in hospital. Another ninety-eight people were seriously injured and more than nine hundred suffered minor injuries, many being tended at first aid stations set up at the scene.

All workers in the munitions plant at the time of the explosion died immediately. The fire-fighters working next to their engines stood little chance. Sub-officer Henry Vickers and Fireman Frederick Sell were killed instantly. Fireman Henry Chapple was seriously injured, Fireman James Yabsley suffered a fractured skull and Fireman James Betts suffered a fractured shoulder blade and other injuries.

Duty fireman Thomas Betts had just telephoned to the West Ham headquarters to ask for extra help when the explosion happened. He was buried in rubble as the station collapsed, but was rescued by men from the Royal Army Medical Corps and escaped with a head injury. The station's living quarters were badly affected and here the victims were less fortunate than Thomas Betts. Fire-fighter Sell's daughter Winifred,

15, Mary Ann Betts, 58 and little Ethel Betts, aged just four months, were all killed. Other family members survived, but most had serious injuries.

A train was passing as the plant exploded, and engine driver George Galloway, 43, was critically injured with multiple fractures of his legs. He died later at the London Hospital. Police constable Edward Green-off's regular beat took him outside Brunner Mond shortly before the disaster. He must have seen the fire, and been well aware of the possible consequences. He stayed to clear as many people from the area as possible, and paid with his life. James Bruce, 62, the Brunner Mond night-watchman, initially decided to run for his life when he saw the fire. He thought better of it, returned to hold the gate for the firemen and other workmen, and was killed.

Many children had been in their beds, and stood little chance of escape as homes collapsed and lethal debris cascaded from the skies. One man lost his wife and four children, all aged between 10 and 13 years old. Another family was devastated by the loss of four youngsters, aged between 2 and 9 years. One mother rushed into the street clutching her baby tightly in her arms until she dropped with exhaustion. On-lookers gently lifted the precious bundle. The child was dead from suffocation.

The *Women's Dreadnought* reported the horrific tale of a young factory girl on 27 January:

> We saw the fire, and went out to look at it. Someone said, 'You'd better run, it'll burst soon!' So we walked away. Then we heard a roar, and we ran; there was a crash and something hit me on the chest. I looked down, and it was a man's head. I couldn't run any further then.

Such harrowing tales were legion. Another young woman rushed from her home with her baby in arms, and met the full force of the explosion as she stepped into the street. The blast wrenched the child from her arms, throwing it backwards and into the rubble of the collapsing house. Late that night rescue workers found the woman sprawled prostrate on top of the debris. She had torn at the rubble to find her baby, breaking four fingers in the process. She had eventually reached down and touched the precious child, and realised it was dead. Her husband had also been in the house. His body was not recovered until Sunday. One worker returned home safely from his factory only to find the body of his 20-year-old daughter lying outside his house. His 23-year-old daughter had also perished. A mill hand identified the

32   Another view of the blast damage. Courtesy Museum in Docklands Project.

33   Soldiers called in to deal with the aftermath. Courtesy Museum in Docklands Project.

battered corpses of his young wife and the couple's two children.

In a hall adjoining the St Barnabas Church a group of between sixty and seventy children were enjoying a Band of Hope treat. Tea had just finished, and the youngsters were about to start their games. Elementary teacher Norah Griffiths stepped outside to go to the parsonage and noticed a flare in the sky. She quickly ran back to the hall and told the vicar, the Reverend Walter Farley, who quickly assessed the situation before telling everyone to "keep cool." They had little time to do anything else before the explosion threw everyone to the ground. The hall was a simple construction of corrugated iron, lined with match boarding, and offered little defence to the blast from a fifty-four-ton bomb. The sides of the building bulged outward. The glare from the fires cast an eerie glow on the scene. Norah realised the roof was about to cave in. She quickly moved to support it on her shoulders to give the children time to escape. Sister Evans, Mrs Burford, Mrs White and Mrs Nobbs joined her and twenty minutes later all the youngsters had been led to safety.

St Barnabas Church and the parsonage were also badly damaged, but that didn't stop the Reverend Farley and his helpers moving quickly to help in the rescue work. The parsonage kitchen was the least affected and most easily accessible room, and was quickly transformed into a first aid point. Bedding and rugs were laid out on the floor and the kitchen became a dressing station and collection point for injured people needing hospital treatment.

As the dazed people of Silvertown recovered their senses and began the desperate rescue work, aid was being hurried into the area. Fire engines from West Ham arrived after about thirty minutes and they were soon reinforced by the Metropolitan Fire Brigade. Fireboats were also at the scene, fighting to control the inferno already raging in the docks and warehouses. Ambulances were a little slower to arrive. During the first hour the injured were rushed to hospital in anything and everything from wheelbarrows and carts to lorries and private cars. Locals commandeered taxi-cabs, throwing out stunned passengers to make space for critically injured survivors. Boats on the Thames were used to ferry more casualties to hospitals across the river. The eventual arrival of a fleet of thirty or more ambulances must have saved many from a tortuous journey.

Special police and soldiers were drafted in, supplemented by voluntary workers, doctors and nurses from across London. First aid posts were set up throughout the district. Doctors, nurses and skilled staff from organisations such as the St John Ambulance Brigade and Salvation Army treated hundreds of victims on the spot, averting the danger of hospitals being overwhelmed by an avalanche of people with minor injuries. Casualties in obvious need of hospital treatment were tended until an ambulance or other transport was available to take them. The Salvation Army, the YMCA and the Invalid Kitchens of London group quickly set up refreshment facilities for the survivors and emergency workers.

The Albert Dock Seamen's Hospital was on the "front line" and reported dealing with more than two hundred patients during the night. Poplar Hospital took more than a hundred casualties, despite having only a hundred beds. Other hospitals on both sides of the river also took a share of casualties. Doctors, nurses and officials used every inch of available space, placing beds in corridors and even basements where necessary. The blast of the explosion rocked the London Hospital at Whitechapel. Staff felt the building shake and 231 windows were shattered. Its role in the calamity is recorded in the log kept by the House Governor, Mr E. W. Morris:

> 6:50 PM—Loud explosion heard. Rather like loud clap of thunder overhead...immediately followed by people running and calling, and falling of breaking glass.... Poplar Hospital rang up. We are dealing with over 100—would send rest to us.... Police station rang up; short of doctors; could we send any? Got five men and three lady doctors; cab of dressings; instruments; morphia; chloroform, etc. One cabman refused to go; abusive; was not going for anybody. Porter took his number.

The hospital prepared to take up to three hundred patients. Beds were brought from the stores and staff made them up. Wards and corridors were packed. Morris continued:

> Injured people soon came up in motor-lorries, butchers' carts—all sorts of vehicles. Treated about 60 then a lull. Some very bad cases and four died during the night. Injuries very terrible, brought up on doors, shutters etc.... One child of eight with baby in arms, and leading child of four. Couldn't find mother. Kindly driver had picked them up in destroyed street.... Little dog came up with one fearfully injured woman. It wouldn't leave her. We let it go into the ward with her.... The taxis returned. 'Could do nothing. Never saw such a night. A square mile burning. Houses by the hundred a mass of bricks. Must be hundreds buried. Heat fearful. Could only get

near by tying shawls round head. No good waiting.' All very upset at sight.

Morris noted it was difficult to get the names of the injured—many were too ill to speak. The fact it was Friday, pay day, helped identification because many had pay tickets in their pockets.

By midnight the bulk of the casualties had been rescued. Work continued throughout the night and by daylight more than thirty bodies had been recovered and placed in temporary mortuaries set up in nearby schools and halls. Hundreds of people were left destitute. In a few moments their homes and belongings were obliterated and they were left with the clothes they stood in. It was a bitterly cold night and there was an urgent need to arrange temporary accommodation.

One factor was in Silvertown's favour. The district was, at the best of times, one of the most deprived in London. Everyday life for most of its people meant a hard and exhausting struggle for survival. But the scale of poverty and the poor quality of life had attracted voluntary workers who had established "settlements," the framework of a community care system that was of inestimable help in the days following the explosion. These settlements, usually run by highly able individuals, were already in place and were rapidly adapted to deal with the catastrophe. The Canning Town Women's Settlement at Lee's Hall, in Barking Road, Plaistow, immediately opened its doors to provide temporary accommodation. Other institutes also offered sleeping space, blankets and food. Local residents lucky enough to have a home in one piece took in friends and strangers from the streets.

Munitions Minister Christopher Addison was working late at his office in Whitehall on 19 January, and heard the blast of the explosion in Silvertown. Like many others, he presumed it was a heavy zeppelin raid. It wasn't until ninety minutes later that he was informed that the tiny munitions works in East London had blown up. He immediately sent his assistant, Keith Price, to investigate. At 11:40 PM he issued a terse statement from the Press Bureau.

> The Ministry of Munitions regrets to announce that an explosion occurred this evening at a munitions factory in the neighbourhood of London. It is feared that the explosion was attended by considerable loss of life and damage to property.

34 *Some of the hundreds of houses damaged by the blast. Courtesy Newham Library Service.*

35 *A first-aid post. Courtesy Newham Library Service.*

Rumours ran riot across London. Thousands had been killed, several square miles had been razed to the ground, it was all the work of a German spy.... Next morning thousands flocked to Silvertown to get a close look at the drama. Some enterprising locals were quick to see the opportunity of "making a few bob." Many with homes overlooking the scene charged the well-to-do visitors a fee for the privilege of passing through their homes to have a good look from their backyards. A cricket ground also offered a good vantage point, and groundsmen happily collected an entrance fee of a few pence.

The appearance of vast numbers of police and soldiers with fixed bayonets to seal off the district did little to quieten speculation. Such precautions were clearly essential as many families had fled leaving what little property they owned in the debris of their homes. Shops and offices had been abandoned and the possibility of widespread looting could not be overlooked. Fires were still burning furiously, bodies and survivors were still being recovered and an influx of several thousand of even the most well-intentioned tourists would have severely hampered the emergency work. Newspaper reporters were given permits to allow them into the district, and people who lived in Silvertown were also escorted through the cordon to salvage what belongings they could. The Ministry of Munitions supplied trucks to carry salvaged furniture to temporary stores. Storage facilities were provided by the council's stables department, the Salvation Army, Church Army and many local firms.

Saturday also saw the inevitable stream of visits by "dignitaries." Prime Minister Lloyd George and Munitions Minister Christopher Addison arrived to offer their sympathy and show concern. Later the King and Queen made an unannounced visit and were taken on a quick tour of the battered dockyards. Early on Saturday morning the Mayor of West Ham called the first meeting of the Explosion Emergency Committee that was to work so hard in the days and weeks to follow. The committee met at Lee's Hall, and comprised of councillors, church and settlement workers. The first priority was to establish temporary accommodation centres and to ensure adequate supplies of food, medical aid, bedding and clothes. By Saturday night, shelter had been provided for more than six hundred people, at centres in The Baptist Tabernacle, Barking Road; the Canning Town Congregational Church; Fairbairn Hall Boys' Club (Mansfield House); the Seamen's Mission; St Matthew's Church and St Margaret's Church. As the hours passed it became clear more accommodation was needed, and more centres were established in other churches and halls in the district. Blankets and bedding were provided by the local poor law authorities, the West Ham Guardians and the Whitechapel and Poplar Guardians; and by the Red Cross.

The 1st Battalion of the Essex Volunteer Regiment did sterling work at the relief centres. It set up a "piquet" night service, from 8:00 PM to 7:00 AM, at all centres. The Battalion's role included distributing blankets, running an ambulance station, calling for doctors when necessary, distributing food for breakfasts and, on the request of the police, searching for relatives to visit patients at Poplar Hospital.

The Emergency Committee established an Information Bureau at Lees Hall. This kept details of those who had died and where their bodies had been taken, patient lists from the different hospitals and the whereabouts of other survivors. Within the first week two thousand people had registered. The service helped reunite many families that had parted in the chaos of the disaster. The Bureau answered letters from all over the country, giving information to friends and relatives of those affected. The Emergency Committee also set up a first aid centre at Lees Hall, which remained staffed by nurses and doctors for several weeks. Recommendations were drawn up for how the aftermath of the disaster should be handled: as far as possible the homeless should be found accommodation within the borough; families should not be separated unless absolutely essential; any attempt to put people in the workhouse would be strongly resented; every effort should be made to help people salvage their furniture and take it to their new quarters; and the scale of relief offered should be generous. These recommendations formed the blueprint for disaster management in Silvertown.

West Ham Council held an emergency meeting on Monday, 22 January. A letter was read stating that the Prime Minister David Lloyd George and Addison had asked the Local Government Board, in co-operation with the Council, to provide temporary assistance to sufferers and to supervise the use of funds made available. A £500 grant from the National Disaster Fund was given immediately. The letter suggested the Council should form a special committee to take responsibility for administration of funds allowed from the Board, and the Silvertown Explosion Committee was elected under the chairmanship of the Mayor. In an effort to ensure good communication, it co-opted three members of the Emergency Committee set up at Lees Hall.

There were three main problems facing the committee. They needed a system to ensure immediate relief was available to all in need; the homeless people needed to be found accommodation until their homes were repaired; and they had to find a way of dealing with the hundreds of children unable to attend school. Around eighteen schools were temporarily closed because of the explosion. The children may have welcomed their unexpected holidays, but Silvertown was like a bombsite, and certainly not the ideal playground for hordes of unoccupied and homeless youngsters.

The government eventually paid out some £3,000,000 in compensation, a figure worth £40,000,000 or more today. The new committee at once approved guidelines for relief payments. Funeral grants of up to £9 were agreed, and sums of up to £10, or in some cases £20, were to be given to help people replace essential furniture destroyed in the explosion. A scale of payments was agreed to those unable to work, either through injury in the explosion or because their workplaces had been destroyed. Amounts received depended on the number of children. A family with seven youngsters was entitled to £2.3s.6d per week, a single adult would get just sixteen shillings. Children aged 16 years or over were treated as adults. Anyone unemployed but capable of work was obliged to register with the Labour Exchange, and those claiming illness had to produce medical evidence stating the sickness was genuine and resulted from the explosion.

A week after the explosion a relief office was set up at the Public Hall in Canning Town and remained open daily for ten days, and then on a part-time basis. This office had the sole purpose of alleviating immediate distress—making payments to those unable to work because of the explosion and giving grants to deal with essential needs. Claims for damages for loss of property or personal effects were dealt with at the Public Library in North Street, Plaistow. Claims to the office were investigated by two council officials, chief of which was one Eric Weddell, who must have become a very familiar face around the streets of Silvertown during the months that followed. As far as was possible, he checked claims to ensure they were genuine. Local firms put temporarily out of business by the explosion were asked to supply lists of employees and to state when they were last paid. Applications to the Public Hall for help ranged from the desperate to the ridiculous, and were dealt with quickly, efficiently and kindly by a staff that included several teachers from schools closed because of explosion damage.

Inevitably, some people found themselves outside the safety net of social care. John Maskell's claim was despairing:

> Sir, allow me to bring before your notice a section of the community called outdoor paupers (like myself) too old and infirm for work but too young for the old age pension, are cruel victims of this catastrophe. Here I am the father of six sons at war on active service, one has given his sight (or nearly so), right eye extracted, left damaged. The youngest is missing others are married (no claim), receiving 8d per week extra for coals during the winter my windows are out upstairs windows all out. The house is very like a refrigerator.... May I add if I were an interned German or convict it would cost my country 25/– per week, because I am a law abiding citizen I have to exist on 6d per day from my blind son and 5/– Guardians, total 8/6d. My rent 2/6d room. My age is 62, one leg and deaf.

Mr G. Fowke of Coolfin Road, Custom House, bemoaned the loss of his cat meat trade:

> I beg to place before you a very great hardship I am now suffering from as a result of the recent explosion. For the past 26 years I have had a cats' meat round extending from Tidal Basin to Silvertown and I gave £100 for the business. As a result of the devastation more than half my living has been wiped out. I have a family of five children all dependent on my business....

Perhaps one of the most bizarre problems faced by staff was the arrival of a cat, along with a note:

> If you please I have sent this cat to you, ask you if you would be kind enough to take it for me. It has had a stroke and I have moved from Emma Street, Silvertown and am in rooms upstairs. The cat cannot get up and down to the back. It is not healthy to have a cat like this upstairs....

Illness which prevented work and entitled an individual to relief had to be attributable to the explosion. Refusing a claim from one young lady, Weddell commented: "...the girl was weak before the explosion, she is a very poor subject...."

Finding an answer to the major housing shortage was the second headache for the council. It appointed a sub-committee to scour the district for suitable accommodation. The scale of the problem was staggering—889 people had been housed in the emergency centre during the first eighteen days after the explosion. Hundreds of houses were uninhabitable and it was obvious the repair and rebuilding work would take some time. Many of the impoverished but generous people of Silvertown took families, friends and strangers into their often already overcrowded homes. The council took over the living accommodation of local shops that had been closed, found other rooms and apartments, and took fifty-three empty houses at Prince Regents Lane, Plaistow, on loan from the Port of London Authority. These homes had been designated to house those displaced by the construction of the King George V Dock, but work had been delayed and fortunately they were still empty.

Meanwhile the government's Office of Works had begun patching up the now derelict Silvertown. Surveyors' reports show twenty-four houses were flattened; another fifty-nine had to be demolished and rebuilt; 765 were severely damaged and needed completely new interiors; and another forty-six homes were slightly damaged. All houses needed to be replastered and decorated and most needed new roofs or extensive reslating, new joinery and considerable joinery repairs. The government was not obliged to take on this work, but felt it would be both expedient and cost-effective to do so. Reconstruction could have taken much longer had individual landlords been left to do the job themselves and the government would have had far less budgetary control. The Office of Works could work on a large scale, negotiate favourable contracts and complete the job at a lower unit cost than would otherwise be possible. The Office also took on the task of rebuilding all council-owned property that had suffered damage. The council received weekly progress reports. By 12 February there were 1,736 men employed on the work. Of the nine hundred damaged roofs, 850 had been replaced or repaired and 450 homes had been made fully weatherproof.

In early March the first families moved back in. There were hiccups in the reconstruction programme. Some families refused to leave their battered homes and some workmen complained they could not do their jobs in homes that hadn't been vacated. At one point painters went on strike, but this was quickly resolved. As time went by workmen, knowing their jobs would soon be coming to an end, left the site and the depleted labour force led to some delays. By August, however, the work was completed and most people had returned to their homes. Critics have argued the explosion offered the ideal opportunity to transform the slum that was Silvertown into a desirable estate. As it was, the government simply rebuilt the existing cramped, poorly designed and substandard accommodation.

Yet there is no doubt the properties were improved, and many unscrupulous landlords were loathe to welcome back their tenants. The refurbished homes, they believed, warranted a better class of tenant—and higher rents. One landlord wrote to the council: "Some of the old tenants were very undesirable, being dirty and objectionable in every way." West Ham's Town Clerk, Hilleary, wrote to all such landlords making it absolutely clear that the original tenants had legal rights to the property until the tenancy had been "determined in the proper legal manner."

The care and education of children was a third major area of concern. The explosion had displaced 18,500 youngsters from their schools. In Silvertown itself the West Silvertown School was virtually demolished. A further eighteen schools in the district were closed until further notice and many more had minor damage that kept them closed for a few days. The problem was solved by switching available schools to a shift system. Half the children would attend in the mornings, the rest in the afternoons. The council ordered that no child should be refused admittance to any school.

Many children had suffered injuries in the explosion, and others were traumatised by the ordeal. Their battlescape home in Silvertown was clearly not an ideal environment, and many were sent to convalescent homes to give them a chance to recuperate away from the chaos. The London Hospital suggested the use of Parkwood, a convalescent home in Swanley, Kent, that had been closed because of insufficient nursing staff. Parkwood was designed to cater for 120 adults from several London hospitals and stood in seventy acres of wooded grounds. The home's generous trustees offered use of the property rent- and rates-free for a period of three months. They also promised the free services of a matron, assistant matron, nursing sister and medical officer. West Ham Mayor Alderman Mansfield and Education Committee Chairman Alderman Enos Smith quickly checked that money to finance the project would be available from the Local Government Board and from unsolicited donations trickling in the council. As soon as it was clear that sufficient funds were at hand, an agreement was signed and the first exodus of Silvertown children to Kent began. Parkwood could take up to three hundred children, and it was decided to send pupils from the devastated West Silvertown School. West Silvertown School headmistress, Miss Emmeline Williams, and nine or ten of her teaching and domestic staff agreed to accompany the children at Parkwood. Personal visits were made to all parents who could be traced, and most agreed to allow their youngsters to take part. The first batch of a hundred children left the Public Hall, Canning Town on 1 March. Two days later they were joined by another 150.

Teething problems started almost immediately. On 5 March a girl and two boys, obviously ill at ease in their new surroundings, attempted to escape. The girl was sent home. We don't know what she had to say when she arrived there, but many of the Silvertown children were suffering homesickness and sent letters to their parents begging to return. Parents, already under great stress and probably upset by sad tidings from their absent offspring, soon had another worry to cope with. Despite medical checks by West Ham Medical Officer Dr Saunders and his colleague Dr Skerrett, a group of children at Swanley promptly developed measles. Measles was regarded far more seriously than it is today. The disease was feared by parents and was well-known as a potential killer. The first case appeared on 5 March. Nine children were nursed in an isolation ward opened at Parkwood, and another thirteen were sent to the Isolation Hospital at Dartford and to the West Ham Fever Hospital.

For at least one group of concerned parents the strain was too much, and a Sunday visiting session on 10 March degenerated into near riot. Ten sets of parents, apparently led by the families Rogers and Letson, insisted on taking their children home with them, not before giving the hapless matron a piece of their undoubtedly irate minds. By 13 March, seventy-eight youngsters had been reclaimed.

Miss Ware, Inspectress of the West Ham Education Department, was furious, and a permit system to control visiting was immediately installed. Parents would only be allowed to see their children on one Sunday per month and access required production of a permit issued by West Ham's Education Department. Any child removed from Parkwood was not allowed to return, or to be admitted to any of the smaller convalescent homes. However, she quickly recovered from her initial anger at the parents' behaviour. On 16 March she wrote to the Town Clerk:

> Some difficulty with parents was inevitable when something they were not accustomed to was being tried. The children were unused to their surroundings and were strange and depressed at first. Their letters no doubt were not very cheerful, but they have settled down quite happily now...

Parkwood remained open until 26 July and dealt with a total of 387 Silvertown children. Local volunteers were enlisted to help with nightly baths for every child, form sewing parties to make and repair the children's clothes, and to stand nightwatch in case of zeppelin bombing raids. Regular school hours were maintained, but whenever possible lessons were held in the open air. The children were encouraged to make the best use of the acres of open space and woodlands, and staff noticed many spent hours constructing "houses" with twigs and branches. Most of these twig palaces, unlike their homes in Silvertown, would feature a bathroom. Many toys, books and games were donated to keep the children entertained. There were so many gifts that the headmistress Miss Williams decided to take some back to Silvertown for distribution at a later date. Just before the project came to an end in July 1917, members of the Silvertown Explosion Committee paid a visit. Their official report commented:

> The Committee...could not help being struck by the wonderful improve-ment in the physique and well-being of the children in general and this was due to the kindly and sympathetic treatment they received...and the splendid regime under which they lived.

Accounts show the Parkwood exercise cost just £2,272.19s.8d. government grants of £2,000 covered the bulk and parental contributions made up most of the deficit. The innovative and successful project was forerunner to the mass evacuations of children from cities during World War II.

Although the government response to individual claims was generous, they were less keen to acknowledge compensation claims from the council. West Ham Council made a claim against the government for compensation to cover loss of rate revenue. Residents in the borough paid the highest rates in the country at the time, and the loss of income from homes and factories destroyed or damaged in the explosion was estimated at £16,500. The government refused to pay up, stating it was sympathetic but that the line had to be drawn somewhere. Ministers insisted the loss was too remote from the initial explosion to be entertained. Claims for loss of electricity revenue, for compensation for school repair work carried out by council staff, and for the salaries of teachers employed when their schools were closed were agreed. The Corporation Electricity Works received £1,544 from a claim for £6,000 and the Education Committee was eventually granted £3,242.0s.5d.

The Silvertown explosion remains the biggest ever recorded in London. It devastated the lives of the people living in the district. Several families were wiped out; scores more decimated. More than seventy people died and a thousand others were injured. Yet despite the scale of this tragedy, it is little known outside East London.

Perhaps the reason is that the government deliberately and methodically played down the incident and its effects. The first press reports on the disaster appeared in Saturday's papers and were brief to the point of being nondescript: "...it is feared that the explosion was attended by considerable loss of life and damage to property." The next day was a Sunday, and the headlines in the *Sunday Times* were almost celebratory: "Losses Not So Heavy As Feared." The official government statement concentrated on the "fortunate" aspects of the incident. The initial fire, it said, gave people the chance to escape. Although a fire engine had been destroyed "only two" firemen had been killed. And while the final death toll was uncertain casualties were "not nearly as heavy as was at first anticipated." The statement contained a damning line: "We are further informed by the Ministry of Munitions that the accident will make no practical difference to the output of munitions." The officials who had argued the desperate needs of the war made it absolutely essential to site a TNT plant in the middle of a densely-populated district, were now stating the annihilation of the factory would make "no practical difference" to the war effort. This point was never picked up by the press. Without exception, the national papers followed the line that the effects of the explosion were less severe than they could have been, that everyone had done a tremendous job and should be thoroughly proud of themselves.

The government wanted to ensure munitions workers were not deterred by the fact some of their peers had been blown to pieces. A *Daily Mirror* headline on Tuesday, 23 January announced: "Searching Investigation Into Great Explosion. No Need For Alarm, Says Munitions Minister." The story briefly reported the government's decision to set up an official inquiry into the Silvertown disaster and reported at length an announcement from Addison that would "be received by the public with feelings of relief and satisfaction." The minister, speaking at a dinner at Mansion House the previous evening, emphasised there was no need for alarm.

I have been astounded as I have seen men many times in these factories handling, without the least fear, even with impunity, the shells that are made therein. The fact is that, apart from the risk of a fire starting in some way, many of these big shells are no more dangerous to handle than so much sand or other similar material.

A story in the next column continued the report on Addison's speech, telling how an extra thirty-four thousand women were needed for munitions work. The Lord Mayor remarked the explosion had brought the excellent work of munitions women to the public eye, and Lord Sydenham commented the victory at the Battle of the Somme was due largely to the work of the "girls at home."

Sir Ernley Blackwell chaired an official inquiry into the explosion. The team made its report on 24 February, but Addison decided it should be kept secret. In 1957 the document became accessible under the "forty-year" rule, but by that time it had disappeared. It was not until 1974 that Newham Librarian Frank Sainsbury located the seventeen-page report at the Public Records Office.

For anyone hoping for an answer to the mystery of exactly what caused the Silvertown explosion the report is a big disappointment. Sir Ernley and fellow investigators Major A. McNeil Cooper-Key and Colonel Sir Frederick Nathan interviewed thirty-six witnesses but could form no conclusive opinion on what caused the disaster. The inquiry looked at the possible explanations; a fire could have started accidentally, or through a malicious act.

The malicious act, or spy, theory was quickly discounted by the committee, although it certainly could not be ruled out. The committee heard there were no "aliens" employed at the TNT plant, and although a German was employed at Brunner Mond's soda crystal plant next door he was a trusted man of good character, who had been in Britain for forty-seven years and had three sons serving in the army. It would have been easy for anyone to blow up the plant. Molten TNT decomposes on contact with strong alkalis, even at relatively low temperatures. All a malevolent individual need do to cause a certain explosion would be to thrust a stick of caustic soda into a bag of crude TNT. When the bag was emptied into the melt pot and heated it would burst into flames and trigger the blast. Caustic soda could be purchased at any ironmonger's store.

The crude TNT destined for Silvertown came from Huddersfield and was transported on open lorries, barges and railway trucks. The journey could take several days and delays were common. Bags were frequently torn and barrels were often without their lids. Tampering with them would have required rather less than the cunning genius of Moriarty and would have been well within the capabilities of the most inexperienced German agent. A thin coating of shellac, varnish or tissue paper would have ensured the desired ignition did not take place until the TNT was in the melt pot. The report comments: "It is obvious that the enemy would be attracted by the project of blowing up a TNT factory situated in a populous part of East London." While the nation's press and government spokesmen were proclaiming there was nothing to substantiate the widespread rumours that enemy sabotage had caused the explosion, the inquiry was revealing how ludicrously simple such acts would have been. If German spies did not cause the disaster it was not because they lacked opportunity.

An accidental fire seemed another strong possibility. It could have been ignited by a carelessly discarded match or by a spark caused by friction. The inquiry discovered that on 29 December 1916, just weeks before the explosion, the Brunner Mond plant had been visited by a government inspector, and had not exactly passed with flying colours. "It is perfectly clear," the report states, "the management at Silvertown did not pay sufficient attention to the explosion risk attached to the handling of TNT." The inspector found precautions against friction sparks—caused by metals or other hard substances—were non-existent. Prompt steps were apparently taken to remedy the situation and, according to evidence, iron tools had been swapped for brass replacements just the night before the explosion. The inquiry decided it was highly unlikely the fire could have been started with a match—none of the staff smoked.

Another potential cause of fire could, again, not be ruled out. TNT could have ignited spontaneously, either because the oily waste had become overheated or because of the presence of impurities. The plant had previously been used to manufacture caustic soda and it was quite possible traces remained on the premises. Such traces could well have caused a deadly reaction. It was impossible for the inquiry team to reach firm conclusions on the cause of the explosion because there were simply too many options, and very few could be ruled out. The inquiry was, however, damning in its criticism of the Silvertown plant. A similar explosion had occurred at a TNT purification plant at Ardeer, Scotland, in 1915. An inquiry after the incident recommended TNT should no longer be exempted from the Explosives Act, and in the meantime special steps should be taken to improve conditions of manufacture and storage. The recommendations included manufacture should take place under danger building conditions, that the bulk of TNT not actually in process should be stored in magazines and that a maximum, stipulated, amount of TNT should be allowed on the premises at any one time. Sir Ernley noted these recommendations had been totally disregarded when the Silvertown plant was set up. The man who supervised the conversion work had never seen a copy of the Ardeer report.

There is little doubt that, had the Ardeer recommendations been taken into account, Silvertown would never have been considered a suitable location for TNT purification. The Crescent Wharf site afforded barely enough room for the plant, let alone the space needed for danger buildings and storage magazines. As the inquiry noted when describing the site of the plant:

> The situation of the works in fact was, from the point of view of explosives manufacture, extremely bad, and in normal times it is certain that no such work would have been undertaken on these premises.

Examining the report leaves the reader with the firm impression the inquiry team felt, wartime or not, Silvertown was a totally unsuitable home for a TNT plant. In addition, it was clear that sabotage of any plant would be simple and that all munitions factory workers were at real risk. Despite Addison's frequent proclamations, it was also apparent that authorities failed to take all possible safety precautions to ensure the safe production of TNT. It is hardly surprising the government decided the report should not be published.

Recommendations made by Sir Ernley and his colleagues were, at least to some extent, taken up. These included that all operations entailing the presence of unmixed TNT must be under danger building conditions; more care to be taken with the packaging and transport of TNT; the bulk of TNT not actually in process to be stored in properly protected magazines; ensuring only the minimum amount of the explosives was kept in a plant at any one time; and the forming of an independent inspectorate at the Ministry of Munitions, to be responsible for safety and maintaining output from Government TNT factories and magazines. This last recommendation was rejected.

Silvertown was not the only plant to suffer an explosion of TNT. Fewer than five months later, on 12 June 1917, the Hooley Hill works at Ashton-under-Lyme were devastated with the loss of more than forty munitions workers. In February 1918 the Government TNT purification plant at Rainham, Essex, with a production rate of some sixty tons per day, was destroyed. But Silvertown stands out as the most destructive and damaging of the explosions. It owes that dubious honour to its location. The other explosions were in country areas where damage was at least limited to the factories. The Brunner Mond plant was at the heart of a tightly packed industrial community and the damage could not possibly be contained.

Locating a TNT factory in Silvertown was a massive and inexcusable error of judgement. Had the explosion occurred at any other time the repercussions would surely have been enormous. But this was wartime, and war waged on an unprecedented scale, evidenced by the zeppelin raids and by the deaths of several million young men. The death toll and suffering in Silvertown were overshadowed by the larger tragedy taking place on the front line. Indeed, when the *Times* of 20 January carried its daily "Roll of Honour" listing the latest war dead there were a staggering twenty-four hundred names, which put Silvertown's death toll into perspective. The bitterness and horror of the war had cast a certain numbness on the British public. Every day brought news of more death and most families suffered personal loss and bereavement. The deaths in Silvertown, a remote working class slum, were insignificant in comparison.

The Establishment message was simple. The people of Silvertown were deemed expendable. The explosion was more notable as a tribute to the excellence of the war effort than as a tragedy that brought destruction and despair to a working-class neighbourhood. Criticism, even questioning, was viewed inappropriate and singularly unpatriotic. Silvertown had done its bit. No more, no less.

CHAPTER EIGHT

Railway Accidents

The Victorian railway system was a tribute to private enterprise. In the early days of the nineteenth century this concept of a new transport system seemed an unlikely candidate for success and the government displayed little interest in its development. The first track for public hire opened between Croydon and Wandsworth in 1801, and consisted of trucks pulled along by horses. It was an inauspicious start, but was soon followed by numerous private companies opening lines in different parts of the country. By 1840 the impact and importance of railways had become clear. Journeys that had taken days could be completed within hours; goods could be dispatched easily and efficiently to far off destinations; market garden produce could be sent to the opposite end of the country with confidence it would arrive fresh and edible; letters could be posted and reach distant addresses by the next day. The English way of life would never be the same again.

The entrepreneurial zeal that took just a few decades to forge Britain's railway revolution had little time for the niceties of public safety. The pace of development was intense, with caution an early casualty. The first locomotives did not come into action until 1825, but just forty-five years later the country was served by a comprehensive rail network utilising some 13,500 miles of track. Engines thundered along at speeds up to eighty miles per hour, without benefit of effective braking or signalling systems, and with calamitous consequences. Timetables were scarcely worth the paper they were written on and frequent but unscheduled "excursion" trains added to the general anarchy. During the four years 1872–1875, some of the bleakest in railway history, accidents on the system killed 5,231 people and injured another 16,944.

The very nature of the railway system caused most of its problems. It was built at speed, by private companies whose prime motive was to run a highly profitable business. Trains were lightly constructed and carriages were liable to be crushed like matchwood at the slightest impact. Third class passengers were usually consigned to compartments with the comforts of a cattle truck, with planks as seats, low sides, no roof and little or no protection from the elements. Any jolt was likely to hurtle the unsuspecting occupants to their deaths. Railway employees were paid a pittance and expected to work at tasks that demanded high concentration for up to fifteen or more hours a day. Passengers were another major source of problems. In the early days many seemed loath to give trains the respect they demanded. Used to stage-coaches, they would insist on travelling on the roofs, often to be smashed to eternity on low bridges. Others thought nothing of leaping out of a carriage in full flight, or attempting to jump in through an open window as a train left the platform. Scenes on railway platforms often became dangerously close to riot, and crowd control was non-existent. Masses of people waiting for a train to take them home would fight each other and cling to any part of the train they could grab in their determination for a return trip.

Railways were highly profitable and the government felt compelled to extend its control and influence. However, the network was so vast that the task of enforcing new procedures was daunting, and only possible over an extended period. The first steps towards regulation came in 1840 and 1842, when Acts of Parliament were passed to establish a railway inspectorate within the Board of Trade. The newly-appointed inspectors, recruited from the Corps of the Royal Engineers, were charged to inspect and report on public lines. No new line was to be opened without their approval, and they were given authority to investigate causes of accidents. In 1844 a Bill was passed giving the government the right to revise all tolls, fares and charges of any railway company whose dividends exceeded 10%. Each railway company was obliged to run at least one train per day that stopped at every station, and carried third class passengers at a rate not exceeding a penny per mile. The Treasury also reserved the right to purchase any railway opened after 1844, although this option was not taken up during the nineteenth century.

The looming prospect of government interference did not deter the railway magnates. By 1855, £300 million of private money had been invested in the system. New routes were established by privately sponsored Acts of Parliament, and by 1867 1,800 Acts had been passed, as well as 1,300 amending Acts. The wheel of progress was difficult to hold back, but the fledgling railway inspectorate and an increasingly anxious public were determined safety must be improved. Even Queen Victoria was alarmed. In December 1864 she instructed Sir Charles Phipps to write to leading railway companies imploring them to take more care with their passengers. "It is not for her own safety that the Queen has wished to provide in thus calling the attention of the company to the late disasters," wrote Sir Charles in his letter of 27 December.

Her Majesty is aware that when she travels extraordinary precautions are taken, but it is on account of her family, of those travelling upon her service, and of her people generally, that she expresses the hope that the same security may be insured for all as is so carefully provided for herself...

Railway workers often took the blame for accidents, and frequently faced charges of manslaughter following major incidents. This suited their employers, who would much rather point the finger of blame at some underpaid and overworked underling than shoulder responsibility themselves. The real fault, the key to the vast majority of accidents, lay in poor managerial organisation and equipment. London escaped the most catastrophic railway tragedies that littered the era, but still saw a number of tragic and preventable accidents with heavy death and injury tolls. A look at a selection highlights the difficulties and frustrations suffered by the Board of Trade as it struggled to persuade—and finally to force—railway companies to adopt basic safety mechanisms. These comprised an interlocking signalling system, a distance "block" to ensure trains on the track maintained safe distances from each other, and a continuous brake system that ran along every carriage of a train.

The North Kent line of the South Eastern railway was always busy, and Sunday evenings were particularly hectic. The trains formed a quick and convenient alternative to the Thames pleasure steamers, and hundreds of people taking a day out from London would pack into carriages bound for Gravesend. Demand for homeward trips in the evening was usually intense, and the company laid on a quick succession of trains to cope with the crowds. The line operated "Tyer's electric signal system." Station masters were instructed to make certain the train leaving their station had passed through the next station along the line before they allowed the departure of any following train. Communication with neighbouring stations was by a simple electronic signal. On

Sunday 28 June, 1857 the system failed.

The tightly packed 9:15 PM train from Strood to London passed through Blackheath Station as normal, but was stopped by danger signals just before reaching Lewisham Station. It was a fast train, and would not normally have stopped at Lewisham. Driver Thomas Hill waited patiently for the signals to change. His train was already running fifteen minutes behind schedule. At the rear of the train, guard William Wiley stepped out of his carriage and stood by the track. Minutes later he heard the unmistakable rumble of another train approaching. He grabbed his hand lamp, which showed a red "danger" light, and ran frantically down the track back towards Blackheath. The *Times* reported his account on 30 June:

> I saw the train approaching, and still continued running towards it, waving the lamp and sounding my whistle. The night was dark, and I could not see whether the driver noticed me. There are two bridges across the line between the Lewisham and Blackheath Stations. I was about 100 yards from the first bridge, but not quite halfway between the two bridges, when the train passed me at a speed of 20 miles an hour. I then turned back towards my own train, and before I got back to the bridge I heard that a collision had taken place. Knowing there was another train coming up the line, I turned back again and ran to the Blackheath Station, and told the station master not to let anything pass up the line.

The 9:.30 PM train crashed into the brake van of the stationary 9:15 PM with a force that pushed it from the rails, into the air and down onto a third-class carriage in front. The frail open carriage and its unfortunate occupants were no match for the hefty five-ton brake van. The carriage disintegrated, and its passengers were left crushed and hopelessly entangled in a mangled confusion of wood and metal. Passengers in other carriages of the train escaped with bruising and shock, and quickly began rescue efforts. A Dr Roberts was travelling on the train and he quickly began to tend those trapped and injured. The passengers were soon joined by railway workmen and officials, including railway manager Mr Eborall who happened to live nearby. Doctors in the district were summoned and a vast crowd of spectators gathered as news of the disaster spread. Organisation was abysmal. The railway company had just one jack at hand, and had to send to London for more equipment. The gathering mass of on-lookers hindered what rescue efforts were underway. Well-meaning but clumsy and uncoordinated efforts to help made matters worse. Meanwhile passengers trapped in the wreckage were dying. The chaotic scene was later described by a passenger who escaped injury but was incensed by the incompetence shown in dealing with the disaster. He wrote a letter to the *Times* on 2 July, penned under the pseudonym "F."

> The confusion from the first to last was frightful, and the delay in procuring the mechanical contrivances which alone could have brought relief to the sufferers was surely needlessly prolonged. Nothing could be done to extract the bodies of some of the sufferers without jacks and powerful pulleys, and levers, for the mass of one carriage had been hurled upon another, and had crushed and buried the wretched travellers in the lower carriage in the most complicated and hideous and apparently inextricable manner. To all our applications to the railway people for jacks we had for a reply that they had been sent for.... One great evil which we encountered in our efforts to extricate the sufferers was the thronging of the mob and the absence of control and organisation. No doubt, we received assistance from the police in certain respects, for they brought more lamps—a thing of material importance, as there seemed at one time a chance of the medley of broken woodwork which enclosed the poor creatures being set on fire by the torches which were improvised...
>
> So foolishly and dangerously, indeed, were some of the mob acting that I had to leave my coadjutors on several occasions on the alarm being given that the carriages were about to be purposely upset, and the crowbars and levers were being fatally introduced into the massive and dislocated ruins of the carriages and the limbs of the wounded.... The immediate neighbourhood of the accident ought to have been kept clear, and, though it is too much to expect the most able commander, or director to be necessarily forthcoming on such an occasion from among the officials, still something may be expected of these people—perhaps to the extent of activity in obtaining the requisite mechanical appliances and free space for the operation of volunteers.

It was three hours before the brake van could be lifted from the carriage. Eleven people died instantly or before they could be released, and another sixty-three were injured. The most seriously hurt were taken by train to St Thomas' Hospital in London. In a move that highlights the almost unbelievable degree of corporate complacency, Mr Eborall, the railway manager, handed the driver and fireman of the 9:30 PM train into police custody, stating they had neglected their duty by passing the danger sign into Lewisham Station. Coroner Charles Carttar presided over the subsequent inquest. He heard how the signalling system on the line frequently broke down and gave inaccurate messages. He heard how the "speaking telegraph" on the line was out of order, and he heard Eborall explain how emergency equipment had not been available because the company "could not expect to have accidents everywhere." The verdict was accidental death. The railway employees were later cleared of blame.

Railway companies were liable to pay damages for injury to the goods or people they carried. The sums involved were generally small, and in the ten years ending in December 1857 the total paid was some £60,500. The companies were exempt from paying compensation to their own employees, although the injury or death of a workman could be devastating for his family. Such accidents were commonplace, and on 2 September 1861 employees of the North London Railway Company organised five excursion trains to Kew to raise money to help injured workmates. Excursion trains were unscheduled, and were slotted into suitable spaces in the day's timetable. The trip down to Kew was uneventful, and the passengers expected to return sometime between 8:00 PM and 9:30 PM. A scheduled train left Kew for London at 6:35 PM, and the crowds of people waiting on the Kew platforms persuaded the station master, James Morse, to set off one of the excursion trains earlier than had been intended. Scheduled trains generally carried warning notices on their end carriage if they were to be followed by an excursion, but the sudden change in arrangements meant that the 6:35 PM had left before this could be done. Morse could not notify stations of the change in arrangements as he had no means of communication. The excursion left Kew at 7:00 PM, with passengers packed into each of the twelve carriages.

Meanwhile engine driver John Perkins had left the nineteen trucks of his ballast train in a siding between Kentish Town and Camden Stations while he went to Camden to fill his engine with water and fuel. Returning to the trucks, he attached his engine to the rear brake van and shunted them onto the up line. He then released the engine and used the track's cross-over points to bring it to the leading truck, ready for his return journey to Bushey, in Hertfordshire. Ballast trains, like excursions, had to time their journeys to fit in with scheduled services. Perkins' manoeuvres had been sanctioned by the Kentish Town station signal-man, George Rayner, a partially deaf lad of 19 who was working a fifteen-hour day for fourteen shillings a week. As Perkins prepared for

36 *The North London Railway excursion train accident, 2 September 1861*

his home run he saw the excursion train rushing towards him at about twenty miles per hour. He immediately realised the danger and tried to pull the trucks over the cross-over points and onto the safety of the down line. There was no time. The excursion engine rammed into the second ballast truck, lurched off the track and careered down a twenty-nine-foot embankment, dragging three carriages and their helpless passengers with it.

The fragile carriages shattered as they landed in the field below the embankment, and the terrified screams of trapped and injured passengers brought locals rushing to the scene. It was about 7:20 PM, and dusk was fast falling. The remains of the front brake wagon were set on fire to give vital light to the would-be rescuers. The blaze illuminated an horrific scene. As the *Illustrated Times* reported on 7 September:

> The glare discovered the wounded men, women and children that lay about, surrounded by little groups who rendered them such assistance as could be procured on the instant. There was the engine on its side, puffing out its hot steam; carriages were hanging in a position that made them appear as if they were just about to fall to the earth; and from under the first carriage that had come over the bridge there were visible the head of one man and the legs and arms of another.

Some shocked passengers ran, screaming, into the surrounding fields and disappeared. Many more were too badly injured to move, and waited for help. Within about twenty minutes police from Kentish Town and Camden had arrived, closely followed by lines of cabs and wagons ready to take the wounded to hospital. The report continued:

> The wounded lay here and there, writhing in agony. Men were engaged in dragging corpses from under wheels and axletrees and out of carriages that had been crushed like pasteboard. Gentlemen and ladies carried water-cans, bottles and other vessels, and were constantly giving those draughts which the mangled so greedily asked for. Many ladies ran about with linen for the doctors to bandage the wounded, and themselves assisted in the kind office. The policemen with their lanterns kept a path for those who were carrying the injured to the cabs, vans and carts, which were now drawn up in a line to the by-road leading out to Kentish Town; and from all sides men, women and children were running with lamps and lighted candles to what, without the slightest exaggeration, may be termed a field of slaughter.

More than three hundred passengers were injured. The most seriously hurt were taken to University College Hospital, the Royal Free Hospital and the Middlesex Hospital. Other casualties went to St Pancras Workhouse and to the homes of local doctors and residents. The death toll reached sixteen, surprisingly light in the circumstances.

More than 150 yards of the railway line had been ripped up or buckled during the collision, and this caused serious delays for hundreds of passengers waiting to return from Kew. News of the disaster quickly spread across London, and soon thousands of spectators were flocking to the scene. Relatives and friends worried by the late appearance of their loved ones added to the mass of people hurrying to look at the carnage. Public interest remained intense over the next few days, especially as this disaster followed close on the heels of an accident in the Clayton tunnel near Brighton. Two trains had collided in the depths of the tunnel, causing the deaths of twenty-three passengers and injury to another 176. Anger and resentment against the inefficiencies and dangerous practices of the railway companies reached fever pitch.

Kentish Town signalman George Rayner was charged with manslaughter and took the brunt of the blame. Inquiries found he had taken off danger signals when he knew the ballast train was shunting across the lines. The excursion had passed through Kentish Town oblivious to the danger waiting just outside the station. The driver of the ballast train was equally unaware the excursion was due. The preceding train had not carried the standard warning sign on its tailboard and excursion trains were not included in schedules. Rayner had only been employed by the railway for eight months, and was near the end of a fifteen-hour shift when he made his disastrous blunder. Once again, the railway company had a scapegoat. However, the demand for government action to improve safety on the railway system was growing. A comment in the *Illustrated London News* of 7 September 1861 is typical of those appearing in the national press:

Fully admitting the principle of self-government in the conduct of our affairs, and deprecating, as a rule, an organised system of government intermeddling in undertakings which are the result of our commercial genius and the natural issues of our national wealth, yet, when it has become clear that the management of railway companies is such that it is inadequate to the due safety of the lives of those who commit themselves to its care, the question arises whether it is not absolutely necessary to create responsibility somewhere. At present responsibility is as shifting as a quicksand, and it is impossible to fix it on any person or body so as to produce any hope of a better state of things...we have lists of killed and wounded that read like bulletins of great battles. Coroners' inquests follow, in the course of which practiced legal ingenuity is allowed to turn personal or corporate responsibility into a will-o'-wisp, which evades the most active pursuit, and in the end perhaps some wretched engine-driver—if one survives—or some miserable pointsman or signalman, has a verdict of manslaughter recorded against him....

Another ballast train figured in a tragedy just three years later. On a damp afternoon on 16 December 1864 the train, pulling twenty-three trucks of bricks and sand, was cleared to pass through a mile-long tunnel between Charlton and Blackheath Stations. Driver Thomas Dowsett met a danger signal at Charlton, and had to stop his train and wait fifteen minutes. This meant his speed on entering the tunnel was lower than usual, and it proved catastrophic. As the train reached a slight upward gradient, it began to slide on the greasy tracks. At first Dowsett managed to keep the train moving at a walking pace, but about three hundred yards from the end, it ground to a complete halt. The signalman in charge of that section of the line was sick and off work. His place had temporarily been taken by a young porter named Jones, who earned sixteen shillings a week. He had worked in the signal box for one full week only and his shifts lasted eleven hours each day. The ballast train had entered the tunnel at about 4:20 PM and the time allowed for a train to pass through was seven minutes. Jones must have decided the ballast train was clear, because he gave an all clear signal that gave an approaching passenger train, travelling at around forty miles per hour, the go-ahead to enter the tunnel.

When the ballast train had come to a standstill, guard William Lancaster had decided to uncouple some trucks to allow the engine to pull a section at a time. Just as he completed his task he heard a crash, felt an ominous jolt and knew there had been a collision. His fears were confirmed as he heard screams from frightened passengers. Driver Dowsett immediately drove the front section of his train on into Blackheath Station and Lancaster ran behind, shouting for help. The men told station officials what had happened and all trains on the line were stopped. A third train, the 4:20 PM from London, was halted a minute before it was due to enter the tunnel. North Kent Railway officials Mr Knight, traffic superintendent; his assistant, Mr Harris; and locomotive superintendent Mr Corner were rushed to the scene in an engine from London Bridge. They were closely followed by company medic Dr Adams and a staff of surgeons. Police, railway workmen and troops from the nearby Woolwich barracks all helped with rescue efforts.

Inside the tunnel five labourers travelling on the ballast train lay dead. The passenger train fireman had suffered severe burns and other injuries and died soon afterwards. One woman passenger had lost both legs, others had broken ribs, fractured limbs, cuts and bruises. Several carriages had been severely damaged by the impact and the rescuers worked in appalling conditions to free the occupants. Conditions inside the tunnel were horrific. There were no lights, so the rescue team set fire to parts of the wreckage to allow them to see what they were doing. The fire would not burn properly in the damp conditions, and the dense smoke it produced added to the discomfort. The wreckage, and the difficulty in using large lifting equipment added to their problems.

After about an hour, a train edged into the tunnel from Charlton Station and passengers on the stricken train were transferred and taken back to Charlton. Here cabs and ambulances from the Woolwich Garrison were waiting to take the injured. Some of the most badly hurt went to the military hospital at Woolwich, others were taken to the Antigallican Arms Tavern or to Blackheath to be cared for by Dr Adams and local doctors. Efforts to recover bodies trapped in the wreckage continued for several hours. It became unbearably hot in the poorly-ventilated tunnel, but work continued until late at night when the last body was released.

The incident was another example of a blunder by an inexperienced railwayman, given duties beyond his capabilities and without essential equipment. Efficient signalling arrangements, and the use of the space block system to maintain distance between trains, would have considerably reduced the risk of human error.

The catalogue of accidents peaked in the 1870s and the Board of Trade's railway inspectorate became increasingly critical of the industry's reluctance to act on its advice. The Board's call for the universal adoption of safer signalling, braking and space block systems became like a battle-cry. But the railway companies remained determined to retain their independence. Many companies preferred to install home-grown but often useless safety devices than accept the recommendations of "interfering" government officials. The frustration of the railway inspectors is apparent in their annual reports submitted to Parliament. In the 1870 report one company, the London and North Western Railway, was singled out for a particularly scathing attack.

On 28 November 1870, eight people died in a collision between the two-engine London and North Western Railway's Euston to Liverpool express and a coal train. The accident happened in thick fog at Harrow. Twenty trucks of the coal train had broken off from the engine as they were being pulled into a siding, and blocked the main line shortly before the express was due to pass. Danger signals were quickly put up, but express driver William Shelvey—who had been sacked from the railway several years earlier for bad behaviour, but had been re-employed—apparently did not see them. As men struggled to clear the coal trucks from the line the express roared towards them. The force of the impact shattered the first engine and tender, threw the second engine off the lines and caused serious damage to several passenger carriages. Shelvey and seven passengers died instantly or shortly afterwards. Work to free the trapped casualties continued for more than four hours, and rescuers included Dr Butler, head of the nearby Harrow School, his sister and a junior master, the Reverend J. Bucknall. Local doctors were called to treat the injured at the scene and a builder, Mr Warne, helped by making splints for some passengers who had sustained fractures. These included Mr Balfour Stewart, Professor of Natural Philosophy at Owen's College, Manchester.

By the standards of the day, the incident was fairly run-of-the-mill, but it was just one of thirty-four on the company's lines during the year. The atrocious record shattered the patience of railway inspector Captain Henry Tyler, a man later knighted for his services. In his annual report he wrote:

> It is hardly possible, indeed, to study the train accidents above enumerated without also considering how it is that the great company to which so vast a proportion of the railway business of this country is entrusted, and which is the principal mail route through the length of the land, has failed during the past year in that important part of its duties which is reference to the public safety. Of the 34 accidents on the lines of the London and North Western Railway, 24 have been cases of collisions at stations,

sidings, junctions or between following trains while running on passenger lines, and five have been in consequence of passenger trains being wrongly turned through facing points.

Tyler went on to criticise the way in which railway employees were frequently used as scapegoats, often facing charges of manslaughter when the real cause of the accidents had been lack of proper equipment. He also commented that it suited the big companies if employees took the brunt of criticism for mishaps when obliged to give evidence at inquests. He called for corporate negligence to receive the publicity it deserved.

> It is under this impression that I have not hesitated, in the present report, to call attention in the plainest manner to the fact that the most important and wealthy, and most powerful railway company, which is also one of the most prosperous in this country has been the most remarkable for its shortcomings on the score of safety; and to lead up to the conclusion that the supreme management of this company is principally responsible for these shortcomings, in so far as the means and appliances by which a maximum, and even a reasonable degree of safety may be secured, have not, as the general result of that management, been provided.

Inspectors' reports were given en masse, and to Parliament. By the time they appeared, and the real cause of the accident could be told, public interest had evaporated.

Escalating accident rates forced the government to take decisive action, and a Royal Commission on Railway Accidents took extensive evidence between 1874 and 1875. Part of the commission's investigation included a trial of braking systems. Testing took place at Newark and resulted in a resounding victory for continuous vacuum braking. This provided brakes for each carriage and was far more effective than the standard system of brake vans at the front and rear of the train. From 1878 all railway companies were obliged to submit half-yearly returns reporting the progress made in fitting rolling stock with continuous brakes. A Railways Act passed in 1889 finally made interlocking signalling systems, the "space block" between trains and continuous brakes on all passenger trains compulsory. Accidents on the railway system continued, but at least after this date most mishaps were caused by faulty equipment or negligence, rather than by a company's failure to provide basic safety apparatus.

Lack of proper signalling, ineffective distancing between trains and poor braking systems were responsible for the great majority of railway accidents during the nineteenth century, but they were not the only cause of calamity. The construction of carriages and trucks often left much to be desired. The Victorians appeared happy to travel in fragile wooden boxes that offered precious little protection in the event of mishap. Broken wheels and faulty couplings caused many incidents during the period, including at least two in London.

The 7:00 AM Eastern Counties Railway train from Cambridge to London was always well filled with millers and farmers making their way to the Metropolitan corn and cattle markets. On 20 February 1860 the train, which had no third class carriages, was packed as usual, but kept good time to reach Ponder's End Station at about 9.10 AM. The next scheduled stop was at Stratford, so ten minutes later driver William Rowell approached Tottenham Station travelling at around thirty-five miles per hour and expecting to pass straight through. As the engine reached the start of the platform there was a loud crash as its left leading wheel suddenly shattered. The engine keeled over and rammed the edge of the brick platform, running briefly along the top before somersaulting back down on to the track. Robert Sinclair was watching from the station platform, and gave a vivid description in a letter to the *Times* (21 February):

> On reaching the platform the engine struck it and turned completely over, the tender flying clean over it. The carriage or van next to the tender was thrown against the engine, and I saw the roof of it broken off; the next carriage was thrown through the platform wall on the up side; the next carriage was off the line, and upright; and the rest of the train was on the rails. I should mention that in turning over the water and steam were discharged from the boiler, and a cloud of steam enveloped the debris as soon as I had noticed what I have described.

The lightly-built carriages were badly damaged, and passengers were trapped in the debris. Luckily, the accident had happened at a station and help was close at hand. Railway staff joined uninjured passengers in working to free casualties and telegraphs requesting help were sent to Stratford Station and the Shoreditch terminus. Senior company officials, including the Superintendent, Mr Robertson and senior engineer Mr Sinclair arrived shortly, along with Dr Luke of the London

Hospital. Other doctors arriving to help included Mr Hall and Mr Fox. The task of recovering the dead and injured was difficult and drawn out. The crumpled carriages had to be dismantled, piece by piece, before all those trapped could be released. Some of the injured were taken to the station waiting room, others were loaded onto ladders or boards and carried off to nearby taverns and private houses. Miller Mr Manston had to have a leg amputated on arrival at the Ship's Tavern, and many other passengers suffered serious cuts and fractures. Seven people died instantly or soon after the crash. These included engine driver William Rowell and fireman George Cornwall.

The Eastern Counties Railway was quick to deny all responsibility. In a letter appearing in the next day's edition of the *Times* the directors wrote:

> The directors deeply lament this very serious accident, which has arisen from causes over which they had no control.

But Board of Trade inspectors and the coroner's jury were not so convinced of the railway's innocence. Each found the wheel tyre that had broken and caused the accident had been faulty. The welding that held it together was defective. Regular inspections would have revealed the danger, but these had not been carried out satisfactorily. The coroner's jury censured the Eastern Counties Railway with the verdict:

> The deceased met with their deaths from the breaking of the tyre of one of the leading wheels of the engine, in consequence of the defective weld; and had proper caution and vigilance been used the same might have been detected.

A similar accident, resulting from faults with rolling stock, killed five people near Old Ford Station in East London on 28 January 1882. Driver William Crabb was taking fifty light trucks on the down-line between Old Ford Station and Fairfield Road bridge in Bow. A drawbar snapped between two trucks near the end of the train, struck a sleeper, and threw several trucks off the rails. Crabb carried on, oblivious to any incident, but brakeman Frank Line was well aware something untoward had happened. He later told coroner Sir John Humphreys: "All at once I found I was left behind, and that the train had parted company."

The abandoned trucks were thrown askew across the track, and in the path of trains approaching on the up-line. The 9:40 PM Broad Street to Poplar passenger train had just left Old Ford Station, and the glancing blow suffered as it collided with the trucks set it careering into the masonry of the bridge wall. The second and third carriages were telescoped together and the cries of the injured and dying passengers soon filled the night air. People from nearby houses, and North London Railway staff from Old Ford Station rushed to help, and burned wood from the shattered carriages to throw light on the scene. Mrs Ellen Snary was badly injured but clasped her two-month-old baby, Charlotte, to her breast as rescuers struggled to free her from the wreckage. The task proved too difficult. Ellen and her baby died before they could be removed.

Accidents caused by faulty rolling stock did not seem to incite the same degree of public outrage and indignation as incidents involving faults in signalling or braking. This may explain why improvements in the design and manufacture of rolling stock took second place to ensuring the more basic safety precautions on the network. Board of Trade inspectors frequently recommended improvements, such as use of the Mansell composite wheel, which was far safer and more resilient than versions that had been welded together. Changes came gradually, helped along by the development of materials capable of withstanding higher stresses, more efficient testing equipment and rigid systems of inspection. The construction of rolling stock remains a subject of hot debate in the railway industry. The Cannon Street train crash that killed two people in January 1991 again triggered arguments on the strength and shock resistance of passenger carriages.

Railway accidents were not restricted to the lines. Organisation at stations was often lamentably inadequate—theatres were not the only buildings where bad design and lack of planning caused deaths among the public using them.

A favourite pastime for Victorian Londoners, including many from the poorer districts who fancied a "day in the country," was to spend a day on Hampstead Heath. On 18 April 1892, a Bank Holiday, an estimated one hundred thousand people flocked to the Heath, and as tea time and rain clouds approached, there was a general rush for home. The London and North Western Railway Company's Hampstead Heath Station was soon besieged by crowds anxious to get back to East London.

The station was normally staffed by nine railway employees, but on holidays Hampstead Heath was notoriously busy, and staffing numbers were increased to around twenty. The staircase down to the station platform was divided into two, each section with twenty-eight steps. At the bottom of the side leading to the up-line there were gates and a ticket collector's box. Just before 6:00 PM the rush of people into the station rapidly increased and the stairway became intolerably packed. Someone—probably a young child—tripped; but the forward rush proved impossible to halt.

John Connor had been on the Heath with his son and daughter. When the time came to return home he bought his tickets at the station and began making his way down the stairs to the platform. His son, John, aged nine, walked in front of him and Connor carried his daughter in his arms. Three steps down the stairway a crush developed and forced him down the stairs with his children. John junior was forced against the side. A policeman later spent an hour trying to revive him, but the child was among the six youngsters and two adults who died.

Mr W.J. Stephenson was returning home from Richmond and stepped from his train as the mayhem reached fever pitch. He later described events in a letter to the *Hampstead and Highgate Express* (23 April):

> A most painful sight met my gaze. The station seemed like a howling wilderness, shrieking, bustling, and cries of women and children made it a scene almost indescribable. On endeavouring to alight on the platform I for some moments found it almost impossible to effect an opening of the carriage door, but at last, with extreme difficulty, I found myself amidst a seething mass of humanity, shrieking and yelling, and amid a scene of wildest confusion.

Stephenson crossed the railway line and made his way upstairs from the opposite platform. As he reached the street he saw "one mass of people all crowding down to the spot, wholly unconscious of the terrible disaster that was being enacted inside."

The ticket collector's box formed an impregnable barrier; four victims were later found wedged against it. The station doors were closed, and police and doctors rushed to the scene. Casualties were taken to the nearby police station where divisional surgeon Dr Payne and his assistant Dr Cooper Rose gave medical care.

As news of the tragedy spread there was a public outcry and railway officials came in for severe criticism. Hampstead Heath Station was known to be dangerously overcrowded on Bank Holidays, and the station officials should have made special arrangements to deal with the hordes of passengers. Mr E. Brodie Hoare, MP, asked a question in the House of Commons about what measures would be taken to prevent future accidents. Board of Trade President Sir Michael Hicks-Beach assured him company officials had promised to institute improvements at the station before the next holiday at Whitsun.

Captain Charles Fox of the Third Battalion, Middlesex Regiment was a noted expert on approaches to public buildings. He told the subsequent inquest that a "very great error of judgement" had been made in locating the ticket box at the bottom of the stairway. The coroner's jury added to the London and North Western Railway Company's public drubbing. Returning a verdict of accidental death on the victims, jurors added the scathing rider:

> And the jurors find that the ticket box was placed in a most dangerous position and further that on the occasion in question the whole of the arrangements made by the company were totally insufficient to cope with the increased traffic on public holidays. And the jurors are of the opinion that further general accommodation should be provided for the public at the said station; that the ticket box should be removed from the bottom of the staircase; that further and more complete arrangements should be made to regulate the traffic of passengers generally to and from the platform and that an extra and separate exit should at once be provided.

By mid-May the improvements to the station were well underway. The ticket collector's box had been re-positioned, an additional entrance provided and the central balustrade on the staircase removed.

The unique character of railway accidents increased the need for some form of disaster management in the evolution of organised disaster response. Voluntary groups played a major role. The traumas of the First World War proved an added stimulus to development, and by the time of the Silvertown Explosion in 1917 statutory and voluntary services were sufficiently geared to deal with a major emergency in a way that would have seemed impossible just fifty years earlier. A brief look at a railway accident in Ilford, on New Year's Day 1915, shows how different organisations had developed to play a role in emergency situations.

The crash happened at about 8:40 AM, when the Clacton to Liverpool Street express smashed into the Gidea Park to Liverpool Street local train. The local train had been given the all clear to cross from its tracks onto the main line. The express driver, travelling at about fifty miles per hour on the main line, failed to see danger signals instructing him to stop. The express careered into the local train as it crossed lines, and shattered two carriages. Ten people died and another five hundred were injured, many seriously. The accident happened on the London side of Ilford Station. The station was immediately closed. Passengers lucky enough to escape harm immediately began efforts to free the trapped and injured. They were soon helped by squads of police constables, the civic guard and territorial army, soldiers and boy scouts. At least half a dozen doctors were called to treat the injured before they could be taken to nearby hospitals. Rescuers were organised into teams to work at different parts of the wreckage. Casualty lists, stating where a particular person had been taken, were posted on local shop windows as soon as possible. The railway company, the Great Eastern, rapidly supplied bandages, splints and other medical equipment.

When the inquest into the deaths was opened at Ilford Town Hall on 5 January, Mr Thornton, general manager of the Great Eastern Railway Company, made a brief statement thanking all those who had helped at the disaster, and added:

> On behalf of the company I also desire to say that the Great Eastern Railway accepts full and complete responsibility for this accident, and all proper claims will be met.

The statement reveals a vastly different attitude to that of Mr Eborall, the railway manager whose immediate response to disaster in 1857 had been to hand two "negligent" employees into police custody. The principle of corporate responsibility coming above the failing of an individual employee had been established.

The trials and tribulations of the early railway system would fill several volumes and this book can only hope to give a brief overview of some of the main problems facing the pioneers. There are many excellent books on this subject and I have included a selection in the list of sources.

CHAPTER NINE

The Albion

The *Albion* launch is probably one of the best documented disasters of the nineteenth century. Scores of those affected—whether severely or trivially—wrote to claim the paltry compensation on offer from the disaster fund. Many wrote long and detailed letters giving full accounts of their role in the incident. Perhaps writing such comprehensive descriptions acted as a kind of therapy to help them cope with the terrible scenes they had witnessed. The sad and sometimes heart-rending correspondence has survived as part of the disaster fund records in the archives at Newham Local Studies Library. They provide today's reader with a unique insight into the lives, attitudes and formidable difficulties faced by people living in the area as the century drew to an end.

The *Albion* was a first class cruiser, a substantial ship around 390 feet in length and seventy-four feet wide. The Admiralty had commissioned her from Thames Iron Works at the height of the "naval race" in Europe. A hurried shipbuilding programme had been instigated in an effort to build up Britain's maritime superiority. The Iron Works had benefitted tremendously from the national—and international—scramble to boost naval power. It won a string of major commissions, building vessels for several nations. It is an ironic fact that many ships spawned in the East End yard went on to fight sea battles on opposing sides.

Work on the *Albion* had been completed slightly behind schedule, partly because the yard was undermanned and partly because the "eight-hour day" engineering union strike had put supplying contractors behind in their deliveries. The Thames Iron Works itself escaped the strikes—Arnold Hills was an enlightened employer and had agreed to an eight-hour day some years earlier. The *Albion* was launched at eight hundred tons less than her intended weight because government-appointed contractors failed to supply sufficient armour plating to clad the ship.

Launches were fairly commonplace at the works. They were all occasions for celebration, but the *Albion* was something special. For a start, the ship was British. It was also to be launched by the Duchess of York and was to be the first "Royal" launch at Thames Iron Works. The fiercely patriotic locals were thrilled at the prospect of catching a glimpse of such distinguished guests. The launch of Her Majesty's warship the *Albion* on 21 June 1898 promised to be an oasis of celebration for East Enders, a welcome break from the drab monotony of their poverty-stricken existence.

The shipyard was festooned with flags and crammed with around thirty thousand spectators as the 3:00 PM launch time approached. Yard workers and local schools were given a day's holiday to attend the celebrations and families dressed in the finest clothes they could muster. Workers received a special bonus on the day—one shilling for apprentices and half a crown and a straw hat for shipwrights. Brilliant sunshine added to the carnival atmosphere and people were determined to enjoy themselves.

Although twenty thousand tickets had been handed out to yard workers, friends and families, the gatemen were instructed to admit anyone who looked respectable. The party atmosphere and *joie de vivre* mounted as launch time approached and spectators jostled for vantage points in the crowded yard. Yard managers had arranged for seventy policemen to be on duty and to help control the crowds. The policemen did their best, but there were too few of them to have much impact among the milling throngs. A little workmen's slipway running by the side of a nearly-completed Japanese warship, the *Shikishma*, provided a perfect view. Yardsmen knew the bridge had not been built to hold large numbers of people, and it had been marked "Dangerous." As launch time drew close and the struggle to find good positions became more intense, the policemen on duty relented in their insistence on keeping the bridge clear. It was soon filled with around two hundred people.

The Duke and Duchess of York arrived at the gaily decorated yard to the cheers of the excited crowds, and enjoyed a lunch with yard director Arnold J. Hills, Lady Mary Lyon, Sir Charles Cust, the Venerable Archdeacon Stevens, Canon Pelly and other dignitaries. The launch was scheduled for 3:00 PM, but after hurried consultation between engineers it was brought forward to 2:50 PM. The dogshores supporting the ship were showing signs of giving way and officials feared they would collapse before the launch could take place.

37   *The Duchess of York christening the Albion*

38   *The launch of the Albion*

The Duke, Duchess and favoured guests took their places on the canopied headstage near the bows of the *Albion*. The Duchess lobbed the traditional bottle of champagne at the great ship's hull. It failed to break. She tried twice more, but the bottle would not crack. Finally she cut the cord signalling workmen to release the dogshores holding the *Albion*. The six-thousand-ton warship was no lightweight, and shipbuilding manager George Clement Mackrow expected her to enter the water at a good speed. He was right. The *Albion* caused a massive surge of water, which smashed against the slipway like a tidal wave, crushing it with the ease of a giant snapping a matchstick tower. The spectators crowded onto the gantry had no time to escape, but their screams of terror were drowned by the hearty cheers that accompanied the *Albion*'s rapid descent into Bow Creek. Few people realised hundreds of spectators on the little slipway had been thrown into the muddy, churning waters around the *Albion*. The Duke and Duchess, oblivious to any problem, returned to their own boat and the crowds began to disperse and make their own ways home.

Meanwhile a desperate struggle was taking place in water just ten feet deep and five yards from the shore. Debris from the slipway crashed onto the mass of people in the water. Many of the thirty-eight to die were trapped beneath timbers, knocked unconscious by floating baulks or simply trampled by other victims struggling to find a footing. It was at least ten minutes before news of the tragedy filtered through to the yard managers, but spectators and shipyard workers who were nearby began immediate rescue efforts. Large numbers of spectators dived into the water to drag out survivors. Thames Police rowed their boats into the mêlée and scooped many from the water. The Metropolitan Police and fire brigade also moved in to help.

The Iron Works had its own ambulance corps, later to become the first West Ham branch of the St John Ambulance Brigade, and its twelve certified members were in action within three or four minutes. Several corps members leapt into the water to help with the rescue, others went in boats to give immediate resuscitation to those hauled out of the water. First Aid workers from the Essex Volunteer Brigade Bearer Company were also quickly on the scene. Several local doctors, including Dr Gregorson and Dr Percy Rose were at the launch and helped treat the injured and confirm death in the less fortunate. They were helped by the nurses of St Katherine's Home, who earned praise from all sources for their skill and gentleness in handling victims and their families.

There were many heroic rescue attempts. Mr E. Offord dragged an unconscious woman to safety. He later wrote to the Disaster Fund committee:

The ship was gliding into the water and the people were wildly cheering their very utmost and from where I stood there came a sound that was totally unlike the other. And then people started running away from the crane towards the entrance that we came in, but the cheering getting less as the ship was launched, the other sound now became the loudest, and there was now no difficulty in finding out from where it came from. I ran with other people to see what was the matter when a most terrible sight met my eyes, thinking and hesitating in the same moment what to do. When a young man rushed past me and into the water he goes, and me after him, but through a piece of wood which caused me to take some of the water down, I was forced to return to some poles that were in the water, but quickly feeling myself alright I went and got a young woman and was taking her to the bank when I touched a body that had just sank with my feet. As I knew the one that was under wanted the most assistance but the one I had was already unconscious that made me keep my hold on her but the fact so unnerved me that instead of taking her to the bank I was forced to make for some poles that was near me, my labour had just now commenced, putting my hand on those poles they sank too low in the water. It meant another struggle which kept on till more help came, but getting safely on the poles at last willing hands put some planks on top of the poles and got us ashore.

Safely ashore, Offord took the woman to "the firemen's place" where she was given some brandy. He added:

Somebody pulled my jacket and vest off while there that I felt so cold without it that I soon put them on again and as I felt rather colder still I decided on going home as quick as I could....

Army Marine Privates Dorrington and McMillan were watching the launch from the slipway, but were agile enough to jump to safety as the wave hit. They helped rescue those floundering, but Dorrington almost became a victim himself. "I was standing on the corner of the bridge that got swamped," he explained to the disaster fund committee:

I was near enough and jumped on shore but dived into the water as I was and brought out a woman and child and two girls when I was struck across the face by a plank and rendered insensible. Private McMillan pulled me out. As soon as I came round I went home as quickly as I could to change my clothes.

Private McMillan gave a graphic account of the accident:

> Myself with another marine named Dorrington and a civilian called
> Warricker were standing almost in the centre of the bridge when the
> accident occurred and as we had not been warned off the bridge by the
> police and as it offered a good view of the proceedings we stayed there.
> When the *Albion* was about three parts in the water I saw by the swell that
> was coming towards us that the bridge must inevitably by swamped.

McMillan leapt to safety on the nearby *Shikishma*.

> I then turned round and seeing a number of people in the water I dived
> in to do what I could. I succeeded in getting one girl to the timber where
> by this time a number of people had congregated and handed her to a
> bystander.Whilst with a second girl a drowning man clutched me by the
> throat and I had to choke him off by pinching his nose. When he let go I
> got hold of the girl and made for the timbers under the Japanese ship, the
> man at the same time catching hold of the tails of my tunic, so I had to
> take the two. People standing by took them to the shed and put them
> under the care of the nurses of St Katherine's Home. I made another
> attempt to rescue a woman but my strength failing me I clambered out
> and cut a rope of a tackle near by and until my friend found me I was
> throwing it, those who had strength and courage to hold it.

George Cuthbertson was another on the slipway who escaped injury. He
told his story to the *West Ham Herald* (25 June):

> Everybody cheered lustily and there was great excitement. Suddenly
> without any warning whatever there came a sudden whirl, the water rose
> up before us, and before we realised what was happening a great wave
> covered our heads. Then everything beneath us collapsed and I, with
> hundred of others found myself struggling in the water.
>
> With considerable difficulty I managed to get my head well above water,
> and to get a gasp of fresh air; but at this critical moment I found someone
> was clinging to me, but whether man, woman or child, it is impossible to
> say. Whoever it was another wash of wave or tide separated us. I had by
> this time swallowed more Thames water than I cared for and I was getting
> exhausted. Finally I somehow got jammed between baulks of timber and
> wreckage and then I managed to grasp a rope and pulled myself well
> above the surface.

Cuthbertson managed to reach the shore:

Had I not been a strong man and a strong swimmer I should in all probability have lost my life. The poor women and children had no chance.

A team of yardsmen, many of them members of the Thames Iron Works' swimming club, rushed to give what help they could. Their efforts were hindered by the dense crowds, many of whom has lost sight of friends and relatives and feared they were among the unlucky ones on the slipway. Unfortunately, their concern hindered rescue attempts. Mr H.J. Hawkins of Forest Gate later told the *West Ham Herald* (25 June):

> Well, to my mind they behaved disgracefully. I was with a friend who is employed at the Thames Iron Works and a member of their swimming club. He made repeated attempts to get near enough to the water to dive but was kept back by a crowd who seemed filled with a morbid curiosity. He is a good swimmer and I have no doubt that he would have saved some persons could he have gained the water.

As those in authority became aware of what had happened a major rescue operation swung into action. The *Albion* was towed further into the creek to allow easier access to rescue boats. Two steam launches crept as close as they dared, and towed away smaller boats filled with casualties.

The organisation was surprisingly like that at scenes of disaster today. Areas were marked out as first aid posts, a mortuary was set up and personal belongings dragged from the water were piled in a heap to await collection by owners, relatives or friends. Some of the St Katherine's Home nurses set up first aid stations where they and doctors gave treatment to those being dragged from the water. The nurses operated a triage system, deciding which sufferers needed urgent attention and which could afford to wait. A few casualties were sent to local hospitals, but most were simply given a change of clothing and, if lucky, a blanket, and sent home. A supply of blankets had been rushed to the scene by Mr Benfield of Victoria Dock Road. He provided nineteen blankets, and later charged the Disaster Fund 2/– for each.

Many people had to make their own way home, but others were driven in a variety of vehicles ranging from coal carts and trucks to cars and taxis. Most were charged for the privilege. The average fare was around 2/6d, in a district where £2 represented a very good weekly wage.

At first nobody realised people had been killed in the disaster. But as the waters cleared it quickly became apparent the death toll would be high. As Sub-Divisional Inspector Dixon of Thames Police later told the inquest, for a time officials thought everyone had been safely recovered...then one, and another, and another body came to the water's surface. Workmen began to drag the river and the shipyard diver, Bill Hodgson, was lowered into the murky water to check for bodies trapped in the mud. By 5:30 PM twenty-four bodies had been recovered and taken to a mortuary set up in an engineering department shed. The St Katherine's Homes nurses and Dr Humphries checked for signs of life. With touching tenderness and respect, the nurses covered each victim with a sheet before washing the body and replacing wet and damaged clothing with one of the clean outfits hurriedly brought to the yard. Pc Lambert had the unenviable task of taking a description of victims before they were covered with a canvas. Clothing was left in a bundle at the feet of each body to help relatives with identification.

A more suitable mortuary was soon needed. The Iron Works employees hurriedly fitted wooden benches in an old galvanising shed, electrician Fred Wilson fitted lights to the building and at 7:00 PM the bodies were transferred from the engineering department shed. When the light was turned on, Wilson saw the lifeless forms of his mother and sister, Matilda Young. Matilda had recently married and had only just returned from her honeymoon.

When news of the disaster spread a great crowd gathered outside the Iron Works. Only those who suspected friends or relatives might be among the dead were admitted. The search for the dead continued as the night drew in. By 11:30 PM thirty-two corpses had been recovered. All but three were identified by distraught relatives.

Other victims died shortly after rescue or in the weeks and months that followed. Amelia Gardner, the 39-year-old wife of a tea grocer, was taken from the river to Blackwall Police Station. She was in a serious condition and despite the efforts of Dr Henry M'Morran, she died after two and a half hours. Mrs Mary Ann Eve, 48, was dragged from the water by Timothy Guilfoyle, but died later in the evening. Guilfoyle later made a claim to the disaster fund to replace his damaged clothing. He wrote:

I went and got a woman of the name of Mary Ann Eve who was apparently dead. I at once started artificial respiration which I kept at for about 20 minutes before there was any sign of life returning but I soon got her right enough to remove her to the refreshment room. I got her around enough to tell me her name and address. I shook hands with her and told her I should call and see how she was but to my surprise I was informed by her son-in-law James Purton that she died at 7 o'clock the same evening.

Mrs Howell died at home within a week of the accident, leaving her husband, Thomas, to care for their seven children. Baby Frank Southgate, aged just three months, fell from the bridge with his parents. The tiny baby never recovered from the ordeal, and died in early August. The father, Samuel, 23, drowned while his wife and son were being rescued. Mrs Forbes, a mother of six children, also died in August. Annie Short, another mother of six, died in September, bringing the known death toll to thirty-eight. However, many victims inhaled water and suffered chest problems that must have caused illness—and ultimately deaths—for years to come. Medical treatment was expensive and many simply could not afford the luxury of a visit to the doctor, let alone the cost of drugs. Antibiotics were non-existent and infections difficult to control. The final number of deaths resulting from this tragedy will never be known.

People who had attended the launching ceremony and left unaware of the tragedy were shocked when they learned so many had died. The Duke and Duchess of York couldn't believe the first reports of the event, and telegrammed to yard director Arnold Hills:

Just heard that accident occurred at launch of the *Albion* today. Trust no truth in such a terrible report. Both Duchess and I are deeply grieved. Should the report be true please express our deep distress and sincere sympathy. It is a sad ending to what seemed a singularly successful day.

Hills telegrammed to confirm the news, and at 9:00 PM received another telegram from the Royal couple:

Have just received your telegram and learn with profound regret that the report respecting which we telegrammed you is true, and beg you to express to the families of the sufferers our sorrow for the calamity and our heartfelt sympathy with them in this terrible disaster.

The day after the accident West Ham Council opened a fund to help survivors and the bereaved. Canning Town was a deprived area and the people involved in the tragedy were desperately poor. Even those who escaped with a ducking emerged with badly damaged clothing. The spectators were dressed in their Sunday clothes—in some cases they were wearing their only complete outfits—and the loss was a serious blow. A notice appeared in local newspapers:

> The terrible calamity at the launch of *HMS Albion* has suddenly plunged into mourning and distress a number of poor families resident in Canning Town and Plaistow and within the borders of the borough of West Ham. I appeal confidently for help in this emergency as a considerable sum will be needed for funeral expenses, maintenance of children etc. A fund to be called the Canning Town Disaster Fund which will be administered by a responsible local committee who will consider all cases upon their merits, has been opened at the London and Coventry Bank, Stratford Branch, Broadway, Stratford. In the event of contributions received being more than sufficient to meet the necessities of the existing distress the balance will be devoted to the assistance of hospitals in the neighbourhood or other local charities.

Thames Iron Works made an immediate contribution of £1,000.

Hills was devastated by the tragedy and in the following days he personally visited the families of the bereaved. He promised to meet all funeral expenses—a burden he knew would prove too much for many families. He wrote in the *Thames Iron Works Gazette* (30 September 1898):

> I went in and out of the homes of those who had lost dear ones, and shared with them of the grief that filled all our hearts, I found the sweetest solace of all. For I met with no shadow of bitterness—no tone of complaint. In some sense I represented the Company at whose doors the responsibility of this great accident lay; but none the less the mother weeping for her child, the husband heartbroken for the loss of his young wife, clasped my hand, and in broken accents told me how sorry they were that this terrible accident should have marred all the joyous festivities of the launch. For such good feeling I can make no fit recompense, but I pray to God that so long as He may spare me I may be enabled to do something for the well-being and happiness of Canning Town.

Within twenty-four hours Hills had purchased a plot of land in the East London Cemetery sufficient for the burial of thirty-two bodies. This cost £104.12s.6d, inclusive of all burial fees and charges. The majority of victims were buried here, though some families opted for private graves

39   *After the accident*
40   *Memorial to the victims. Courtesy Newham Library Service.*

elsewhere. These responsibilities were later assumed by the disaster fund committee, but the initial gesture came from Hills.

Arnold Hills was an untypical Victorian employer. He seems to have had a genuine compassion for his workers and if he was an autocrat he was, at least, a benevolent one. Not only was Thames Iron Works one of the first yards in the country to adopt an eight-hour day four years before the strike that won the privilege for engineers working elsewhere, but the yard operated a "good fellowship" bonus system that gave employees benefits for completing work in good time. There were a vast number of workmen's social and leisure clubs, ranging from the drama and operatic societies to swimming and athletic clubs. The works had its own sportsground and swimming pool, and men were encouraged to use the facilities on offer. The Thames Iron Works' football team later achieved fame as West Ham United. The club's "Irons" nickname derives from its Iron Works pedigree and the "Hammers" from the rivetting hammers used in shipbuilding. The works produced its own newspaper, the *Thames Iron Works Gazette*, and in the June 1898 issue— published too early to feature the launch—Hills commented:

> I have before me a beautiful ideal, which I desire to see realised; I desire to see the Thames Iron Works celebrated not only for its world renowned engineering triumphs, but for the happy, healthy, hearty capacity of its men in every possible field of distinction.

The Iron Works closed on the day following the tragedy as a mark of respect for the dead. Workmen received a half-day's pay. Hills may have been relatively generous, but this was Victorian England.

There was a widespread feeling the victims were to some extent to blame for their fate. A report in the *Illustrated London News* on 25 June, for example, commented:

> It appears that notices of warning were posted near the fatal gangway, but the East End crowd is more wilful than its western counterpart.

Alderman William Ivey was Mayor of West Ham and chaired the Disaster Fund committee. Hills, the Venerable Archdeacon Stevens, the Reverend Canon Pelly, the Reverend Canon Buckley, the Reverend Partner and George Mackrow, the shipbuilding department manager, accepted invitations to sit on the committee. Mackrow was responsible for a large part of the organisation this work entailed. The Town Clerk, Fred Hilleary, acted as committee secretary. The first Disaster Fund committee meeting was on 28 June. A set of standard payments was agreed. All those bereaved were to receive £5 towards mourning expenses. Burying a loved one meant wearing black as a mark of respect. These impoverished people had the bare minimum of clothing and most had to buy special garments to attend the funerals. Only one payment was made to each family. The Simms family had lost three children, but their £5 had to stretch to purchase mourning clothes for the mother, father and surviving child. Funeral expenses to a maximum of £7.10s.0d were met from the fund. This was to provide two mourning carriages and a hearse. The various undertakers sent their bills into the fund committee. Most provided a standard funeral for £7.10s.0d, supplying an elm coffin with brass handles, two horses in head feathers and velvet hangings. The committee acted with discretion and in some cases agreed payments slightly in excess of the limit.

The *Albion* had been launched on a Tuesday and the dead were buried the following Saturday, Monday and Tuesday. Most were interred in the communal grave at East London Cemetery, but others were buried in individual graves in other parts of the cemetery or in other graveyards. The police had been criticised for having too few officers at the launch—although the inquest later heard numbers were decided by the Iron Works management—and were taking no chances at the funerals. Reports reveal fifteen thousand officers attended the cemetery on Saturday, seven thousand on Monday and a relatively modest four to five thousand on the Tuesday.

Scenes at the funerals were harrowing. Vast crowds gathered along the routes of the various funeral cortéges. Mrs Eliza Tarbot, at 64 the oldest victim, was first to be buried. She was followed by Mrs Isabel White, 30, and her children Lottie, 5, and Queenie, 2. When Mrs White had been dragged from the water, rescuers had found her two little daughters still clinging to her frock. All were dead. Albert Hooks, 30, had been a Salvation Army bandsman and his fellow musicians turned out to play at his funeral and comfort his widow, left virtually destitute and with two babies aged 1 and 2 years.

The tragic Simms family were charged £22.10s.0d to bury their children. Simms commented bitterly to the Disaster Fund committee:

> The three children were buried together and £10 or £12 would have amply paid for the funeral. Apparently the only person to benefit from my misfortune is the undertaker....

Two separate inquests were held. Amelia Gardner had died at Blackwall Police Station and her death came under the jurisdiction of the Poplar coroner, Mr Wynne Baxter. Inquests on the other victims were heard by Mr Hilleary at the public hall in Canning Town.

The juries had to decide the cause of the deaths and whether anyone was to blame. They heard the slipway bridge had been constructed for workmen and had not been intended for use by spectators at the launch. It was only five or six feet wide and about eighty feet long. At the time of the launch—high tide—it would have been between three and six feet above the water level. The bridge had been constructed by foreman labourer Thomas Reed. Reed had realised it would not be strong enough to hold spectators and had warned police to keep it clear. By all accounts the bridge was kept clear until about 2:00 PM, but by that time the crowds had grown so large the police reluctantly decided to allow people on to the footway. The seventy policemen on duty were dealing with a situation on private property and were present by invitation. An identical number of officers had been "ordered" for the launch of the previous ship to leave the Iron Works, the *Fuji*. On that occasion there were no problems with crowd control. This was not the case at the launch of the *Albion*. Mackrow told the Poplar jury a regiment of soldiers would have been needed to keep people off the slipway.

No one had realised the backwash from the *Albion* would be as substantial or as devastating as it was, although there had been a similar incident twelve years previously. The launch of HMS *Benbow* at the yard in 1886 had caused a backwash that swept nine people into the water, but all had been saved.

Wynne Baxter's twenty-one-man jury deliberated for more than two hours before reaching a verdict of accidental death. They reflected the public outrage when they added the rider:

> We are of the opinion that the visitors to the yard acted contrary to instructions in going and remaining on the footbridge, but that the said bridge was of a very unsubstantial character and that sufficient precautions were not taken to prevent visitors using it and also that owing to the great concourse of people the police were unable to carry out their instructions.
>
> We are further of the opinion that there was a great lack of judgement in allowing such large numbers of people admission to the works in addition to the accommodation provided by the specially erected stands. We therefore recommend that on all further occasions it would be desirable for

the safety of the public that the police should have thorough control and responsibility and that no person should be allowed upon any structure or platform which had not been properly tested and certified by a competent authority.

The jurors donated their fees—a total of £4.10s.0d—to the Disaster Fund.

Hilleary's jury reached a similar verdict, finding Rose Elliott, 18, and "32 others" had died through drowning and that no one was to blame. The jurors' rider was more tempered than that of their colleagues in Poplar.

> ...the jury would suggest that on further occasions greater precautions should be taken by the company to keep the public from such dangerous positions which are well known to exist at the launching of large vessels.

If money didn't exactly pour into the Disaster Fund it did collect in a steady trickle. Hills set the fund off to a good start with a £1,000 donation. Queen Victoria sent £50 and another £26.5s.0d (twenty-five guineas) came from the Duke and Duchess of York. Several local companies subscribed to the fund, including the Great Eastern Railway and brewers Charrington's and Courage. George Mackrow made a personal donation of £25, "Frankie and his mother" sent 2/6d, "six servants" collected 4/6d and the Infants' department of the Star Lane School, Canning Town sent 10/-. Many individuals, most of whom would have been among the poorest in the country, made donations. Men had collections at work and several departments at the Thames Iron Works sent substantial contributions. The music hall proprietor Mr Charles Relf staged a benefit performance at the Royal Albert Music Hall in Canning Town and raised £161.19s.2d for the fund. The "Penge Poet," Mr Joseph Gwyer, penned a few verses and sold his work at a penny a time to raise £2.10s.0d. Long lists of donors appeared in the local press.

Naturally, there was a wealth of sympathy and good intent, but the Disaster Fund committee decided to close the appeal on 18 July. By this time a total of £2,762.0s.11d had been raised and Alderman Ivey and his committee believed this would be sufficient to deal with the needs of those affected by the disaster. How these good and well-intentioned men came to such a conclusion is difficult to understand. They knew how many had been killed and injured, and how impoverished the vast majority of those affected were. Yet they grossly underestimated how much money would be needed. This may be due to the creed of self-reliance which Victorian England epitomised: that people should look after themselves, that the future of individuals and their families lay in their own hands. There is no doubt the *Albion* Disaster Fund was closed prematurely, and many donations and offers of help were turned away as unnecessary when in reality they were desperately needed.

One spurned offer came from Samuel Gammon. Gammon represented the ship and insurance brokers who had insured the *Albion*'s launch. He wrote to Hills:

> I have approached some of the underwriters on the launching risk of this ship and in consideration of the fact that it appears that there can be no possible claim against them in this matter, I think the majority of them would be prepared to make a suitable and substantial present to the relief fund.

He asked how much would be required, and added:

> It sometimes occurs that subscriptions to such funds are overdone, and happily there are not many breadwinners' lives lost by this accident.

Gammon sent a personal donation of two guineas, but was told the underwriters would not be required to contribute as the funds collected would be sufficient.

There is little doubt a more skillfully managed fund would have relieved much heartbreak suffered by the innocent victims of the disaster. The district's workers lived from hand to mouth. Any event bringing extra expense created real hardship. The traumas at the launch were compounded by the mounting difficulties and struggles that followed. Funerals and inquests over, and funds collected, the hard work of dealing with the inevitable suffering and desperation began.

George Mackrow seems to have been responsible for much of the fund's organisation. He produced a map of Canning Town and marked in red the places where disaster victims lived. The area was divided into three districts and committee members were paired and allocated districts in which they dealt with all claims from the fund. Mackrow and Buckley dealt with the area south of Barking Road, home of sixteen bereaved families. Ivey and Partner concentrated on the north side of Barking Road, where there were eleven bereaved families. Stevens and Pelly dealt with all cases falling outside those boundaries. Mackrow comes across as a humane and kindly man. On 30 June he wrote to Ivey:

> I hope we shall be provided with funds tomorrow, in cash, that we may commence to dispense where we find actual need, as for instance in two

such cases as were mentioned on Tuesday evening last, as these poor creatures may be at their last resources....

He added a postscript:

> We have just heard of another death at Greenwich, a Mrs Howell, who was one of the rescued. We had sent over our Mr Atkinson with £5 before we heard of the death as we were informed of there being great need.

People affected by the disaster sent their claims to the committee. These were investigated by committee members or their representatives and payments were made in cases considered genuine. The payments were usually meagre and rarely covered the losses suffered. Limited medical expenses were paid from the fund, and those who had clothing damaged by the water were able to claim a maximum of £5. In reality few were paid more than a standard £1.10s.0d in compensation. Higher sums were paid to victims who had lost items of greater monetary value, and little consideration was given to whether or not such victims could afford the loss more easily than those who had lost their old, shabby but only set of clothing. The tragedy left many families in dire straits. Most of the victims were young and had children. Husbands were left without wives, wives without husbands. In the days before the welfare state this created immense problems. Mothers had no income, fathers had no one to care for the children while they worked, and could ill-afford a childminder.

At a Disaster Fund committee meeting on 3 January 1899 members discussed provisions to be made for single-parent families. They decided that, for a period of six months, widows would receive £1 per week plus five shillings for the first child and half a crown for each subsequent child. They also agreed that in cases where the mother had died and the father had been obliged to employ outside help, he would be entitled to a maximum payment of 15/– per week, again for a period of six months.

The committee dedicated small sums of money—the maximum received was £150—to benefit families after the six months. These sums were paid to various committee members who then took responsibility for making regular monthly payments to the families until the kitty had dried up. The payments were almost derisory, in some cases around 10/– per month. The committee offered to place children into homes, and several distraught parents had no option but to accept. Victorian orphanages and children's homes were not noted as places rich in the delights of childhood.

There was little choice for orphans like the three McGoldrick youngsters. Their mother, Margaret, died at the launch of the *Albion* and their father was killed at sea a few weeks later. The two boys were sent to the St Vincent's Home in Harrow and the girl went into the care of The Sisters of Charity.

Annie Short was seriously injured at the launch. The family struggled to pay medical bills and a Silvertown missionary, Mr Emmerson, wrote to the committee asking for the family to receive financial help. They received just £4. Annie died in September, leaving her husband with six young children to care for. Not surprisingly, he felt unable to cope. "I am left with six children averaging from 18 months to 15 years and have not anyone to look after them," he wrote to the committee. "I should be much obliged if you could assist me in getting some of them into a home." Charles Short, aged two, went to the Home of the Church Extension Association and Ellen and Alice Short were sent to a Mrs Tennyson in Brightlingsea. Mrs Tennyson was asked to take all three children, but insisted her home was for girls only.

Thames Iron Works employee James Dives lost his wife Ann, 38. He was left with five children: Martha, 9, Florence, 8, Ada, 6, Mabel, 3 and Sylvia, 2. He was determined they would not be taken into homes:

> The proposal to send some of them away I cannot agree. I was sent to a school myself so know what they are. I am only a labourer, but as long as I am able to work I prefer to keep them at home.

Just £100 was set aside to help Dives keep his family together. His struggle ended when he died from "congestion of the lungs" on 6 January 1900, aged 37. We cannot know if his death was related to the *Albion* disaster, but it must be a distinct possibility. The Dives children did not end up in a home. The family rallied round and the orphans were raised by their aunts and uncles.

Another Iron Works labourer, Edward Hodgkinson, 35, died while trying to rescue others floundering in the water after the slipway capsized. His pregnant wife was left with two toddlers aged 9 months and 3 years. She was clearly distraught at the prospect of having to care for a third child and, while declining the committee's offer to put her existing children into homes, wrote:

> ...if you could do anything as regards the one that I am expecting I should be most thankful to you, so that I know it would be well cared for, as that will be my greatest burden.

The committee would not help, but agreed the sum of £150 set aside for her family should be paid at a rate of 10/– per week. Mrs Hodgkinson's third child was born on 21 December and she realised she had little chance of being able to feed her family. She pleaded again with the committee:

> ...if it is in your power, if you would kindly help me by trying to get the youngest, a boy, into a home or institution, if only for 15 months or two years, till the second child is more off my hands and so enable me to earn a little. Trusting dear sirs, that you will do what you can to help me in this respect.

The committee was powerless to help. Funds were exhausted.

Sarah Hooks fared little better. Her husband Albert, 30, was drowned, leaving her with two children aged under three years. She was clearly appalled at the offer to put them into homes:

> Owing to the tender ages of both I could not think your enquiry would include them. Seeing Victor is just 2 years and Harrold 14 months you must kindly pardon me but I hope the gentlemen of the committee will not try and force this understanding the ages of the children. And if some other arrangement can be made, so that I could have my children with me, which are my only comfort, they would help heal the wound this sad affair has caused me.

The "other arrangement" amounted to a woefully inadequate £150, paid at 10/– per week. Sarah was clearly distressed. "You must not think I am ungrateful," she wrote to the committee.

> But the future comes before me. According to the decision in your letter the £150 at 10 shillings per week will not cover six years. My children will be only 5 and 6 years respectively. What must I do then? I shall be obliged to appeal to the Parish for relief. I see nothing else. Considering the amount collected I did not quite expect this.

The Simms family of Canning Town were among the worst affected. Their lives were shattered by the tragedy. Mr Simms, his heavily pregnant wife and their four children—two of them from Mrs Simms' first marriage—were thrown into the water. Ernest, 12, Kitty, 10, and Alfred, 5, died. The parents and 2-year-old Edith survived, though not without injury. The Simms received the standard £5 "mourning payment" from the fund, a sum barely sufficient to purchase mourning clothes for one, let alone three.

The surviving family were all seriously ill in the weeks that followed. Mr Simms worked at the Iron Works and went back to his job in July. He was forced to return home as he was too weak to work. A doctor's certificate shows he was suffering from "pulmonary disability." There was no such luxury as sickness pay. If a man could not work, he was not paid. The fact he could not work because of a catastrophe at his workplace that had made him ill and killed his three children made no difference. The family went for a much-needed rest in Southsea, near Portsmouth. The break was another disaster. On his return home, Simms enlisted the help of coroner's officer Fred Rosen to write an appeal for help from the disaster committee:

> I am an employee of the Thames Iron Works and on 21st June attended with my wife and family to see the launch. When the ship went off and the wave struck the bridge the whole of us were precipitated into the water. Me, my wife and daughter Edith, aged two and a half years, were rescued the others being drowned.
>
> After the inquest was opened and the children buried, me, my wife and child were compelled to go away to the seaside on account of our failing health. We went to Portsmouth. When there three days Edith was taken bad and was attended by Dr Emmett who certified her to be suffering from gas poisoning. She was ordered to be kept in bed and stayed there for a fortnight. Extra expenses for doctor, nursing and nourishment were incurred. When the doctor pronounced it safe we brought her home and she is still under the care of Dr Lawrence as is also my wife. I myself am still on the sick list and unable to work consequent upon the shock and immersion.
>
> When at Portsmouth I wrote to Mr Mackrow of Thames Iron Works who sent me £5 in addition to that I had from Mr Hills for the purpose of buying mourning which was not sufficient by £2.10s.0d to supply myself and little one.
>
> Owing to being out of work and expenses incurred in doctor's fees, extra nourishment for us all, my funds are quite exhausted. I made application to Canon Buckley and have been awarded the sum of £2 which will nothing like pay for my family loss. We were all wearing our best clothing which was entirely spoiled.
>
> I was informed by Mr Ivey the mayor that the sum of £22.10s.0d was paid to Mr Cribb the undertaker of Hallsville Road which sum I consider an exorbitant one. The three children were buried together and £10 or £12

would have amply paid for the funeral. Apparently the only person to benefit from my misfortune is the undertaker. In these circumstances I respectfully beg that the committee reconsider my case and allow me some further sum from the fund.

Mackrow wrote to Alderman Ivey:

As suggested in my last to you, I paid over to Alfred Simms the sum of £2.14s.6d. He has shown me a certificate from the doctor, and his wife is evidently very ill. The water got into her lung and has done great mischief, and the poor woman though slowly recovering from her confinement, it is feared will go into consumption. He is a very quiet reserved man, and I do not think he has received any help from anyone but through myself.

He has received the following sums: £5 for mourning June 23, £5 June 8 upon representation of Mr Payne, our chief time keeper and Simms and surviving child were sent away to Southsea for a few weeks. August 5 he received another £2, September 8 £5, December 10 £1, January 16 £2.14s.6d making a total of £20.16s.6d. He is and has been engaged at these works for some time, and has called at my office now and again, and I presume that is how I have dealt with the case.

Simms eventually received a total of £22.14s.6d from the fund. At the last we hear of him, January 1899, his wife was still very ill after her confinement.

The committee seemed rather more generous to wealthier claimants. Miss Lizzie Shakespeare was dressed in fine and expensive clothes as she watched the launch from the ill-fated slipway. Her father wrote on her behalf to the committee:

The loss of her hat and the damage done to her clothes I have reckoned up and it cost me about £4 for them as the velvet dress is completely spoilt and stands up stiff as a poker. Then again it has cost my missus a tidy bit for her daughter....

Lizzie was sent £6.6s.0d (six guineas)—as much as many Canning Town labourers could earn in a month. Dr Edwin Gill claimed on behalf of Mrs Endicott and Mrs Corbett, two relatively well-off ladies. He commented both had been fully recovered within twenty-four hours of the accident, and their medical expenses amounted to 5/– each. "A small sum would I think satisfy...as they could not be called poor people." They received £2.5s.0d each, comparatively large amounts. The committee was less generous to Mrs Annie Pearse. When Annie and her baby were thrown into the water their clothes were ruined and Annie lost her purse containing her "little all." She received just £2 from the fund.

The fund covered some medical expenses, but even then payment was haphazard. The sufferings of the Young family were typical. A family group had attended the launch. Elsie Young and her younger brother were rescued, but their sister-in-law, Matilda, 23, drowned. Elsie was seriously injured and suffered severe illness for months after her lucky escape. She was treated by Dr Beadle, and his bills were forwarded to the committee. His charges—12/– per week for four weeks—were considered excessive and the committee delayed payment. It seems Dr Beadle was annoyed and refused to give Elsie further help. Alderman Ivey was in charge of the case and in October 1898 Mackrow wrote to him:

> If you are dealing with it I would advise your worship to do so early as the poor girl seems very unwell and needs attention.

Mrs Matilda Thompson, 60, was lucky to survive her day out at the launch. She was seriously injured by the floating timbers and was initially expected to die. Doctors at Poplar Hospital amputated her leg and she eventually made a good recovery. The committee was informed a wooden leg would cost about 50/– and an artificial limb £12. Mrs Thompson received a £5 grant from the fund, plus £50 to purchase the more expensive artificial limb and provide her with a small weekly grant.

Those who had damaged their clothes or sustained injury whilst helping with the rescue efforts were also entitled to claim from the fund, though the sums given were again minimal. William Angus dragged eight people from the treacherous waters, including fellow rescuer Albert Sandell, who had been struck by a timber after saving seven people. William wrote to the committee:

> I must state I have been very ill ever since I came out of hospital where I was conveyed on the night of the accident. My clothes of course were damaged to some extent. I was working for Mr Robinson Bange and Lea Shipbuilders of Old Canning Town where I have been earning an average £2.4s.6d per week, having a wife and three children to support. I am in a penniless condition....

William received £4, barely enough to cover a couple of weeks off work and certainly nowhere near enough to keep his family fed until he had recovered. John Downey rescued seven people and was awarded £1 to replace damaged clothing. The cheque was sent to his wife but returned to the committee with the note:

> I am sorry that I must explain that the reason of the delay in not sending a receipt of the cheque for £1 payable to my husband John Downey is that shortly after the Blackwall incident he left me and is gone on the drink.

Some claims made following the disaster were highly suspect. Frederick Robinson won fame and acclaim in the national newspapers of the day, being hailed a hero. He claimed to have rescued fifteen conscious casualties, six unconscious sufferers and retrieved ten dead bodies. His exploits apparently included giving artificial respiration to three people at the same time. Clement Mackrow took a dim view, reporting to the committee: "As regards this case I can say nothing, except that his statement is improbable." Robinson received no compensation from the fund, but was later awarded one of twenty bronze medals awarded to rescuers by the Royal Humane Society.

The families and orphans of the thirty-eight people killed shared the grand total of £2,187.5s.1d, and well over £500 of this went to cover funeral expenses and the cost of the memorial stone. The committee paid out just £519.3s.0d to the 193 who suffered non-fatal injuries and loss as a result of the disaster. The rest of the money went on miscellaneous expenses such as doctors' bills, clerical help and postage costs.

Arnold Hills, Iron Works director, had planned an opulent memorial for the plot of land purchased at the East London Cemetery. He had commissioned designs from Italy and printed a sketch of the proposed monument in the *Thames Iron Works Gazette* on 30 September 1898. It featured a rolling wave and an angel, cast in carrara marble and Aberdeen granite—and a price tag of several hundred pounds. Within two months of the disaster Mackrow realised the plans were beyond the fund's means. On 15 August 1898 he wrote:

> I don't think we ought to spend £300 or £400 on a memorial and leave honest claims unmet. We are stewards of the generous public and I think we must meet all genuine cases of need.

In February 1899 the committee decided to complete the memorial with a marble panel and marble chips. Hills' plan to launch a second appeal to raise funds for the original memorial design was rejected by the committee. Hills was furious and resigned. At the committee's final meeting, in May 1899, Mackrow raised the subject of the second appeal again. This time it was agreed to proceed and it was decided the appeal should be signed by all committee members. Alderman Ivey, the chairman, refused to have anything to do with it. The Reverend Partner, a committee member and a pastor at Plaistow Congregational Church, was not at the meeting, but wrote in protest.

> As I could not conscientiously vote for the Appeal I would not consent to my name being attached to it. If after dealing with all the cases of hardship and distress caused by the disaster we had been in possession of ample funds one would have gladly voted for the monument, but as we are not it seems to me that the only proper course is to finish the enclosure according to our means. Nor have I any doubt that the subscribers as a whole would commend us for spending money on the sufferers rather than on a very costly monument. However, the committee have resolved to send forth the appeal, and after so much pleasant work together I am heartily sorry that in this matter I cannot go with them, but though my name would count for very little one way or the other, I could not, after the people have been so generous, allow it to be connected with the appeal for something which is not really needed.

The angel and the wave never appeared in the East London Cemetery. To this day the memorial is marked only be slabs listing the names of those buried. The sole decoration is a simple anchor.

The suffering at the *Albion*'s launch was possibly surpassed by the emotional and physical pain endured by victims and their relatives in the weeks, months and years to come. The *Albion* disaster must go down as one of the saddest and most badly-handled tragedies in Victorian London.

Appendix: Disaster Casualties

These are lists of people who died in the major incidents described in this book. Unfortunately, the publicised lists of those killed were not always complete. Casualties often returned to their own homes after accidents, and sometimes died from their injuries several weeks later. Researchers should also note mistakes in christian names and in the spellings of surnames were common.

Explosion at Firework Factory, Lambeth Butts, February 1842

Mr D'Ernst	Mrs Hampshire	John Whiting
Georg Gibbets		

Explosion at Woolwich Arsenal, 17 September 1845

Robert Burbage	John Crake, 74	Alexander Leonard
Henry Butters senior	Samuel Kendley	Michael Purtill
Henry Butters junior		

Explosion at King Street, Lambeth Butts, January 1846

Mr Holmes	William Kenyon

Explosion of Firework Factory, Westminster Road, 6 March 1854

Mr Coton	unidentified boy

Explosion at Woolwich Arsenal, 3 December 1855

Thomas Holland, 40	Henry Langham, 25	James Wallace, 25
John Kirwin, 40		

Panic at Surrey Gardens Music Hall, 19 October 1856

Harriet Barlow, 30	Harriet Johnson, 20	Elizabeth Mead, 48
Samuel Heard, 24	Harriet Mathew, 16	Grace Slipper, 40

Fall of Houses, Tottenham Court Road, 9 May 1857

Frederick Byng
Ann Driscoll, 26

John Garnett
James Kivil, 29

Joseph Taylor, 26
Richard Turner, 29

Train Crash, Lewisham, 28 June 1857

Edith Bellinger, 9 months
Elizabeth Bellinger
John Bellinger, 31
Thomas Dalton

Francis Drake
Thomas Franklin, 15
Mary Anne Howe
William Nightingale

Horatio Turner, 18
Thomas Turner, 7
Mrs Wilcox

Fire and collapse of house, Gilbert Street, 29 March 1858

Eliza Hedger, 50
John Hedger, 13
William Hedger, 20
William Hedger, 53
Alfred Smith
Alfred Smith, 14

Harriet Smith, 15
Harriet Smith, 41
Harvey Smith
Henry Smith
Jessie Smith, 2

Mary and Maria Smith
(twins), 5
Richard Smith, 17
Richard Smith, 40
Thomas Smith, 7
Walter Smith

Explosion of Firework Factory, Westminster Road, 12 July 1858

Caroline Bridges, 11
Madame Coton

Sarah Anne Vaughan, 11
two others killed

over 300 injured

Panic at Royal Victoria Theatre, 26 December 1858

Charles Barber, 14
Charles Buchan, 14
John Cobley, 16
George Craig, 14
William Hammond, 20

Patrick Handrahan, 15
Thomas Herring, 15
Moses Holford, 17
William Jennings, 13
Thomas Lewen, 15

Walter Maizey, 12
Henry Marks, 17
Charles Morvin, 23
James Newman, 16

Train Crash, Tottenham Station, 20 February 1860

George Cornwall
William Rowell

Mr Satchell

Mr Stokes

Train Crash, Hampstead, 2 September 1861

Elizabeth Allen
Eroda Bowby
Clara Clements, 44
Emma English
Master Greenwood, 12

Master Greenwood, 8
Edward Hills
Rhoda Oliver
David Saunders

Mary Sillis
Miss Stacey, 10
Charles Standing
John Yeoman

Erith Explosion, 1 October 1864

Luke Barker
John Dadson
John Eaves, 26
John Hubbard, 53

Walter Jemmett
Eliza Osborne, 8
George Rayner, 39
Daniel Wise

Elizabeth Wright, 13
James Wright
Mr Yorke
John Yorke, 13

Blackheath Tunnel Train Crash, 16 December 1864

Edward Allum
William Jones

William Morris
William Seeby

Henry Smith
William Wade

Collapse of first floor, Catholic Free School Rooms, 26 January 1865

Adelaide Fallen

Mary Hefferson

Collapse of Six Ely Court, Holborn, 16 August 1866

Guiseppe Carlo Casartelli

Elizabeth Davis

Ice disaster in Regent's Park, 15 January 1867

Frederick Beer
R. Born, 12
John Broadbridge, 10
J. Bryant
H. Chadwick
John Claridge
James Crawley
William Davies
Henry Gambell
James Glanfield, 15
James Griffon
R. Haarnack
Henry Hardiman
Thomas Hardy Jr

Thomas Harries
James Jobson
Charles Jukes
J. Justice
Thomas Justice
C.E. Luckman
Mr M'Intyre
James Mitchell
David North, 14
Samuel Olley, 20
W. Parkinson
Edmund Pullen
Edward Pullman

George Rhodes
William Robertson, 40
Lt R. Edwin Scott
Charles Smith
William Smith
Arthur Stevens
Edward Thurley
John Vincent
Mr Waite
Charles Wake
Thomas Whately
J. Spencer Woods
H. Woodhouse

Explosion at Woolwich Arsenal, 5 October 1867

Charles Keightley, 13
Garrett McCallaghan, 14

Herbert Newby, 16
William Pigge, 14

Henry Webb, 14

With Disastrous Consequences...

Bomb Explosion, Clerkenwell, 13 December 1867

Minnie Abbott, 7	Humphrey Evans, 67	Sarah Hodgkinson, 30
William Clutton, 47	Martha Evans, 65	Martha Thompson, 11

A memorial at the Parish Church of St James, Clerkenwell states nine other people died soon after the explosion.

Explosion of Firework Factory, Moscow Road, October 1869

Mrs Jack and three children	Elizabeth Titheradge, 9	Emma Titheradge, 7
Edward Titheradge		

Train Crash, Harrow, 28 November 1870

Miss Bell	J.H. Jordan	William Shelvey, 40
George Bell	Mr Rowley	Mr Smith
J.W. Jeffreys		

The Princess Alice—Collision with Waterman's Boat, October 1873

George Gray, 64	Patrick Lanna, 16	Thomas Smith, 50
Joseph Jocelyn, 65	Patrick Martin, 45	Henry Tanner, 25
Samuel Jones, 26	William Piper, 39	John Taylor, 15

The Goliath Fire, 22 December 1875

William Burrell, 14	Clement Harris	Alfred Powney, 15
Frederick Cook, 14	Charles Leggett, 13	Alfred Scarfe, 13
Joseph Denholme, 10	Peter Leonard, 14	George Skinner, 14
James Dickerson, 15	Richard Mc'Kay, 14	Alfred Smith, 13
William Giddings, 14	William M'Grath, 14	Richard Wheeler, 20

From a list compiled by Thurrock Local History Society.

Sinking of The Princess Alice, 3 September 1878

South London

Identified	George Bailey, 25	Henry Butcher, 27
	John Bailey, 25	Lucy Brady
Ann Aldridge, 16	Mrs Baker	Clement Butt
Eliza Aldridge, 32	Ben. Frederick Baker	Harriet Calton, 20
Ellen Anckorn, 47	Frederick Basten	Frederick Carter
John Anckorn, 49	Mary Ann Basten	Sarah Carter
Frances Andrews, 31	William Bridger, 40	Ernest Chabot
William Andrews, 27	Thomas Botrill	Harold Chabot
Frank Aylen	William Bottrill	Josephine Chabot, 40

William Childs
George Chittlebury
John Clymick
Jane Crawford, her mother,
  brother and two children
Emma Dormer, 60
Henry Dormer
Mary Jane Cutler Drake, 20
Ethel Durrant
George Edridge, 29
Mary Ann Elliott
William Elliott
Flora Fricker, 3
Mrs Forsdyke
Edmund Forsdyke
Eliza Forsdyke
Sydney Forsdyke
Jane Amelia Frost, 46
Robert Frost, 48
Emily Furneaux, 21
Mary Drew Furneaux, 60
Mr Freeman
Harry Gissing
Sarah Green
George Greenwood
Joseph Greenwood
Rebecca Greenfield and
  infant daughter
Sarah Greenwood
Ellen Grimsay
Mrs Gyde
Clara Louisa Gyde, 18
  months
Hannah Haggar
Maria Hallett
Dinah Hand
Thomas Hand
Walter Harris
Henry Hawkins
Alfred Head
Alice Head
Mary Ann Hilson
Mary Hollis
Elizabeth Hollingsworth
George Hollingsworth
Maud Hollingsworth
Frances Hoskins
Henry Hoskins
George Howard
Henry Hughes
Edith Hunt
Rose Marie Hurwood

Eliza Hutley
James Ivory, 60
Mary Ann Ivory, 55
Charles Jardine, 48
Elizabeth Jones
Florence Jones
Martha Jones
William Jones
Mr Kempe
Mrs King
Edward King, 6 months
Francis King
Arnold Larchin
Harriet Larchin
Kate Lambert
Lucy Lambert
W.J. Lambert
Samuel Larner
Albert Leaver, 15
Ben Leaver, 18
Ruth Leaver, 14
Amy Lee
Caroline Lewis
Amelia Lynn
Alice Mansfield
Jane Mansfield
Ebenezer Marks
Esther Marks
Frank Marks
John Marks
Frederick Martin
Fanny May
Joseph M'Geary, 54
Emily Morrison, 24
Evelyn Morrison, 15
Anna Muncey
Blanche Muncey
Charlotte Nares
Alfred Orr
Emily Page
Frederick Page
Thomas Page
David Palmer
Susan Pearson, 22
Anne Pickerell
George Pickerell
Jane Pickerell
Emma Potter, 42
Kate Ralph
Mary Ann Ralph
Sarah Ralph
Mary Randall

Alfred Sabine, 30, wife and
  four children
Joseph Sedgwick, 43
Jane Shand
Martha Sims
Ann Slocombe
William Slocombe, 74
Kate Smith
Lilian Smith
Maria Smith
Arthur Spencer
Victor Stahr, 22
John Standish
Susannah Standish
Grace Steele, 12
Hannah Steele
Louisa Steele, 27
Sophia Steele
Annie Summers, 29
Florence Summers, 5
Sydney Summers, 13 months
Anne Swan
James Swan
Mary Elizabeth Swan
John Taylor
Alice Wallis
Anne Wallis
Jane Wallis
Louisa Ward, 16
Mrs Wark, 38
John Wark
William Wark
Mrs White
Aaron White, 50
Sarah White
Sarah White, 45
Emily Weightman, 14
George Whiten
Mary Whiten
Harry Wickens
Rebecca Wickens

Missing

Maria Bandy
Mr Greenfield
Mrs Hagger, and daughter
Mr Hallett
Mr and Mrs Hollingshead
  and two children
Mr and Mrs Hunt and one
  daughter

Mr and Mrs Jones and two
    children
Mr and Mrs Jones and
    daughter, Alice, 6

Mr James Jenkins
Miss Marson, 56
Mrs Pearson
Elizabeth Reuter

Herbert Russell, 18
Anne Stubbings, 39
William Stubbings, 41
William Welby, 18

Greenwich, Woolwich, Plumstead etc

Identified

Mary Barker
Mary Ann Best
Ann Bing
Frederick Boncey
James Burton, 9 and two
    other children
James Burton, 38
Maria Burton, 36
Ada Catlin, 3
Ann Catlin
Thomas Catlin, 3 months
Nellie Collis, 12 months
Theresa Collis, 27
Caroline Constable, 44
Mary Ann Coombes, 67
Amelia Crofts
Charles Curtis
Valentine Dunkley
Jane Ferguson

John Grinstead
William Grinstead
George Halliday
John Harrison
Eugenie Hawkes
Henry Hawkins
Mr Hock
John Holliday
Eliza Hooper, 63
Mrs Ralph Jobling, 22
Thomas Jobling
Alfred King, 19
Edward King
Elizabeth King
William King
Annie Rowley, 14
Walter W. Rowley, 12
Nelly Louisa Sans
Mary Ann Searle, 24
Hannah Smith
Grace Summers

Emily Turner, 18
Barnard Towse, 14 months
Edgar Towse, 13
Emily Towse, 32
Frederick Towse
Winifred Towse, 10
Louisa Ward
Ellen Warmy
Frederick Watson
Helen Wearing
James Westhall
Frederick Whomes

Missing

Willie Collis, 18 months
Fanny King and infant son
Mr Saury, 40 and son
Maria Smith, 25 and infant
Mrs Vanderbilt

East London

Identified

Alfred Alesbury
Edith Alesbury, 5 months
Eliza Alesbury, 58
Elizabeth Alesbury, 21
Jaber Alesbury, 2
Jessie Alesbury, 9
Louisa Alesbury, 5
Jane Green, 17
Catherine Allan
George Allan
Edmund Aslat
Mr W. Aslat
Francis Beadle
Harriet Belcher
Henry Belcher
James Bilton
William Bishop
Jessie Blackburn
Louise Blackburn
Thomas Bledger

Jane Bridges
Philip Burman, wife
    Charlotte and three
    children
Alfred Butler, 28
Elizabeth Butler
Joseph Butler, 48
Henry Clifton
Charles Cole
Mr F. Conway
Emily Jane Crocker
Lewis Crocker
Matilda Crocker
Flora Crouch
Frank Crouch
Frederick Crouch
Florence Crouch
Thomas Davis, wife and four
    children
Robert Everest, wife and two
    children
Florence Finnett

Sophy Finnett
W.A. Fisher
Sarah Freeman, brother and
    two children
George Hallett
Alice Hammond
Frederick Hammond
Mrs Harden
Jane Harris, 15
Kate Harris, 7
Sarah Harris, 44
Sarah Alice Harris, 17
Bessie Howlett, 25
Walter Howlett
Eliza Huddle
Ernest Huddle
George Huddle
George Michael Huddle
Henry Huddle
Amelia Johnson, 29
William Johnson, 38
Mrs Filmer Kidston

Rosina King
Alfred Lewis
Mary Ann Lewis
William Magiff
Catherine Meeks
Caroline M'Geary
Catherine Mulhern
James Mulhern
Margaret Mulhern
Elizabeth Newman, 40
John Northey
Katharine Penney
Disney Perou, 51
Annie Piddell
George Piddell
Flora Piper
Harriet Rackley, 24
Mr J. Richardson and son
   William, 11

George Richmond
Arthur Riddell, 12
Edward Riddell, 18
Mrs Roberts
Emma Roberts
Thomas Savage
Michael Scurr
Jane Sinclair
Mary Jane Sinclair
George Skelton
William Skillington
William Sutton, 56
Henry Velcher and two
   children
Ann Watson
Emily Mary Watson
Frederick Wyatt
Susan Wyatt

Missing

Mrs Allan
Mrs Billing and child
Mr Crouch
Jane Grinstead
Mrs Hallett
Hannah Jackson
Jane King, 40
Thomas Macgiff
Mitchel
Charles Newman
William Potter, 33
Mrs Sutton
Mrs Skelton
Eliza Taylor

North London

Identified

John Arnstead, 21
Emma Jane Baker
William Baker
Emma Ball, 58
Jane Bange
Elizabeth Bardens, 63
Cornelius Briscoe
Jane Briscoe, 23
Sarah Briscoe, 5
Eliza Brodrib, 52, John
   Brodrib, 18, and two
   children
Emma Bull
Hugh Burns
Emma Campbell
W. Campbell
Julia Cattermole
Elizabeth Chapman
Craven Proctor Cobham
Elizabeth Cobham
Mildred Cobham
H.J. Cochren
Maria Copping
Charles Rowe Dillon
Sarah Dillon
Hannah Donald
Elizabeth Drew
Mary Ann Drew

Miriam Drew
Joseph Ellis
Mary Ellis
James Emmett
Ada Farnum
Gertrude Finney
Phyllis Flatman
Sarah Fricker
George Garrard
R. William Ginn
Charlotte Golding
Annie Gristwood
Harriet Gurr, 40
Ella Hambury, 20
William Harrison, 24
Ross Hennessy
William Hill
Mary Ann Hollings
George Hughes
Mrs Hunt
Edgar Hunt
Eliza Hunt
Ethel Hunt
Sarah Jane Hunt
George Ingram
James Ledamun
Leonard Ledamun
Mary Ann Ledamun
Samuel Lowry
Eliza Maynan

Edward Moore, wife and two
   children
Harry Muddock
Henry Muddock
Ross Muddock
John Notman, 50
Kate Notman, 21
Hannah Nunn
Charlotte Oakley
George Oakley
Emily Phillips, 37
S. Pitt
W.L. Pitt
Kezia Rolt
Sarah Rolt
Alfred Rouse
Kate Rouse
Sarah Rouse
Maria Scholz
Annie Stubbins
W. George Stubbins
Miss Teesdale
Mrs Teesdale
Charles Teesdale, 24
Kate Thompson
Rosa Warburton, 23
Louisa Ward
Albert Watson
Alfred Watson
Bess Watts

George Watts
Wiliam Watts
Alfred Wayman, 18 months
Drusilla Wayman, 16
Elizabeth Wayman, 14
Harriet Wayman, 26
Augusta Wheatley
Fanny White, 15

Mary White, 13
Thomas White
Annie Wool, 42
Annie Bird Wool, 14
Emily Wool, 5
Kate Wool, 16 months
Lydia Wool, 13
Minnie Wool, 11

Charles Worsfold
Charlotte Worsfold

Missing

Benjamin Briscoe, 18 months
Mary Jane Emmett, 36
Mrs Hughes
Charlotte Turner

West and North West London

Identified

Norman Barnes
Mary Bishop
Walter Bishop
Minnette Bishopp, 26
Eliza Besley
Lucy Bridgeman, 25
William Bridgeman, 35
Mrs Brown
Charles Channel
Alice Childs, 6
George Childs, 3
William Codling
James Coulman
Mrs Hayes
Harry Henderson, 26
Louisa Henderson, 23
Mrs Hill
George Hill
F.H. Hollingsworth
George Howard
Thomas Lamborne
Mary Ann Leverton, 40
Eliza Lee
Edith Legg
Egmontina Little, 14
William Little

Maria Loder
Eustace Marsh
Susan Marsh
Annie Marshall
Ellen May
Harry May
Michael May
Minnie May
Robert Mekins
Florence Milsom
Caroline Murphy
Harriet Murphy
Emily Ridout
T. Chapman Ryall
Thomas Ryalls
Martha Russell
Lucy Silvester
Rosa Silvester
Alice Small
Edwin Smith
Frances Smith and child
Prudence Smith
Elizabeth Somerville, 25
Elizabeth Teesdale, 7
Joseph Teesdale, infant
Sarah Tidy
Harriet Usherwood
Mary Ann Usherwood

Fanny Wakeham
Jane Weaver
Ann White
Louisa Whittington, 13
Susan Whittington, 9
Maria Wilkins
Robert Wilkins
Betsey Wilson, 43
John Wilson, 43
Robert Wood, 63

Missing

Frank Ackroyd, 29
Mrs Beaver, 64
John Clynch, 45
Mrs Cocks, 50
Susan Dawes, 55
Philip Flatman
Eliza Ingram
William Little
Mr and Mrs Milsom and two
    children
Winifred Sims
Mr A.J. Smith
Edward Wilson
Florence Wilson
Samuel Wilson

Central London

Identified

Ann Aldridge, 65
William Aldridge, 35
Mary Ball, 26
William Beecher, 43
Elizabeth Bird
Elizabeth Boddington
Mary Ann Bolam
Susan Bryant

Christopher Denham
Caroline Dyble
Sarah Fricker
Mrs Frith
Thomas Fuller
Mary Ann George
Mrs Gulliver
Matilda Gulliver
Eliza Haist
Eleanor Haist

Matilda Haist
William Haist
Elizabeth Harris
Arthur Harrison, 20 and
    brother, 12
Mrs Hayes
Sarah Ann Holmes
Frederick Hunt
James Jenkins
Thomas Jones

Mary King
John Kitt
Rachael Kitt
Jane Law
Alexandre Mouflet
Annie Mouflet ·
Louis Mouflet
Nancy Mouflet
Mary Ann Neale
Lucy Quick
Eliza Rich

George Roberts
Elizabeth Ropkins, 72
Alice Senior
Elizabeth Sewell
Christina Smith
Emma Stoneman
Mr Thurgood
Mrs Eliza Thurgood
Eliza Thurgood, 2, and sister
Richard Thurgood
Emma Vivash

Maria Wakley
Zillah Waddilove
Harriet Warren
George Webb, 10
Ellen Willemot, 40

Missing

Edward Hogwood, 74
Caroline Smith, 62

Suburban and Provincial

Identified

Harold Bell, Barnet
W.E. Bell, Barnet
Walter Bell, Barnet
Arthur Bonsey, Chertsey
Elizabeth Bools, Sheerness
William Creed, Gravesend
Jane Cully, Croydon

Sarah Dewell, Surbiton
Arthur Harrison, York
Emma Hosken, Balham
James Hosken, Balham
Jessie Hosken, Balham
James Huddart, Hampton
Mary Ledger, Chobham
Thomas Ledger, Chobham
Lawrence Marshall,
  Birmingham

Mrs Martin, Huntingdon
Richard Welch, Tonbridge

Missing

Elizabeth Bowles, Sheerness
Mrs Leech and three
  children, Hertfordshire
Elizabeth Room, 44,
  Birmingham

This list is compiled from Edwin Guest's book *The Wreck of the Princess Alice*. Most of those buried unidentified were later identified by police photographs and by personal clothing and effects.

Train Crash, Old Ford, 28 January 1882

James May, 25
Charlotte Millar, 28

Charlotte Snary, 2 months
Ellen Snary, 32

Phillis Warwick, 19

Explosion at Woolich Arsenal, 24 Septembeer 1883

Arthur Carlick

Richard Stevenson

Hebrew Dramatic Club, 18 January 1887

Kate Baum, 19
Pessi Cohen, 15
Esther Ellis, 16
Elizabeth Eisen, 28
Isaac Gilberg, 12
Millie Gilberg

Jane Goldstein, 24
Lewin Kratofsky, 13
Soloman Kratofsky, 15
Mrs Levy, 47
Isaac Levy, 74
Rachel Levy, 22

Raina Mannikendam, 44
Goa or Eva Marks, 9
Sarah Renalde, 20
Esther Rosenfeld, 24
Kate Silverman, 22

Fire at Forest Gate School, 1 January 1890

Gilbert Allison, 10
Charles Biddick, 12
Frank Chalk, 7
William Dawson, 7
Augustus Flowers, 10
Theophilus Flowers, 9
Thomas Hughes, 11
William Hume, 9
John Jones, 7

John Joyce, 10
Edmund Kilburn, 9
Thomas North, 12
Richard Page, 7
Arthur Pidgeon, 9
James Potts, 10
James Rolfe, 8
Herbert Russell, 10
Frederick Scott, 7

Walter Searle, 9
William Sillitoe, 9
Albert Smith, 12
Frederick Smith, 9
Henry Sowerbutts, 10
John Taylor, 6
Michael Vassum, 8
Frederick Wigmore, 8

Crush at Hampstead Station, 18 April 1892

James Ansell, 12
John Connor, 9
Annie Eaton, 40

James Gorrie, 12
Susan Hamilton, 47
Charles Holloway, 12

Thomas Langford, 14
Alfred Lathey, 13

Food Poisoning, Fores Gate School, 24–27 June 1893

Hannah Fish

Edward Puttick, 14

An additional 143 children suffered from serious food poisoning, but survived.

The Albion Launch, 21 June 1898

Rose Andrews, 22
Beatrice Bishop, 24
Beatrice Bradshaw, 20
Rosa Brown, 25
Harold Cadman, 9
George Claydon, 14
Eliza Coutts/Tarbot, 64
Lena Dearle, 23
Ann Dives, 38
Rose Elliott, 18
Mary Ann Eve, 48
Mrs Forbes
Mrs Gardiner, 39

Amelia Gardiner, 14
Edward Hodgkinson, 35
Albert Hooks, 30
Ernest Hopkins, 12
Kitty Hopkins, 10
Mrs Howell
Moses James, 14
Ada J. King, 23
Jane Langford, 21
Margaret McGoldrick, 38
John Petty, 21
Mary Redfarm, 13
William Riley, 12

Mrs Short
Sarah Simmonds, 12
Alfred Simms, 5
Frank Southgate, three
  months
Samuel Southgate, 23
Isabel White, 30
Lottie White, 5
Queenie White, 2
Sarah Whitehouse, 31
Mary A. Williams, 41
Mary Wilson, 65
Matilda Young, 23

Explosion at Woolwich Arsenal, 18 June 1903

C. Adams
G. Case
Mr Connor
Frank Curran
William Edwards
J. Finham

Alfred Greenlees
Mr Herbert
S. Johnson
J.P. Larkins
Mr Marshall
S. Morley

E. Newton
G. Remington
A. Swords
James Usher

Collapse of Berners Hotel, Oxford Street, 9 April 1908

George Albrecht, 27
Joseph Cremery, 23
Revel Firranti, 21

Aradl Gloie, 25
John Jordan or Jorgan, 21
F. Keoch, 24

Gustav Rigoletti, 21
Frederick Tischaner, 23

Train Crash, Ilford, 1 January 1915

H.W. Bird
Miss Bertha Christie, 34
S.H. Daniels

J. Delfgron or Defron
August Lambert
George Maylin

G. Richardson
E.L. Simmons
Alexander White

Explosion at Silvertown Munitions Factory, 19 January 1917

John Acton
Thomas Henry Acton, 62
Andrea Angel
Henry Badcock, 26
Walter Baker, 35
Sidney Benstead, 26
Ethel Betts, four months
Mary Ann Betts, 58
Ellen Boyce, 32
James Bruce, 62
John Chandler, 27
Edward Craft
Frederick Craft, 36
Thomas Crickmar, 67
Croft, a baby boy, 18 months
E. Croft
Lillian Davey, 15
Charles Downing
John Enness, 25
Edward Forshaw, 30
Frederick Forshaw, 30
Harold Foster, 21
George Galloway
Norman Gardner, 5
Edward Goodsmark,15
William Gray, 39
Robert Greenleaf, 17
Edward Greenoff, 30

Alfred Harlow, 39
Alexander Hart, 25
Charles Hiscock, 57 or 45
Charlotte Hiscock, 76
Catherine Hodge, 16 (also
    called Lizzie Lawrence)
George Hopkins, 24
John Howard, 36
John Royal Howard, 21
Ernest Jenkins, 34
Agnes Jennings, 23
May Jennings, 20
Edward Kidd, 49
William Lambert, 34
Eliza Lettson
Henry Lidbury, 60
Hugh McCoombs, 44
Hugh McMarsh, 24
Walter Manger, 26
John Mason, 9
Ellen Noakes, 29
Francis Oates, 20
Thomas Oates, 8
Thomas Pasture, 53
Rosa Patrick, 4
Roydon Patrick, 2
Ruby Patrick, 6
William Patrick, 9

Dorothy Preston, 11 months
Elisabeth Preston, 28
George Preston, 3
Hannah Preston, 68
Alfred Prior, 35
James Reeve, 44
Frederick Robinson
Henry Rogers, 23
Samuel Saunders
Frederick Sell, 45
Winifred Sell, 15
Ernest Sharp, 36
Frances Simpson, 50
Katharine Smith, 16
William Sinden Smith
Thomas Tasker, 53
David Earl Taylor, 69
Albert Tyzack, 38
Henry Vickers, 49
Sophia Villiers
Geoffrey Wainwright, 17
George Wainwright
Alice Wass, 10
Elsie Wass, 13 or 10
Mary Wass, 32
Stanley Wass, 10 or 13
Walter Wass, 13
George Wenborn, 49

This list is taken from records compiled by Newham Local Studies Library, and is based on research in the Times and the Stratford Express.

The official death toll was 73, but a total of 82 names have come to light. Some of these may be errors in reporting, but all have been listed.

List of Sources

Archives and Primary Source Material

Accident Reports of the Railways Inspecting Officers, Board of Trade, Ministry of Transport and Department of the Environment, 1856–1892.

Annual Report of HM Inspector of Gunpowder Works, 1874–1875.

Annual Reports of the Royal Humane Society, 1831, 1866–1868.

Bank Book of the Clerkenwell Explosion Relief Fund Committee.

Brunner Mond Official Company History.

Clerkenwell Guardians of the Poor Letter Book, 1868.

Clerkenwell Vestry Minute Book, 1868.

East and West India Dock Company, Half Yearly Report, July 1867.

Forest Gate School District Annual Reports and Statement of Accounts, 1888–1895.

Forest Gate School District Minute Books, 1875–1876, 1889–1897.

Forest Gate School District Staff Book.

Forest Gate School District Superintendent's Report and Journal, 1889–1890.

General Register of Subscriptions, Clerkenwell Emergency Relief Fund Committee.

Greater London Public Records Office—Archives and records relating to the *Princess Alice* inquest.

Greenwich Union Minute Books, 1866–1867.

Letter Book of the Clerkenwell Emergency Relief Fund Committee.

Metropolitan Board of Works. Report by John Hebb into the Panic at the Hebrew Dramatic Club.

Ministers' Queries on the Silvertown Report. 1917.

Minute Book of the Clerkenwell Emergency Relief Fund Committee.

Minutes of the Woolwich Board of Guardians, 1878.

Newham Local Studies Library—Albion Archives.

Newham Local Studies Library—Silvertown Explosion Archives.

Official Report by Mr Marsh Nelson, Architect, on the Calamity in Gilbert Street, 1858.

Official Report by Mr Marsh Nelson, Architect, on Fall of Houses in Tottenham Court Road, 1857.

Archives and Primary Source Material (continued)

Poplar Board of Guardians Minutes Books, 1866–1867, 1893–1894.

Port of London Shipmasters' Guide.

Report by Lt Col Boxer RA and Correspondence Relating to the Explosion of Gunpowder at Erith and the Condition of Magazines and Manufacturies of Gunpowder.

Report into explosion at Local Government Board Offices and The Times, March 15, 1883, by HM Inspector of Explosives Col. Majendie.

Report into explosions at Scotland Yard and St James' Square, May 30 1884 by HM Inspector of Explosives Col. Majendie.

Report into explosion at Victoria Railway Station, Pimlico, February 26 1884 and the attempted explosions at Charing Cross, Paddington and Ludgate Hill railway stations by HM Inspector of Explosives Col. Majendie.

Report of the Committee appointed by the Home Office on the Silvertown Explosion, 1917.

Report of the Departmental Committee Appointed by the Local Government Board to Inquire into the Existing System of Maintenance and Education of Children Under the Care of Managers of District Schools and Boards of Guardians in the Metropolis, 1896.

Report of the Investigation held at the Board of Trade Court into the circumstances attending the collision between the steamships *Princess Alice* and *Bywell Castle*, 1878.

Report of the Regent's Park Explosion Relief Fund.

Report of the Select Committee on Explosive Substances, 1874.

Report of the Select Committee on Theatres and Places of Entertainment, 1892.

Report of the Silvertown Explosion Committee, 1917.

Royal Commission into Accidents on Railways, 1875.

St. Marylebone Board of Guardians Minute Books, 1866–1867.

Select Committee Report on Accidents on Railways 1858.

Statements of Witnesses to the Silvertown Explosion Committee. 1917.

Vestry Minutes, Parish of Erith, 1864.

Whitechapel Board of Guardians Minute Books, 1866–1867, 1893–1894.

Whitechapel Union Minute Books, 1866, 1886–1887.

Legislation

Building Act 1774
Building Act 1844
Explosives Act 1875
Gunpowder Act 1860
London Building Act 1894
London County Council Theatres
Bill 1889

Metropolitan Building Act 1855
Metropolitan Commissioners for
Sewers Act 1848
Metropolitan Management and
Building Act 1878
Public Health Amendment Act 1890

Contemporary newspapers and periodicals

Camden and Kentish Town Gazette
Daily Mirror
Daily News
East London Observer
Globe
Graphic
Hampstead and Highgate Express
Hansard
Illustrated London News
Illustrated Times
Jewish Chronicle
Kentish Independent

Kentish Mercury
Mail
Standard
Stratford Express
Sunday Times
Thames Iron Works Gazette
Times
Times Weekly Edition
Tower Hamlets Independent
West Ham Herald
Women's Dreadnought

Secondary Sources

Acworth, W.M. *The Railways of England*. John Murray, 1890.
Blythe, Richard. *Danger Ahead*. Newman Neane, 1951.
Davenport-Hill, Florence. *Children of the State*. 1867.
Dickens, Charles. *Household Words*. 1857.

Secondary Sources (continued)

Guest, Edwin. *The Wreck of the Princess Alice.* 1878.

Holt, G. *Railway Accidents.* Institute of Railway Signal Engineers, 1923.

Magnus, Laurie. *The Jewish Board of Guardians 1859–1909.* 1908.

Nock, O.S. *Historic Railway Disasters.* Ian Allen, 1966.

Quinlivan, Patrick and Rose, Paul. *The Fenians in England 1865–1872.* 1982.

Rolt, L.T.C. *Red for Danger.* The Bodley Head, 1955.

Shaw, Eyre. *Fire in Theatres.* 1876.

Thurston, Gavin. *The Great Thames Disaster.* Allen and Unwin, 1963.

Vincent, W.T. *The Records of the Woolwich District.* Jackson Press, 1888–1890.

White, H.P. *The Regional History of the Railways of Great Britain. Volume 3, Greater London.* Phoenix House, 1963.